Lecture Notes
in Business Information Processing 189

Series Editors

Wil van der Aalst
Eindhoven Technical University, Eindhoven, The Netherlands
John Mylopoulos
University of Trento, Povo, Italy
Michael Rosemann
Queensland University of Technology, Brisbane, QLD, Australia
Michael J. Shaw
University of Illinois, Urbana-Champaign, IL, USA
Clemens Szyperski
Microsoft Research, Redmond, WA, USA

More information about this series at http://www.springer.com/series/7911

Karl-Heinz Krempels · Alexander Stocker (Eds.)

Web Information Systems and Technologies

9th International Conference, WEBIST 2013
Aachen, Germany, May 8–10, 2013
Revised Selected Papers

 Springer

Editors
Karl-Heinz Krempels
RWTH Aachen University
Aachen
Germany

Alexander Stocker
Virtual Vehicle Research Center
Graz
Austria

ISSN 1865-1348
ISBN 978-3-662-44299-9
DOI 10.1007/978-3-662-44300-2

ISSN 1865-1356 (electronic)
ISBN 978-3-662-44300-2   (eBook)

Library of Congress Control Number: 2014945218

Springer Heidelberg New York Dordrecht London

Printed on acid-free paper

Springer is part of Springer Science+Business Media (www.springer.com)

Preface

This book includes extended and revised versions of a set of selected papers from WEBIST 2013 (the 9th International Conference on Web Information Systems and Technologies), held in Aachen, Germany, in 2013, which was sponsored by the Institute for Systems and Technologies of Information, Control and Communication (INSTICC) and the German Federal Ministry of Economics and Technology by the grant "econnect Germany – *Stadtwerke machen Deutschland elektromobil*" (econnect Germany – public utility as electric mobility providers in Germany). This conference was also co-organized by RWTH Aachen University. The conference was held in cooperation with Association for Computing Machinery/Special Interest Group on Management Information Systems (ACM SIGMIS) and technically sponsored by the European Research Center for Information System (ERCIS).

The purpose of the WEBIST series of conferences is to bring together researchers, engineers, and practitioners interested in technological advances and business applications of Web-based information systems. The conference has five main tracks, covering different aspects of Web Information Systems, including Internet Technology, Web Interfaces and Applications, Society, e-Business and e-Government, Web Intelligence and Mobile Information Systems.

The conference program included two specialized tutorials. The first tutorial titled "Cross-Platform App Development: Options and Strategies" was provided by Tim Majchrzak and Hennig Heitkötter, University of Münster, Germany. The second tutorial titled "Usability 101: What Makes Interactive Products Easy to Use – And How to Design Them" focused on human–computer interaction and was provided by Gero Herkenrath, RWTH Aachen University, Germany. Furthermore, the three keynotes provided by Emer Coleman, Harald Schöning, and Brian Donnellan addressed cutting-edge questions in open discussion with the conference members. Emer Coleman, Government Digital Services, UK, addressed "Open Data and Reflections from the London Datastore" in her keynote. Harald Schöning, Software AG, Germany, focused on the big data problem in his keynote titled "See the Wood for the Trees." Last but not least, Brian Donnellan, National University of Ireland, Maynooth, Ireland, discussed "IT and Sustainability" in his keynote.

WEBIST 2013 received 143 paper submissions from 43 countries in all continents. A double-blind review process was enforced, with the help of 190 experts from the international Program Committee, all of them with a PhD in one of the main conference topic areas. From these paper submissions only 27 papers were selected to be published and presented as full papers, i.e., completed work (10 pages in proceedings / 30-min oral presentations) and 30 additional papers, describing work-in-progress as short papers for 20-min oral presentation. Furthermore 29 additional papers were also presented as posters. The full-paper acceptance ratio was 19 %, and the total oral paper acceptance ratio was 39.9 %. The papers included in this book were selected from those with the best reviews also taking into account the quality of their presentation at the conference, assessed by session chairs. Therefore, we hope that you find these papers interesting, and we trust they may represent a helpful reference for all those who need to address any of the research areas mentioned.

We wish to thank all those who supported and helped to organize the conference. On behalf of the conference Organizing Committee, we would like to thank the authors, whose work mostly contributed to a very successful conference, and the members of the Program Committee, whose expertise and diligence were instrumental in ensuring the quality of the final contributions. We also wish to thank all the members of the Organizing Committee, whose work and commitment was invaluable. Last but not least, we would like to thank Springer for their collaboration in getting this book to print.

December 2013   Karl-Heinz Krempels
                                                      Alexander Stocker

Organization

Conference Chair

Karl-Heinz Krempels   RWTH Aachen University, Germany

Program Chair

Alexander Stocker   Virtual Vehicle Research Center, Austria

Organizing Committee

Marina Carvalho	INSTICC, Portugal
Helder Coelhas	INSTICC, Portugal
Bruno Encarnação	INSTICC, Portugal
Ana Guerreiro	INSTICC, Portugal
André Lista	INSTICC, Portugal
Andreia Moita	INSTICC, Portugal
Carla Mota	INSTICC, Portugal
Raquel Pedrosa	INSTICC, Portugal
Vitor Pedrosa	INSTICC, Portugal
Susana Ribeiro	INSTICC, Portugal
Sara Santiago	INSTICC, Portugal
Mara Silva	INSTICC, Portugal
José Varela	INSTICC, Portugal
Pedro Varela	INSTICC, Portugal

Program Committee

Josep Domingo-Ferrer, Spain
Atilla Elci, Turkey
Vadim Ermolayev, Ukraine
Larbi Esmahi, Canada
Davide Eynard, Switzerland
Alexander Felfernig, Austria
Anna Fensel, Austria
Miriam Fernandez, UK
Alberto Fernández, Spain
Josep-Lluis Ferrer-Gomila, Spain

Filomena Ferrucci, Italy
Pasi Fränti, Finland
Britta Fuchs, Germany
Giovanni Fulantelli, Italy
Martin Gaedke, Germany
Ombretta Gaggi, Italy
John Garofalakis, Greece
Irene Garrigos, Spain
Panagiotis Germanakos, Cyprus
Massimiliano Giacomin, Italy

Claudio Schifanella, Italy
Hamida Seba, France
Jochen Seitz, Germany
Weiming Shen, Canada
Marianna Sigala, Greece
Anna Stavrianou, France
Alexander Stocker, Austria
Giorgos Stoilos, Greece
Hussein Suleman, South Africa
Jiao Tao, USA
Christoph Terwelp, Germany
Dirk Thissen, Germany
Thanassis Tiropanis, UK
Riccardo Torlone, Italy
Raquel Trillo, Spain
T. Tsiatsos, Greece
George Tsihrintzis, Greece

Athina Vakali, Greece
Jari Veijalainen, Finland
Maria Virvou, Greece
Petri Vuorimaa, Finland
Mohd. Helmy Abd Wahab, Malaysia
Chen Wang, Australia
Fan Wang, USA
Luyi Wang, USA
Jason Whalley, UK
Manuel Wimmer, Austria
Viacheslav Wolfengagen,
    Russian Federation
Guandong Xu, Australia
Yeliz Yesilada, Turkey
Daniel Dajun Zeng, USA
Christian Zirpins, Germany
Amal Zouaq, Canada

Additional Reviewers

Jose Alfonso Aguilar, Mexico
Christophe Bobineau, France
Paul Bogen, USA
Marcin Davies, Austria
Paul Heiniz, Germany
Oluyomi Kabiawu, South Africa
Mehdi Khouja, Spain

Vikash Kumar, Austria
Isaac Lera, Spain
Diego Magro, Italy
Christian Samsel, Germany
Samir Sebahi, France
Cleyton Slaviero, Brazil

Invited Speakers

Emer Coleman
Harald Schöning
Brian Donnellan

Government Digital Services, UK
Software AG, Germany
National University of Ireland, Maynooth, Ireland

Contents

Society, e-Business and e-Government

Web Intelligence

Mobile Information Systems

Internet Technology

Networked XML Compression by Encoding Pre-order Traversals

Tyler Corbin[1], Tomasz Müldner[1](✉), and Jan Krzysztof Miziołek[2]

[1] Jodrey School of Computer Science, Acadia University,
Wolfville, NS B4P 2A9, Canada
[2] IBI AL, University of Warsaw, Warsaw, Poland
{tomasz.muldner,094568c}@acadiau.ca, jkm@ibi.uw.edu.pl

Abstract. The advantages of the eXtensible Markup Language, XML, come at a cost, especially for huge datasets or when used on small mobile devices. Several known XML-conscious compressors used in real time environments compress data during data streaming. This paper presents a study of new real time algorithms that exploit local structural redundancies of pre-order traversals of an XML tree. These algorithms focus on reducing the overhead of streaming data while maintaining load balancing between the sender and receiver. Our algorithms have similar or better performance than existing algorithms, while emphasizing low memory and processing overheads.

Keywords: XML · XML compression · Real time environments

1 Introduction

The eXtensible Markup Language, XML [1], is a World Wide Web Consortium (W3C) endorsed standard for semi-structured data. However, XML's usefulness is limited, in particular for very large datasets and for simple data sets, such as for AJAX requests, and when used on commercial mobile devices that rarely meet the necessary bandwidth and resource requirements. A naive solution to reduce the XML format overhead uses a general-purpose data compressor, e.g., GZIP [2]. However, such compressors do not reveal redundancies in the tree structure, nor do they distinguish an element tag from a text segment, thereby increasing the entropy of the data. There has been considerable research on *XML-conscious compressors*, e.g., XMill [3], XGrind [4] and XQueC [5], that take advantage of the semi-structured organization of XML data (for more, see [6]).

Permutation-based XML compressors separate structure from content and then apply a partitioning strategy to group content nodes into a series of data containers compressed using a general-purpose compressor (a *back-end compressor*). Another class of XML compressors consist of *queryable* XML compressors, which allow querying the compressed contents as if it were a space-efficient database, e.g., [7–9]. Querying XML is based on path expressions, see [10,11]. Another type of XML compressors, which we focus on in this paper, are designed for real-time network activities.

K.-H. Krempels and A. Stocker (Eds.): WEBIST 2013, LNBIP 189, pp. 3–20, 2014.
DOI: 10.1007/978-3-662-44300-2_1

Online, or *real-time*, XML compressors are a subset of XML compressors that only apply backward adaptive compression techniques. Using these techniques, the compressor may either predict the next input, or develop a model, based only on prior inputs. In general, it is assumed that the overhead induced by applying foreword adaptive compression techniques, i.e., developing a model, or prediction, based on both past and present inputs, is prohibitive for real time environments. In summary, the encoder (or decoder) processes chunks of data whenever possible rather than doing it *offline* when the entire document readily is available, and foreword adaptive compression techniques are available. Real time and backward adaptive compressors allow the compression of data even if the entire document is not readily available, or local to the machine in question. In particular, these stream-based compressors receive an input stream of XML data and process the data as if they were executing a pre-order traversal of the XML tree (even though this tree is never stored in memory). The efficiency of real time algorithms include several factors, such as compression ratio, encoding and decoding times, memory and processing overheads, and network bandwidth. Therefore, it is often beneficial that one should be able to tune these algorithms depending on its environment for optimal performance.

Contributions. We present a study of new online algorithms, which exploit local structural redundancies of pre-order traversals of an XML tree focusing on reducing the overhead of sending data blocks and maintaining load balancing between the sender and receiver. Four new approaches were studied: (1) a SAX-Event based encoding scheme; (2) its improvement using bit packing; (3) path-centric compression, which alleviates some overhead of the first two algorithms; and (4) deferred text compression with variable sized buffers. For testing, we designed a suite consisting of 11 XML files with various characteristics. In order to take into account network issues, such as bottlenecking, and to analyze certain properties of each encoding, we took two measures of each encoding process. Ten encoding techniques were compared, such as GZIP, EXI, Treechop, Online-XSAQCT, an improvement of Online-XSAQCT, and the algorithms proposed in this paper. Testing indicates that our new algorithms have similar or better performance than most existing online algorithms with the exception of EXI for files with a substantially large amount of character data, which can be attributed to the different philosophies of memory overheads vs. compression performance.

Because of space limitations, for a brief description of related work see [6]. This paper is organized as follows. Section 2 describes our new algorithms and traces of some algorithms. Section 3 includes a brief description of the implementation and results of testing aimed at evaluating the efficiency of our algorithms. Finally, Sect. 4 provides conclusions and describes future work.

2   Online Algorithms

Our work on real time compression is partially based on the offline XSAQCT [12] compression process. Therefore for the sake of completeness, Sect. 2.1 recalls from [13] the basic terminology, definitions and examples, and adds several new definitions. Section 2.2 recalls XSAQCT's examples of real time compression, while the following sections present a study of several new *real time algorithms*, and form the main part of our paper. Sections 2.4 and 2.5 present two algorithms, a lightweight SAX parsing, which sends encoded SAX events to be executed by the receiver, and an improvement that uses bit packing. Finally, Sects. 2.6 and 2.7 present algorithms that alleviate the requirement of sending extra bytes and an improvement using deferred text compression. Each algorithm focuses on reducing the overhead of sending data blocks by way of transformations that provide high compression ratios at the expense of total number of bytes sent. This is why no substantial pre-processing or alteration will be done to the semantic data during encoding. It is assumed that general backend compressors can be configuratively changed with respect to the amount of sophistication required given specific environmental factors.

2.1   Introduction to XSAQCT Compression

In the first phase of offline compression – compression local to the client computer – the compressor transforms the original XML document into a more compressed form, called an *annotated tree*. Then it strips all annotations to a separate *container* and finally compresses all containers using a back-end compressor.

Definition 1. *Similar paths are paths that are identical, possibly with the exception of the last component, which is the data value. An **annotated tree** of an XML document is a tree in which all similar paths are merged into a single path labeled by its tag name and each node is annotated with a sequence of integers, referred to as an **annotation list**.*

Definition 2. *Character data is the actual semantic data of the XML document that must be associated with the correct parent node regardless of the transformation of the input XML document used. Conversely, **Markup Data** is data used to provide the self documenting structure of the character data. A **text container** of an XML path P is a list of all **syntactic or semantic** data (ASCII zero delimited) for all paths similar to P.*

Given the XML document shown in Fig. 1(a), its associated annotated tree is shown in Fig. 1(b). Because of space limitations, we refer the reader to [12] for the algorithms to create an annotated tree and to [14] for the description of how cycles, i.e., consecutive children X, Y, X and contradicting child orderings X, Y, X vs. Y, X, Y are dealt with. For an XML document to be faithfully represented by a single annotation tree, it has to satisfy the full mixed content property; for more details see [6]. Another important property is that the annotated tree represents a permutation-based representation of an XML document while also being a lossless representation of any XML document.

One of the reasons that foreword adaptive compression techniques are not well suited for networked environments can be explained by considering the following example. Given an XML document, the encoder will build an annotated

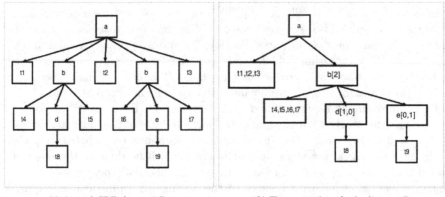

(a) A sample XML document D.   (b) The annotated tree for the document D

Fig. 1. An XML document and its associated annotated tree.

tree that compresses the original XML document; the decoder decompresses the annotated tree and restores the original XML document in its entirety. This type of processing is inherently singular, i.e., the encoder (and decoder) will be inactive for the time it takes for decoding (and encoding), and the network would be inactive during both encoding and decoding. For *querying* XML contents, the encoder performs the same compression operation, while the decoder stores the compressed data and queries it. Conversely, there exists one common scenario where the benefits of foreword adaptive compression can vastly outweigh backward adaptive algorithms. In such a case, a networks latency or bandwidth bring about such a severe hindrance to an applications performance that the benefits received from more extreme compression will only provide performance gains.

Definition 3. *Real Time Compression is defined as an encoding or decoding scheme where the encoder operates on data as it is being received and the decoder is not forced to wait until the entire encoded document has been received. Instead, decoding of the document can be started as soon as the beginning of the encoded data stream is received.*

Existing work on real time compression have focused on maximizing compression ratios, while processing-time and, least frequently considered, bottleneck effects caused by network latency and bandwidth have not been a primary concern. This is because it is assumed the less data being sent across a network, the less bottlenecking will occur. However, this only happens to be true when the encoder is sending data uniformly over time. Another important factor that should be considered in designing real time compression is the usage of the data at hand. Specifically, if the receiving node is piping XML content directly into an application, the character data should be transferred as rapidly and frequently as possible into the client. However, in a networked environment to achieve optimal, or near-optimal, processing and transfer times, a plethora of external conditions may have to be considered. These conditions range from (A) the intended use of the data; (B) the networking backbone (WANs, LANs, Mobile Networks, Wireless Sensor Networks, etc.); and (C) the available resources of each participating node. Therefore, most real-time approaches are often considered as a highly configurable bundle of algorithms, with each configuration emphasizing some specific need.

Definition 4. *There are two basic applications of the decoder: (1)* **restoration**, *in which the decoder restores the original XML document, and (2)* **querying**, *in which the decoder saves the data or it transforms the data into a representation suitable for subsequent queries.*

For *restoration* the encoder node produces encodings while the decoder node receives this encoding and outputs (to an application or storage device) the original XML document, or in most of our applicative cases, the annotated representation of the original XML document because it allows a more succinct representation and provides efficient query functionality. From a network's perspective, three situations can occur: (1) Perfect network utilization, in which the encoder and decoder are never bottlenecked by a network, or by the processing loads of one another; (2) Decoder starvation, in which the decoder (or its associated process) is often located on its associated operating systems I/O wait queue, which happens when the encoding process or the network bandwidth is slow or limited; (3) Encoder starvation, in which the encoder (or its associated process) is often located on its associated operating system I/O wait queue, which can arise when the decoding process (or bandwidth) is slow and the encoding socket is waiting for a RR or ACK request for specific TCP/UDP packet/frame before it is allowed to send more data. Cases (2) and (3) often occur at the same time on low-bandwidth networks. However, in terms of processing load, real time algorithms have *non-disjoint processing loads* since processing can happen on both ends at the same time. For *querying*, the encoding node produces encodings while the decoding node translates these encodings into a format that can be used to answer specific queries. An encoding can also be translated back into its original XML representation and be queried using tools such as SOAP [15], the encoding can directly interface with the *Query Streams* design pattern as described in [16]. Simply put, a query stream receives a list of queries to resolve before an XML download occurs and before the XML data is sent to its destination (i.e., a disk or application). The XML data is filtered through the query stream, which attempts to answer queries given the decoded data at the current point. Finally, the encoding could also be directly converted into the annotated representation for querying. Regardless of the situation, the processing load negatively favours the decoder.

2.2 Real Time Compression

The offline XSAQCT compression algorithm described in [12] will be used as a baseline for comparison. Under most circumstances, the client receiving this data will be building the annotated tree for future querying and use. Therefore, if a real time algorithm can transfer less encoded data than what an annotation algorithm produces, the real time algorithm can be described as *maximally space efficient*. Hence, the strictly backward adaptive algorithm is more efficient than the foreword adaptive offline algorithm. This goal is plausible and can be explained by considering the "scope of compression". Even though the scope of compression is greater for the annotated algorithm, i.e., a compression model is developed for the entire XML document, while for real time compression an encoding is created for only *specific branches* of tree. The resulting compression may not necessarily be optimal for entire document modelling. For example, the zero annotations in Fig. 1(b) tell the decoder that this specific subtree has no tag element and this, generally speaking, can be considered strictly overhead. The comparison between offline and real time algorithms will mostly revolve around the number of bits in representing the XML file.

2.3   Example of Real Time Compression

Figure 2 depicts the encoding generated by the algorithm discussed in [13] for the document shown in Fig. 1(a). The encoding is created by a pre-order traversal on the non-text nodes with the caveat of whenever there is traversal back up the tree (stack-pops in a pre-order traversal) a new encoding block is formed; initialized with an integer representing the number of traversals back up the XML tree (usually one).

Within an XML document, tag names will often be repeated many times. The example shown in Fig. 2 has only one tag repetition ('b'), but tag names are often long and also dependant on the character set of the data. Using a tag-name dictionary that can be synchronously built on the fly by both the encoder and the decoder, the encoder will only have to send indices within the dictionary. This will substantially decrease the overhead of sending tag names, and more specifically, substantially decrease the amount of markup usually witnessed in XML documents. An example of synchronous dictionaries is shown in Fig. 3. A dictionary in this instance would be a suffix-tree (or trie), which has, at worst, linear (with respect to the string being searched) insertion and access times. To handle XML attributes in a pre-order encoding, all attribute data can be encoded along with a dictionary index. For example, if the "d" node in Fig. 1(a) had an attribute "href", a standard encoding would be {...3, d, attrEncoding(d)...}.

---

   i. {-1, a, t1, b, t4, d, t8}
  ii. {1, t5}
 iii. {1, t2, b, t6, e, t9}
 iv. {1, t7}
  v. {1, t3}
 vi. {EOF} // End of File

Fig. 2. Example of XSAQCT real time encoding.

i. {-1, 1, a, t1, 2, b, t4, 3, d, t8}	D={a,b,d}
ii. {1, t5}	D={a,b,d}
iii. {1, t2, 2, t6, 4, e, t9}	D={a,b,d,e}
iv. {1, t7}	D={a,b,d,e}
v. {1, t3}	D={a,b,d,e}
vi. {EOF} // End of File	D={a,b,d,e}

Fig. 3. Node name dictionary.

In addition, this technique can be conceptually simplified by declaring attributes as a special type of node, rather than an attribute of a node, allowing attributes to be included in a standard pre-order traversal of an XML tree.

2.4 Lightweight SAX Parsing

For compressing data we can describe an XML document as having four major components: (1) The XML Declaration; (2) Start Element Tags; (3) End Element Tags; and (4) Character Data, which can be sub-categorized as parsed character data, unparsed character data (processing instructions, comments), and intermittent namespace definitions. An XML declaration only occurs once, start and end tags define the pre-order traversal of a tree, and character data (recall Definition 2) encompasses everything else. Since we assume full-mixed content [6], all Start Element and (non-child) End Element events are followed with a text string which is, at minimum, an ASCII zero byte (also used to inform the decoder of an end of string); this data is often the structure or whitespace data of an XML document.

Encoding. Define the following two elements, both encoded by single bytes: (1) Start Element, encoded by 0x0; and (2) End Element, encoded by 0x1. The description of Lightweight SAX is provided in Algorithm 1. Running this algorithm on the document from Fig. 1(a) will produce the encoding shown in Fig. 4 with Table 1 showing a part of the sample execution. Note that the synchronous dictionary techniques (described in Sect. 2.2) can be used to reduce the overhead in sending node names.

2.5 Bit Packing Improvement

Introducing bit-level operations can reduce each start and end declaration by, at maximum, seven bits. The encoding bytes 0x0 and 0x1 can be represented using a single bit, which changes the encoding shown in Fig. 4 to the one shown in Fig. 5. Here, a low-level design choice must be made for this technique: either (1) the entire encoding will be done on the bit level, i.e., one bit will be written for start/end declaration followed by multiple bytes that include tag index, character data, etc., or (2) an algorithm is forced to *buffer* eight bits, each representing a SAX event. While both techniques may induce extra processing and memory

Algorithm 1. Lightweight SAX.

Require: n is the Root on initial function call
1: **function** ENCODE(Node n)
2:     send(0x0); // Start Element
3:     send(handleAttributes(n)); // send name+attribute
4:     send(getText(n)); // send text
5:     // Pre-order Traversal
6:     **for** Each Child Node **s** Of **n do**
7:         Encode(s);
8:         // Full mixed content, so text exists between all children.
9:         // This data resides between two siblings, e.g., t_2 in Fig. 1.
10:         send(getText(n,s))
11:     **end for**
12:     send(0x1); // End Element
13: **end function**

---

   i. {0x0, a, t1, 0x0, b, t4, 0x0, d, t8}
  ii. {0x1, t5, 0x1, t2}
 iii. {0x0, b, t6, 0x0, e, t9, 0x1, t7}
 iv. {0x1, t3, 0x1=EOF} // End of File

Fig. 4. Encoding with lightweight SAX

   i. {00011001_2, a, t1, b, t4, d, t8, t5, t2, b, t6, e, t9, t7}
  ii. {11_2, t3, EOF }

Fig. 5. Encoding using two bits.

overheads, (e.g., using the second technique, the corresponding tag-dictionary keys and associated character data must be buffered until a byte is packed and the amount of data to buffer is undefined), the second method is preferred for the following reason. By packing bits, the entropy of the entire encoding block will be smaller than the former block because no character data (the most common form of data) is being bit-shifted before the encoder outputs it, and by extension, this technique allows more separation between structure and content.

2.6   Path-Centric Compression

To satisfy the full-mixed content property while avoiding the potentially large overheads of sending ASCII zeros, we extend the algorithm from Sect. 2.4, by introducing an additional *text element*, encoded by 0x2 (10 in binary). By allowing this new element, an encoding sequence with no intermediate 0x2 value (e.g.,

Table 1. Sample execution of lightweight SAX encoding.

	Line	Execution	Stack	Output
1	1	Encode(A)	{}	{}
2	3	send(0x0)	{Encode(A)}	{0x0}
3	5	send(a)	{Encode(A)}	{0x0, a}
4	7	send(t1)	{Encode(A)}	{0x0, a, t1}
5	9	for (s = {B_{left},B_{right}})	{Encode(A)}	{0x0, a, t1}
6	10	Encode(B_{left})	{Encode(A)}	{0x0, a, t1}
7	3	send(0x0)	{Encode(A), Encode(B)}	{0x0, a, t1, 0x0}
8	5	send(b)	{Encode(A), Encode(B)}	{0x0, a, t1, 0x0, b}
9	7	send(t4)	{Encode(A), Encode(B)}	{0x0, a, t1, 0x0, b, t4}
10	9	for (s = {D})	{Encode(A), Encode(B)}	{0x0, a, t1, 0x0, b, t4}
11	10	Encode(D)	{Encode(A), Encode(B)}	{0x0, a, t1, 0x0, b, t4}
12	3	send(0x0)	{Encode(A), Encode(B), Encode(D)}	{0x0, a, t1, 0x0, b, t4, 0x0}
13	5	send(e)	{Encode(A), Encode(B), Encode(D)}	{0x0, a, t1, 0x0, b, t4, 0x0, e}
14	7	send(t8)	{Encode(A), Encode(B), Encode(D)}	{0x0, a, t1, 0x0, b, t4, 0x0, e, t8}
15	9	for (s={})	{Encode(A), Encode(B), Encode(D)}	**{0x0, a, t1, 0x0, b, t4, 0x0, e, t8}**
16	16	send(0x1)	{Encode(A), Encode(B), Encode(D)}	{0x1}
17	13	send(t5)	{Encode(A), Encode(B)}	{0x1, t5}
18	16	send(0x1)	{Encode(A), Encode(B)}	{0x1, t5, 0x1}
19	13	send(t2)	{Encode(A))}	**{0x1, t5, 0x1, t2}**

---

  i. {0x0, a, 0x2, t1, 0x0, b, 0x2, t4, 0x0, d, 0x2, t8}
  ii. {0x1, 0x2, t5, 0x1, 0x2, t2, 0x0, b}
 iii. {0x2, t6, 0x0, e, 0x2, t9, 0x1}
 iv. {0x2, t7, 0x1, 0x2, t3, 0x1=EOF} // End of File

Fig. 6. Encoding using three special bytes.

0x0, 0x1), informs the decoder to insert empty text where necessary (instantaneously, with no additional buffering). Using these three elements, the pre-order encoding from Fig. 4 will change to one in Fig. 6. In addition, each of these three elements can be encoded using a pair of bits, so four encodings can be packed into a single byte (a more complex packing of bits would use the following prefix codes (0_2, 10_2, 11_2)). However, most XML documents are well structured, and so most subtrees satisfy the full-mixed content constraint, implying there would be a large number of 0x2 identifiers. Therefore, this approach is not used and instead a modification of this idea is introduced, named context driven compression.

2.7 Introducing Context

Recall that for offline XSAQCT a text container for path P contains a list of text data for all paths similar to P. This technique provides a favorable compression ratio because the types of data for each path are typically related (e.g., an ID tag will only have characters defined by the class $[0-9]^+$) and thus will have a smaller entropy in comparison to all of the text in total. Consider the two algorithms provided in Sects. 2.3 and 2.4. For both algorithms, every encoded block focuses on a single (or few, if using bit packing) pre-ordered branch of the XML document, which makes it more difficult to deal with text data. Extending this idea, if a number of text nodes of each similar path are buffered and that buffer is compressed before transfer, the compression ratio will be improved by exploiting character locality properties used by permutation-based XML compressors.

For storing XML content which could later be queried upon, and for improving the compression ratios on the encoder-side especially when the encoding node has superior processing resources another approach can be used. Specifically, the same text containers used for offline compression could be losslessly constructed on the sending node instead of the receiving node during an online compression process by using a technique which we call a "Deferred Text Compression".

Deferred Text Compression. As described above, each unique path discovered in the encoding stage will contain its own statically defined character-buffer. When a buffer becomes full, the encoder writes 0x2 (or 10_2) and the contents of the buffer are written to the output stream, allowing data that are known to be alike to be grouped together. One slight modification to the algorithm would allow variable sized buffers that expand or contract depending on the frequency of usage of the text container. This allows sparsely used containers to be sent more frequently and more frequently used containers to be compressed even "more". In the following example let square brackets [text] denote a buffer with a maximum capacity of two elements (in our implementation the buffer's capacity is actually based on a specified number of bytes). Algorithm 2 provides a complete description of this technique (it can also use the bit-packing techniques). Following this algorithm, with a part of the sample execution shown in Table 2.

Figure 7 gives the output of encoding for the document in Fig. 1(a). The last encoding line in Fig. 7, includes all leftover buffered text data, sent in a commonly

---

   i. {0x0, a, 0x0, b, 0x0, d, 0x1}
  ii. {0x2, [t4,t5], 0x1, 0x2, [t1,t2]}
 iii. {0x0, b, 0x0, e, 0x1, 0x2, [t6,t7]}
 iv. {0x1, 0x1, [t3], [\0], [t8], [t9]}

Fig. 7. Buffering text.

Algorithm 2. Deferred Pre-order Encoding.

Require: n is the Root on initial function call
1: **function** ENCODE(Node n)
2:     preorder(n);
3:     **for** Each Unique Path **q do**
4:         buffer(q).finalize().close(); // Any trailer data in the buffer
5:         send(compress(buffer(q)));
6:     **end for**
7: **end function**
8: **function** BUFFER(Path path, Text t)
9:     buffer(path, getText(n));
10:     // Check if a flush is required.
11:     **if** buffer(path).isLimitExceeded() **then**
12:         send(0x2);
13:         send(compress(buffer(path))); // Offload the full buffer
14:         buffer(path).clear(); // Reset the buffer
15:     **end if**
16: **end function**
Require: n is the Root on initial function call
17: **function** PREORDER(Node n)
18:     send(0x0); // Start element
19:     send(handleAttributes(n)); // Send name+attribute information.
20:     buffer(p, getText(n)); // Buffer left-most text node
21:     // Pre-order traversal
22:     **if** not isChild(n) **then**
23:         c = LeftChildOf(c);
24:         **while** $c \neq$ null **do**
25:             preorder(c);
26:             // This is the data that resides at the right-most position.
27:             // For example, this is t_3 in Fig. 1.
28:             buffer(p, getText(n));
29:             c = RightSiblingOf(c);
30:         **end while**
31:     **end if**
32:     send(0x1);
33: **end function**

---

agreed upon ordering (for this example, a depth-first fashion, while our implementation uses the synchronous dictionaries natural ordering).

3 Implementation and Results

3.1 Testing Environment

All algorithms described in this paper were implemented using Java version 1.7 [17]. To create a test suite described in the following section, we first analyzed previous research on the varying characteristics of XML files. Based on these results, we chose to consider the following characteristics: (1) Document Unspecific Measurements, such as size of the document and its information entropy,

Table 2. Sample encoding of deferred encoding.

	Line	Execution	Stack	Buffers	Output
1	1	Encode(A)	{}	{}	{}
2	2	Preorder(A)	{Encode(A)}	{}	{}
3	23	send(0x0)	{Encode(A), Preorder(A)}	{}	{0x0}
4	25	send(a)	{..., Preorder(A)}	{}	{0x0, a}
5	27	buffer(/a/, t1)	{..., Preorder(A)}	{{t1}}	{0x0, a}
6	30	c=B	{..., Preorder(A)}	{{t1}}	{0x0, a}
7	32	Preorder(B)	{..., Preorder(A)}	{{t1}}	{0x0, a}
8	23	send(0x0)	{..., Preorder(A), Preorder(B)}	{{t1}}	{0x0, a, 0x0}
9	23	send(b)	{..., Preorder(A), Preorder(B)}	{{t1}}	{0x0, a, 0x0, b}
10	27	buffer(/a/b/, t4)	{..., Preorder(B)}	{{t1}, {t4}}	{0x0, a, 0x0, b}
11	30	c=D	{..., Preorder(B)}	{{t1}, {t4}}	{0x0, a, 0x0, b}
12	32	Preorder(D)	{..., Preorder(B)}	{{t1}, {t4}}	{0x0, a, 0x0, b}
13	23	send(0x0)	{..., Preorder(B), Preorder(D)}	{{t1}, {t4}}	{0x0, a, 0x0, b}
14	25	send(d)	{..., Preorder(B), Preorder(D)}	{{t1}, {t4}}	{0x0, a, 0x0, b, 0x0}
15	27	buffer(/a/b/d/, t8)	{..., Preorder(B), Preorder(D)}	{{t1}, {t4}, {t8}}	{0x0, a, 0x0, b, 0x0, d}
16	39	send(0x1)	{..., Preorder(B), Preorder(D)}	{{t1}, {t4}, {t8}}	{0x0, a, 0x0, b, 0x0, d, 0x1}
17	35	buffer(/a/b/, t5)	{..., Preorder(A), Preorder(B)}	{{t1}, {t4, t5}*, {t8}}	**{0x0, a, 0x0, b, 0x0, d, 0x1}**
18	14	send(0x2)	{..., Preorder(A), Preorder(B)}	{{t1}, **{t4, t5}***, {t8}}	{0x2}
19	16	send(buffer(/a/b/)	{..., Preorder(A), Preorder(B)}	{{t1}, {}, {t8}}	**{0x2, [t4,t5]}**

* – Requires extraordinary amount of RAM. Crashes with 16 GB of allocated memory.

with emphasis on free-formed English text; (2) Grammar Specific Measurements, such as XML-syntax-data versus XML-semantic-data; (3) Tree specific measurements such as the number of elements and attributes, the number of paths, and the number of distinct paths. For encoding, two measures were taken: (1) an ordinary encoding of the entire document, which represents the number of raw bytes generated by the encoder; (2) A compression of the encoding by using a general purposed back-end compressor. GZIP [2] was chosen as the back-end (and text) compressor because many bandwidth aware transfer protocols (including HTTP, see [18]) use GZIP or a DEFLATE variant for speedup. While the first measure may provide insights as to how efficient each encoding is in comparison to the original data, the second measure describes compressibility and provides a loose description of the entropy of each encoding. Recall from Sect. 2 that the main approach in dealing with character data is by re-organizing data in such a way that a general back-end compressor can be changed with the level of sophistication required. This philosophy is quite different from the EXI standard that tries to perform an initial dictionary-based compression scheme on common subsequences of text. Thus, EXI follows the philosophy of pre-compressing specific pieces of data at the cost of reducing the overall compressibility.

In total, ten complete encoding techniques are compared. First, we measured a naive solution of using GZIP (or no compression depending on the measure), followed by an EXI implementation [19] (using all fidelity options, default encoding options, and a compression-oriented coding mode). Next, we measured performance of Treechop [16], the original Online XSAQCT algorithm as discussed in [13], its leaf node improvement [13], followed by the new proposed algorithms.

3.2   Characteristics of Test Suite

Our experiments used the following 11 files listed here in the order of their sizes (from 5,685.77 GB to 159 KB): enwiki-latest-stub-articles.xml from [20], 1gig.xml (a randomly generated XML file, using xmlgen [21]), enwikibooks-20061201-pages-articles.xml, dblp.xml, SwissProt.xml, enwikinews-20061201-pages-articles.xml, lineitem.xml, shakespeare.xml, uwm.xml (all from the Wratislavia corpus [22]), baseball.xml (from [23]), and macbeth.xml (from [24]). For more details of characteristics of XML files in our corpus, see [6].

3.3   Results of Testing

Reducing Markup Data. Table 3 compares the efficiency of each algorithm described in Sect. 2 in terms of encoding *only* the markup of an XML document. The compression ratio is calculated as the size of the encoding divided by the size of the markup data (column two). Note that for each real time compression algorithm, the size of the markup includes all occurrences of ASCII Zero to satisfy the full-mixed content property and all additional data required to describe text data – for example, block lengths, text terminators/delimitations, etc. Each row in Table 3 has its smallest compression ratio underlined and Fig. 8(a) provide two measures: (1) A grey bar with a white bar stacked on top, which represents the best compression of markup a real time algorithm could achieve, while the white bar stacked-upon it represents the size of its GZIP'd encoding; (2) A grey bar with a black bar stacked on top, which represents the number of bytes required to encode an annotated tree, while the black bar stacked-upon it represents the size of its GZIP'd encoding. For the real time algorithms, we achieve over a 25 % compression ratio (or a space savings greater than 75 %) for all files. For the offline algorithm, some files produce encodings that contain many zero annotations and thus contain large portions of overhead. However, there is no decisive winner when one compares both compressed encodings as these encodings produce compression ratios of over 98 % of the original markup. Comparing the two encodings after compression is quite misleading, yet it still provides interesting information nonetheless as to how compressible and random the data is. This is because for our proposed algorithms these encodings are not continuous as large portions of intermittent character data separate portions of this markup, thus not allowing us to encode markup data as one contiguous sequence.

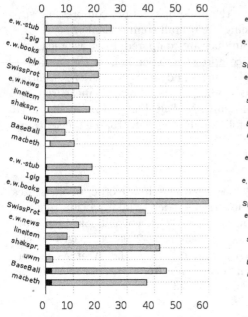

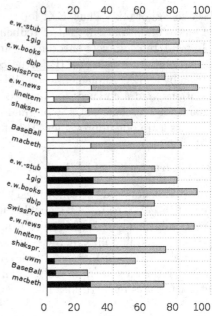

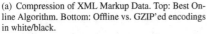

(a) Compression of XML Markup Data. Top: Best On-line Algorithm. Bottom: Offline vs. GZIP'ed encodings in white/black.

(b) Compression of Actual XML. Top: Best Online Algorithm. Bottom: Offline vs. GZIP'ed encodings in white/black.

Fig. 8. Compressing XML markup and actual XML.

Table 3. Compression ratio of structure: number of bytes to encode markup/original markup size.

File	Markup data	XSAQCT	Leaf imp.	SAX	Bit pck.	Path	Defer
enwiki-lat.	2.59E+09	0.331	0.304	0.359	<u>0.244</u>	0.376	0.26
1gig	3.04E+08	0.282	0.249	0.312	0.216	0.325	<u>0.181</u>
enwikibooks	9.03E+06	0.279	0.277	0.312	0.208	0.317	<u>0.167</u>
dblp	5.86E+07	0.294	0.214	0.305	0.206	0.312	<u>0.191</u>
SwissProt	6.38E+07	0.302	0.244	0.316	0.235	0.37	<u>0.194</u>
enwikinews	4.89E+06	0.27	0.264	0.3	0.2	0.305	<u>0.123</u>
lineitem	2.59E+07	0.193	0.128	0.197	0.128	0.197	<u>0.099</u>
shakespeare	2.71E+06	0.308	0.25	0.332	0.216	0.332	<u>0.163</u>
uwm	1.30E+06	0.233	0.213	0.257	0.167	0.257	<u>0.077</u>
BaseBall	5.96E+05	0.234	0.152	0.238	0.155	0.238	<u>0.072</u>
macbeth	5.99E+04	0.312	0.252	0.335	0.219	0.336	<u>0.104</u>

Switching focus to only the real time algorithms, the first general trend is that as the file gets bigger the worse the compression ratio of markup data seems to be. The four documents with the highest number of tag elements are also the four least-compressed documents (enwiki-latest, 1gig, dblp, and SwissProt). This phenomenon can be attributed to two issues: (1) The full-mixed contents

Table 4. Encoding the entire XML document (sizes in bytes*E+07).

File	Offline	EXI	Treechop	XSAQCT	Leaf	SAX	Bit pck.	Path	Defer.
enwiki-lat.	409	*	466	412	406	421	391	425	394
1gig	94.7	47.9	1.24	94.8	93.8	95.7	92.8	96.1	91.7
enwikibooks	14.9	13.9	14.5	14.3	14.3	15.0	14.9	15.0	1.41
dblp	12.6	8.69	10.7	9.24	8.78	9.31	8.73	9.35	8.63
SwissProt	8.26	4.37	8.46	7.03	6.66	7.12	6.60	7.46	6.25
enwikinews	4.27	3.95	4.27	4.18	4.17	4.30	4.25	4.30	4.10
lineitem	0.83	0.73	1.19	0.11	0.96	1.14	0.96	1.14	0.94
shakespeare	0.64	0.59	0.64	0.58	0.56	0.58	0.55	0.58	0.52
uwm	0.12	0.077	0.15	0.13	0.13	0.14	0.13	0.14	0.084
BaseBall	0.039	0.018	0.15	0.021	0.016	0.021	0.017	0.025	0.004
macbeth	0.013	0.012	0.013	0.02	0.018	0.012	0.012	0.012	0.0006

* – Requires extraordinary amount of RAM. Crashes with 16 GB of allocated memory.

Table 5. Using a backend compressor on the encodings (sizes in bytes*E+06).

XML file	Offline	EXI	Treechop	XSAQCT	Leaf	SAX	Bit pck.	Path	Defer.
enwiki-lat.	695	*	914	887	886	895	939	699	695
1gig	329	157	390	371	371	370	374	332	331
enwikibooks	44.5	43.9	45.2	45.1	45.1	45.4	45.6	44.4	43.8
dblp	19.4	18.6	23.6	22.7	22.7	22.9	23.4	19.4	19.2
SwissProt	7.63	7.71	1.33	1.23	12.3	12.4	13.6	7.74	7.77
enwikinews	12.6	12.6	12.9	12.8	12.8	12.9	13.0	12.6	12.5
lineitem	1.43	1.44	2.34	2.33	2.20	2.34	2.44	1.45	1.44
shakespeare	1.89	1.99	2.07	2.02	2.03	2.03	2.05	1.91	1.90
uwm	0.10	0.11	0.15	0.14	0.14	0.15	0.17	0.10	0.10
BaseBalll	0.047	0.039	0.053	0.05	0.0483	0.055	0.05	0.035	0.035
macbeth	0.043	0.045	0.046	0.045	0.045	0.045	0.045	0.043	0.043

* – Requires extraordinary amount of RAM. Crashes with 16 GB of allocated memory.

assumption, in which for larger documents more ASCII zero delimitations are required; (2) each algorithm also requires ASCII zeros to delimit its text so that the decoder knows when each character portion ends. In our future work, more compressible text delimitation and full mixed content techniques will be studied.

Reducing XML Data. Tables 4 and 5 and Fig. 8(b), which follows the same structure as Fig. 8(a), encompass an entire XML encoding and transfer process. Each element in the table represents the number of bytes physically transferred over a socket. The results of compressing enwiki-latest-stub with EXI were not reported due to hardware limitations. However, this brings up an important issue not discussed before: memory overheads. Our analysis incorporated a very open restriction in that the amount of internal memory allocated to a process can never exceed twice the file size. Not only did EXI exceed this, it also exceeded three times the original file size. This problem can be attributed to the fact (described in Sect. 3.1) that EXI also performs some manipulation on the text to allow better compression ratios by storing commonly occurring character substrings, similar to LZW. Disabling this functionality often drastically reduces the compression ratio, while the techniques proposed in this paper use GZIP natively – allowing other general back-end compressors to be used – and has an opposite memory footprint. For example, using "SAX Bit Packing" compression, the overhead is equivalent to the following four additional costs: (1) parsing the data (SAX Parsing typically requires a few megabytes of overhead); (2) the maximum amount of data to buffer (to pack an entire byte); (3) the dictionary (which usually stores less than 250 strings); and (4) the single instance of a GZIP compressor (usually 32/64 KB buffer plus a Huffman Tree). Thus, other than the 'Deferred' compression technique (which requires an additional buffer for each path, which still is not on the scale of EXI), they easily scale to data of all sizes.

Relating each individual algorithm to the baseline transfers (Offline and GZIP) we see that in each case all real time algorithms perform better than GZIP. However, in each case as we relax the "real time constraint" – i.e., the more data are allowed to buffer – the better and more significant results we receive. Comparing Offline XSAQCT, which requires processing the entire document before transfer, to Lightweight SAX, which processes on the fly, the Offline XSAQCT performs on average 15 % better. However, comparing Offline XSAQCT to the Deferred algorithm, the former algorithm performs on average 2 % better, with the Deferred algorithm beating its offline counterpart in five cases. This also implies that the Deferred Algorithms are very close to satisfying the space efficiency property discussed in Sect. 2. This is significant because the Path-Centric algorithms do not require a full document scope, making it well suited for the domain of large-scale XML streaming.

In comparison to Treechop, the original and lightweight SAX variants also prove to be quite competitive and once again, the Path-Centric algorithms beat Treechop. Finally, in comparison to EXI, the Path-Centric algorithms tend to be similar for documents smaller than 1 GB. However for 1gig, a document which contains ample character data, EXI is better than "all" algorithms by a substantial margin. Note that this comes at a trade-off of substantial memory and processing overheads.

4   Conclusions and Future Work

This paper provided a study of different schemes of XML compression suited for real time environments, which exploit local structural redundancies of preorder traversals of XML trees. These schemas focus on reducing the overhead of streaming data and maintaining load balancing between the sender and receiver with respect to encoding and decoding. For testing various algorithms, a suite consisting of 11 XML files with various characteristics were designed and analyzed. In order to take into account network issues, such as bottlenecking, and to provide additional insights into each encoding scheme, two measures of each encoding process were considered. In total, ten encoding techniques were studied, including GZIP, EXI, Treechop, Online-XSAQCT, an improvement of Online-XSAQCT, and the new algorithms proposed in this study. Our experiments indicated that our new algorithms have similar or better performance than existing real time algorithms, such as XSAQCT, Treechop and EXI, while being very competitive with its offline counterparts.

In our future work, we will provide more extensive analysis of the amount of memory overhead of performing each encoding as well as the amount of resources required for encoding. Finally, more techniques will be introduced to alleviate the vast overhead of sending ASCII zero characters to delimit text and to satisfy the full mixed content property.

Acknowledgements. The work of the first and second authors are partially supported by the NSERC CSG-M (Canada Graduate Scholarship-Masters) and NSERC RG-PIN grant respectively. We would like to thank the anonymous reviewers for their detailed and helpful comments used to improve the final version of our paper.

References

1. XML: EXtensible Markup Language (XML) 1.0, 5th edn. (2012). http://www.w3. org/TR/REC-xml/. Accessed 20 June 2013
2. GZIP: The gzip home page (2012). http://www.gzip.org. Accessed 20 June 2013
3. Hartmut, L., Suciu, D.: XMill: an efficient compressor for XML data. ACM Special Interest Group on Management of Data (SIGMOD) Record **29**, 153–164 (2000)
4. Tolani, P., Haritsa, J.: XGRIND: a query-friendly XML compressor. In: International Conference on Data Engineering (ICDE)' 02, pp. 225–234 (2002)
5. Arion, A., Bonifati, A., Manolescu, I., Pugliese, A.: XQueC: a query-conscious compressed XML database. ACM Trans. Internet Technol. **7**, 1–35 (2007)
6. Corbin, T., Müldner, T., Miziołek, J.: Pre-order compression schemes for XML in the real time environment. In: SciTePress Digital Library - WEBIST 2013 - 9th International Conference on Web Information Systems and Technologies, Aachen, Germany, pp. 5–15. SciTePress Digital Library (2013)
7. Skibiński, P., Swacha, J.: Combining efficient XML compression with query processing. In: Ioannidis, Y., Novikov, B., Rachev, B. (eds.) ADBIS 2007. LNCS, vol. 4690, pp. 330–342. Springer, Heidelberg (2007)
8. Lin, Y., Zhang, Y., Li, Q., Yang, J.: Supporting efficient query processing on compressed XML files. In: Proceedings of the Symposium on Applied Computing (SAC) '05, pp. 660–665. ACM, New York (2005)
9. Ng, W., Lam, W.Y., Wood, P., Levene, N.: XCQ: a queriable XML compression system. Knowl. Inf. Syst. **10**, 421–452 (2006)
10. XPath: XML Path Language (XPath) (2012). http://www.w3.org/TR/xpath/. Accessed on 20 June 2013
11. XQuery: XQuery 1.0: An XML Query Language, 2nd edn. (2012). http://www. w3.org/TR/xquery/. Accessed 20 June 2013
12. Müldner, T., Fry, C., Miziołek, J., Durno, S.: SXSAQCT and XSAQCT: XML queryable compressors. In: Böttcher, S., M. Lohrey, S.M., Rytter, W. (eds.) Structure-Based Compression of Complex Massive Data. Dagstuhl Seminar Proceedings, vol. 08261, Dagstuhl, Germany. Schloss Dagstuhl - Leibniz-Zentrum fuer Informatik, Germany (2008)
13. Müldner, T., Fry, C., Miziołek, J.: Online Internet communication using an XML compressor. In: The Seventh International Conference on Internet and Web Applications and Services, Stuttgart, Germany, pp. 131–136. International Academy, Research, and Industry Association (IARIA) (2012)

14. Müldner, T., Fry, C., Miziołek, J., Durno, S.: XSAQCT: XML queryable compressor. In: Balisage: The Markup Conference 2009, Montreal, Canada (2009)
15. soap: SOAP Version 1.2 Part 1: Messaging Framework, 2nd edn. (2012). http://www.w3.org/TR/soap12-part1/. Accessed 20 June 2013
16. Leighton, G., Müldner, T., Diamond, J.: TREECHOP: a tree-based query-able compressor for XML. In: The Ninth Canadian Workshop on Information Theory, pp. 115–118 (2005)
17. Java: Java version 7 (2012). http://www.oracle.com/technetwork/java/javase/7u-relnotes-515228.html. Accessed 20 June 2013
18. HTTP: HTTP RFC 2616 (2012). http://www.w3.org/Protocols/rfc2616/rfc2616.html. Accessed 20 June 2013
19. Peintner, D.: EXI: EXIficient (2012). http://exificient.sourceforge.net. Accessed 20 June 2013
20. enwiki dumps: enwiki-latest.xml (2012). http://dumps.wikimedia.org/enwiki/latest/. Accessed 20 June 2013
21. xmlgen: The benchmark data generator (2012). http://www.xml-benchmark.org/generator.html. Accessed 20 June 2013
22. Corpus: Wratislavia XML corpus (2012). http://www.ii.uni.wroc.pl/~inikep/research/Wratislavia/. Accessed 20 June 2013
23. Baseball: baseball.xml (2012). http://rassyndrome.webs.com/CC/Baseball.xml. Accessed 20 June 2013
24. Macbeth: macbeth.xml (2012). http://www.ibiblio.org/xml/examples/. Accessed 20 June 2013

Generating XACML Enforcement Policies for Role-Based Access Control of XML Documents

Alberto De la Rosa Algarín[1]([⊠]), Timoteus B. Ziminski[1],
Steven A. Demurjian[1], Yaira K. Rivera Sánchez[1],
and Robert Kuykendall[2]

[1] Department of Computer Science and Engineering,
University of Connecticut, Storrs, USA
{ada,tbz,steve,yaira}@engr.uconn.edu
[2] Department of Computer Science, Columbia University, New York, USA
rrk2136@columbia.edu

Abstract. Ensuring the security of electronic data has morphed into one of the most important requirements in domains such as health care, where the eXtensible Markup Language (XML) has been leveraged via standards such as the Health Level 7's Clinical Document Architecture and the Continuity of Care Record. These standards dictate a need for approaches to secure XML schemas and documents. In this paper, we present a secure information engineering method that is capable of generating eXtensible Access Control Markup Language (XACML) enforcement policies, defined in a role-based access control model (RBAC), that target XML schemas and their instances, allowing instances to be customized for users depending on their roles. To achieve this goal, we extend the Unified Modeling Language (UML) with two new diagrams: the XML Schema Class Diagram, which defines the structure of an XML document in UML style; and, the XML Role-Slice Diagram, which defines roles and associated privileges at a granular access control level. We utilize a personal health assistant mobile application for medication and chronic disease management to demonstrate the enforcement component of our work.

Keywords: Security and policy modeling · Security policies · XML · XACML · Role-based access control

1 Introduction

Securing sensitive and private information has evolved into a needed requirement in domains such as healthcare informatics, where the daily workflow depends on the secure management and exchange of information, often in time-critical situations. In healthcare informatics, the eXtensible Markup Language (XML) is used for data and information exchange across heterogeneous systems via XML standards such as Health Level Seven's clinical document architecture (CDA) [10] for health information exchange and the Continuity of Care Record (CCR) for capturing clinical patient data. In such settings, security protection must be insured so individuals have

K.-H. Krempels and A. Stocker (Eds.): WEBIST 2013, LNBIP 189, pp. 21–36, 2014.
DOI: 10.1007/978-3-662-44300-2_2

the appropriate credentials to access all of the required data (clinical, genomic, other phenotypic, etc.) in accordance with the Health Insurance Portability and Account-ability Act of 1996 (HIPAA) [1]. For the purposes of our work, we propose a secure information engineering method using the Unified Modeling Language (UML) to define and enforce XACML role-based access control (RBAC) security policies that allow XML schemas to be controlled and instances customized based on role, time, and usage.

The main objective of this paper is to create security policies defined and realized in XACML that target XML schemas and their instances to provide granular docu-ment-level security. The enforcement of these policies permits document instances to look different to authorized users at specific times based on the user's role. In contrast to the general research done in XML security, which typically embeds security pol-icies as part of the XML schema's definition, our approach allows policies to be evolved and applied to an application's XML instances without changes to instances and schemas. This approach results in a separation of concerns for facilitating security policy evolution without impacting XML instances.

To support this process, we have defined a security framework for XML in prior work [9] as shown in Fig. 1. The general approach is to have a set of XML schemas corresponding to an application (middle right in Fig. 1), which will be instantiated for the executing application (bottom right of Fig. 1). From a security perspective, our intent is to insure that when users attempt to access the instances, that access will be customized and filtered based on their defined user role and associated security privileges (role restricted, or RR, bottom left of Fig. 1). To achieve this in a secure information engineering context, the framework in Fig. 1 contains two new UML diagrams: the XML Schema Class Diagram (XSCD) that represents the structure of an XML document in UML style design artifacts; and, the XML Role-Slice Diagram (XRSD) that supports RBAC through the definition of granular access to XML schemas (and associated instances) based on role.

This paper to extends our earlier work [9] by concentrating on the left hand side of Fig. 1 (the XACML Policy Mapping box) for the definition and generation of XA-CML security policies and their enforcement at the runtime level on XML instances to insure that filtered, correct, and required data is securely delivered. The emphasis of this paper is on the generation of XACML security policies from XRSD diagrams that allow for the enforcement of those policies at runtime, which changes to the policy able to be made so that there is no impact on the original XML schema and its existing instances. Our proposed security framework will be applied to the health care domain, specifically to the CCR schema, using a case study of a mobile health application, Personal Health Assistant (PHA), for general health management.

The remainder of this paper is organized as follows. In Sect. 2, we present related work on XML security and access control, focusing on the approaches of embedded security and general access control. Section 3 provides background information on NIST RBAC, XML and XACML, the CCR standard; and a review of the key facets of our XML security framework that are needed to explain XACML policy generation. In Sect. 4, we present the mapping process and rules that generate XACML policies process from the XRSDs of a given XML schema, including an algorithm. In Sect. 5, we demonstrate the XACML policy interplay and enforcement with PHA, describing

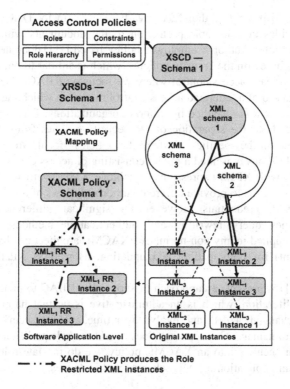

Fig. 1. Security framework for XML.

in detail the way that the patient and provider use them for information sharing and the achievement of enforcement. We finish the paper by offering concluding remarks and ongoing work in Sect. 6.

2   Related Work

The work of [5] presents an access control system that embeds the definition and enforcement of the security policies in the structure of the XML documents in DTDs in order to provide customizable security. This provides a level of generalization for documents that share the same DTD, similar to our work where security policies act against XML schemas to control XML instances. Two differences are: their work targets outdated XML DTD's while ours utilizes schemas, and their polices are embedded into both DTD and instance, requiring changes to instances when policies change; our work allows changes with no impact on instances.

Another effort [6] details a model that combines the embedding of policies and rewriting of access queries to provide security to XML datasets. The XML schema is extended with three security attributes: access, condition, and dirty. While this work is similar to our work by targeting security in XML instances via policies, it differs by requiring changes to instance when the policy is modified and does not consider XML document writing (see Sect. 5.3).

Efforts by [2, 3] present Author-X, a Java-based system for DAC in XML documents that provides customizable protection to the documents with positive and negative authorizations. Author-X employs a policy-based DTD document that prunes an XML instance based on the security policies, which is similar to our approach, but focuses on discretionary access control where we focus on RBAC. The work of [14] considers the scenario of a federated access control model, in which the data provider and policy enforcement are handled by different organizations. This approach relates to ours with regards to the separation of the security policies from the data to be handled, but differs in the specifics of where the policies' details are stored.

The work of [13] has presented a model consisting of access control policies over outmoded DTD's with XPath expressions to achieve XML security. Their model is similar to ours, as it aims to provide different authorized views of an XML document based on the user's credentials. However, the significant difference is that this approach combines query rewriting and authentication methods, whereas our approach can be applied to any non-normative XACML architecture (having a policy enforcement point) for both reading and updating, as well as XPath or XQuery queries.

The work of [15] presents an approach of supporting RBAC to handle the special case of role proliferation, which is an administrative issue that happens in RBAC when roles are changed, added, and evolve over time, making security of an organization difficult to manage. Our approach doesn't address role proliferation; however, by separating our security into an XACML policy, we do insulate role proliferation from impacting an application's XML schemas and instances.

3 Background

The NIST RBAC [12] standard has permissions assigned to roles which are assigned to users. NIST RBAC has four reference models. In $RBAC_0$, policies can be defined at the role level instead of the individual level. In $RBAC_1$, parent roles can pass down common privileges to children roles. In $RBAC_2$ the separations of duty (SoD) and cardinality constraints are provided, ensuring the role that grants permissions (authorization role) exists in a different entity to the other roles. The last reference model, $RBAC_3$, introduces the concept of sessions (lifetime of a user, role, permission and their association for a runtime setting).

XML facilitates information exchange across systems by providing a common structure to information that is hierarchically structured and tagged, where tags can be used to represent the semantics of the information. XML offers the ability to define standards via XML schemas, which serve as both the blueprint and validation agents for instances to comply and be used for information exchange purposes. The Continuity of Care Record (CCR) standard allows the creation of documents with patient information (demographics, social security number, insurance policy details, medications, procedures, etc.) and a common structure for uniform information exchange across institutions. The CCR schema contains elements for virtually all health information items, and is represented with extended granularity for better detail keeping. For example, Fig. 2 shows a subset of the official CCR schema

```
<xs:complexType name="StructuredProductType">
  <xs:complexContent>
    <xs:extension base="CCRCodedDataObjectType">
    <xs:sequence>
      <xs:element name="Product" maxOccurs="unbounded">
        <xs:complexType>
        <xs:sequence>
          <xs:element name="ProductName"
          type="CodedDescriptionType"/>
          <xs:element name="BrandName"
          type="CodedDescriptionType" minOccurs="0"/>
          <xs:element name="Strength" minOccurs="0"
          maxOccurs="unbounded">
          <xs:complexType>
          <xs:complexContent>
          <xs:extension base="MeasureType">
          <xs:sequence>
            <xs:element name="StrengthSequencePosition"
            type="xs:integer" minOccurs="0"/>
            <xs:element name="VariableStrengthModifier"
            type="CodedDescriptionType" minOccurs="0"/>
          </xs:sequence>
          </xs:extension>
          </xs:complexContent>
          </xs:complexType>
          </xs:element>
          <xs:element name="Concentration" minOccurs="0"
          maxOccurs="unbounded">
          <xs:complexType>
          <xs:complexContent>
```

Fig. 2. Segment of the CCR schema's StructuredProductType.

corresponding to the complexType element StructuredProductType, which is utilized to represent medications and their attributes. This StructuredProductType is used throughout this paper to explain the modeling and policy generation in an example health care scenario.

Our prior work has defined new UML security diagrams for supporting RBAC [16] via the UML meta-model. Using this as a basis, we have extended this work to define two new UML artifacts [8, 9]: the XML Schema Class Diagram (XSCD), which contains architecture, structure characteristics, and constraints of an XML schema; and the XML Role Slice Diagram (XRSD), which has the ability to add permissions to the various elements of the XSCD. Figure 3a shows the StructuredProductType complex type of the CCR schema modeled as an interconnection of UML classes. We represent each xs:complexType in the schema as a UML class with their respective UML stereotype. If an xs:element is a descendant of another schema concept, then this relation is represented as an equivalent class – subclass relation. This holds true for xs:sequence, xs:simpleType, etc. XML schema extensions (xs:extension) are represented as associations between classes. Data-type cardinality requirements (minOccurs, maxOccurs) and other XML constraints are represented with a «constraint» stereotype on the attribute. The xs:element type is represented with a «type» stereotype. Due to space limitations, we only show the Product xs:element and three main sub-elements: BrandName, ProductName, and Strength.

The next step is to apply security policies to the XSCD (top left of Fig. 1) by defining an XRSD that is capable of defining role-based access control policies or permissions on the attributes of the XSCD based on role, thereby achieving fine grained control. We note that permissions on XML documents are read, no read, write, and no write, represented in the XRSD as the respective stereotypes, «read/write», «read/nowrite», «noread/write», and «noread/nowrite». As an example, Fig. 3b defines Physician and Nurse XRSDs with permissions against the XSCD in Fig. 3a. Note that in Fig. 3b, the CCR complex type StructuredProductType element Product allows a role to have read and write permissions (Physician) or only read permissions (Nurse). While a Physician role can get all of the information regarding a drug and be able to create new instances following the schema, a Nurse role may be limited to read the drug details and cannot create new records.

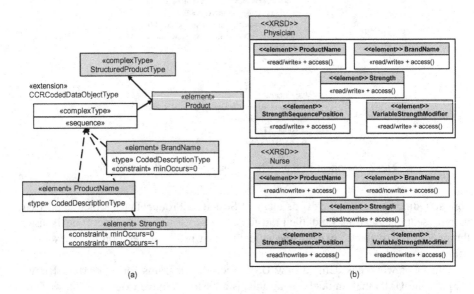

Fig. 3. XML Schema Class Diagram (a) and XML Role Slice Diagram (b).

4   Generating Policies from the XML Role Slice Diagram

In this section, we describe the generation of an XACML security policy (see Fig. 1 again) in order to allow XML instances to be customized and delivered to users based on role. As a result, security privileges defined at a schema level do not impact the XML instances of an application when privileges evolve, separating the security concern from the application data. By extracting the security policies targeting XML schemas and their instances into an external component of the framework, our approach avoids the high cost of updating XML schemas and instances when security policies change, in contrast to those approaches which embed the security policies as part of the XML schema and instance structure [5, 6].

To accomplish this, we present an approach to generating XACML security policies from the XRSD (see Fig. 3b). Towards this objective, Sect. 4.1 presents a process and architecture for the mapping of XRSDs that are used to generate a XACML policy for the schema based on the roles, using a portion of the CCR schema and its attributes; this achieves fine-grained control on CCR and results in an XACML policy that enforces the security as defined in XRSD against XSCD. Then, in Sect. 4.2, we present and explain an algorithm for this mapping process, which revolves around a set of equivalence rules between the XRSD and XACML structures; again, we use CCR as an example to illustrate the algorithm.

4.1 Mapping the XML Role Slice Diagram to the XACML Policy Construct

As given in Fig. 1, XRSDs (Fig. 3b) act as the blueprint of the role-based access-control policy for reading and writing permissions for a specific element or component of an XML schema for any given role, and represent the portions of the application's XML schemas that are to be allowed (or denied) access at an instance level. To map the XRSD into an XACML policy, we use XACML's language structure and processing model which consists of a PolicySet, a Policy, and a Rule. An XACML PolicySet is utilized to make the authorization decision via a set of rules in order to allow for access control decisions. A PolicySet can contain multiple Policy structures, and each Policy contains the access control rules. As a result, the Policy structure acts as the smallest entity that can be presented to the security system for evaluation. Based on our understanding of XACML and its usage, we are taking an approach that each XRSD must be mapped into a XACML Policy structure with its own set of rules that represent the appropriate enforcement for roles against a schema. Note that multiple XACML Policy structures may be generated, resulting in a PolicySet for a specific set of XML schemas that comprise a given application.

The collection of Policy structures is contained in a PolicySet, combined via an algorithm specified by the PolicySet's PolicyCombiningAlgId attribute that targets the particular XML schema. The XACML specification defines four standard combining algorithms: Deny-overrides (in which a policy is denied if at least one of the rules is denied); Permit-overrides (in which a policy is permitted if at least one of the rules is permitted); First-applicable (in which the result of the first rule's evaluation is treated as the result of all evaluations); and, Only-one-applicable (in which the combined result is the corresponding result to the acting rule). For our intent with XML instance security, and the way we map the XRSD into an XACML Policy, the combining algorithm of choice is Deny-overrides. With this algorithm, if a single Rule or Policy is evaluated to Deny, the evaluation result of the rest of the Rule elements under the policy is also Deny. While this might be the case when focusing on access control for XML instances in the document-level, as in our approach, other higher-level systems (e.g., software applications that utilize the XML instance, etc.) can very well deploy security policies with different combining algorithms.

In Fig. 5, we present the main sections of the mapped XACML policy for the Physician XRSD in Fig. 3b that is utilizing data as defined in the XSCD in Fig. 3a.

To create an XACML Policy structure per each XRSD, we present the following mapping equivalences and rules.

Policy and Rule Descriptors and Structure:

- Policy's PolicyId attribute value is the XRSD's Role value concatenated to AccessControlPolicy (e.g., the Physician role in Fig. 3b)
- Rule's RuleId attribute value is the XRSD's Role value concatenated to the XRSD's higher order element (e.g. in Fig. 3b it would be Product as defined in the XSCD in Fig. 3a), also concatenated to "ProductRule".
- Rule's Description value is the XRSD's Role concatenated to "Access Control Policy Rule".
- There are two XACML Rules under a higher level Target element, one for allowed and one for denied permissions.
- XACML Policy and Rules target and match the role (Subject, e.g., Physician in Figs. 3b and 4), the schema elements (Resources, e.g., ProductName, BrandName and Strength in Figs. 3a, b and 4), and the permissions (Actions, e.g., read and write in Figs. 3b and 4).

Rule Target's Subject (Fig. 4a):

- Only one XACML Subject and SubjectMatch per Rule.
- SubjectMatch's MatchId uses the function "string-equal" to evaluate the user's role as modeled in the XRSD.
- AttributeValue of the Subject is a string, and the value is the XRSD's Role (e.g., Physician in Figs. 3b and 4).
- SubjectAttributeDesignator's AttributeId is the role attribute.
- While more than one Rule per Policy might exist, the Subject is equal in both cases. This means that the role to be considered for policy evaluation is the same for operations that are allowed or denied.

Rule Target's Resources (Fig. 4b):

- One XACML Resource per permitted XRSD element.
- Each Resource's ResourceMatch has a MatchId that determines the usage of the function "string-equal".
- Resource's AttributeValue's is the XRSD's element names from the XSCD (e.g., ProductName, BrandName and Strength in Figs. 3a, b and 4).
- Resource's ResourceAttributeDesignator is an AttributeId that determines the target-namespace and datatype of the element.

Rule Target's Actions (Fig. 4c):

- One XACML Action per operation permitted exists (e.g., read and write in Figs. 3b and 4).
- ActionMatch's MatchId uses the function "string-equal".
- ActionAttributeDesignator's AttributeId value is action-write or action-read.

```
<Subjects>
  <Subject>
    <SubjectMatch MatchId="...:function:string-equal">
      <AttributeValue
        DataType="http://www.w3.org/2001/XMLSchema#string">
        Physician
      </AttributeValue>
      <SubjectAttributeDesignator AttributeId="...:attribute:role"
        DataType="http://www.w3.org/2001/XMLSchema#string"/>
    </SubjectMatch>
  </Subject>
</Subjects>
                                    (a)
```

```
<Resources>
  <Resource>
    <ResourceMatch MatchId="...:function:string-equal">
      <AttributeValue DataType=" XMLSchema#string">
        ccr:schema:product:productname
      </AttributeValue>
      <ResourceAttributeDesignator
        AttributeId="...:resource:target-namespace"
        DataType=" XMLSchema#string"/>
    </ResourceMatch>
  </Resource>
  <Resource>
    <ResourceMatch MatchId="...:function:string-equal">
      <AttributeValue DataType="XMLSchema#string">
        ccr:schema:product:brandname
      </AttributeValue>
      <ResourceAttributeDesignator
        AttributeId="...:resource:target-namespace"
        DataType=" XMLSchema#string"/>
    </ResourceMatch>
  </Resource>
  <Resource>
    <ResourceMatch MatchId="...:function:string-equal">
      <AttributeValue DataType=" XMLSchema#string">
        ccr:schema:product:strength
      </AttributeValue>
      <ResourceAttributeDesignator
        AttributeId="...:resource:target-namespace"
        DataType=" XMLSchema#string"/>
    </ResourceMatch>
  </Resource>
</Resources>
                         (b)
```

```
<Actions>
  <Action>
    <ActionMatch MatchId="...:function:string-equal">
      <AttributeValue DataType="XMLSchema#string">
        read
      </AttributeValue>
      <ActionAttributeDesignator
        AttributeId="...:action:action-read"
        DataType="XMLSchema#string"/>
    </ActionMatch>
  </Action>
  <Action>
    <ActionMatch MatchId="...:function:string-equal">
      <AttributeValue DataType="XMLSchema#string">
        write
      </AttributeValue>
      <ActionAttributeDesignator
        AttributeId="...:action:action-write"
        DataType="XMLSchema#string"/>
    </ActionMatch>
  </Action>
</Actions>
                                    (c)
```

Fig. 4. Mapped XACML Policy for the Physician role from the XRSD.

– ActionMatch's Attributevalue is the permission, read or write, depending on the stereotypes of the XRSD (e.g., read and write in Figs. 3b and 4).

Collectively, our approach presents three types of mappings: a *role mapping* (Fig. 4a) which maps a specific role (e.g., Physician) to a Policy's Subject; an *element mapping* (Fig. 4b), which maps an attribute (e.g., ProductName, Brand, Strength) to a Policy's Resource; and a *permission mapping* (Fig. 4c) which establishes permissions for the element (read and/or write) as Policy Actions. These mapping equivalences and rules permit each XACML Policy to capture the information modeled on the XRSD, while simultaneously limiting the amount of policies needed to only one per role. While each policy will have two high level Target elements, each with its own rules for those permissions that are allowed, the Effect of the Rule will be Permit, while those that are denied will have an Effect of Deny. Note that a special case is given to those roles where the permissions are all positive (a «read/write» stereotype in the XRSD) or all negative (a «noread/nowrite» stereotype in the XRSD). In these cases, only one higher-level Target element with one Rule is necessary, and the positivity or negativity of the stereotype determines the Effect of the rule (if «read/ write», then Permit, else if «noread/nowrite», then Deny).

4.2   Algorithm for the Mapping Process

The process of mapping the XRSDs to an XACML Policy can be automated, as shown by Fig. 5. The XRSD and schema to be secured serve as the parameters, while the XACML schema is used as template for the resulting instances. The first step of the algorithm determines whether or not all of the permission stereotypes in the XRSD are all positive or negative (either «read/write» or «noread/nowrite», respectively). If they are, then only one Target and Rule is needed to completely generate an equivalent Policy, and the algorithm proceeds down the left side branch. In this case, the algorithm proceeds through a series of steps. First, the template of the XACML Policy is created (based on the XACML schema) with one high-level target and rule. Depending on the permission stereotypes from the XRSD, the Policy Rule is set with an effect of Permit («read/write») or Deny («noread/nowrite»). Then, as shown in

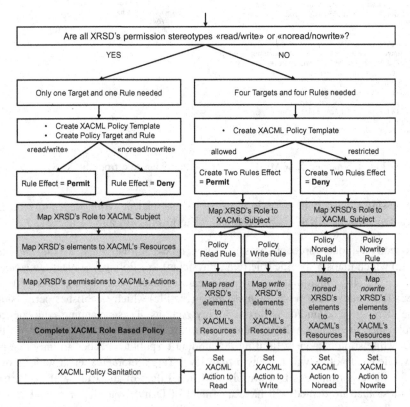

Fig. 5. Mapping from the XML Role Slice Diagram to the XACML Policy.

Fig. 4, a threefold mapping is performed between: the XRSD role and Rule's Subject; the XRSD elements and the Rule's Resources; and, the XRSD permission stereotypes and Rule's Actions; this finalizes the XACML Policy.

However, if not all permission stereotypes in the XRSD are all positive or negative, then the XACML Policy will require multiple high-level targets and rules, and the algorithm would proceed down the right side branch in Fig. 5. In this case, the first step is also creating the template XACML Policy, but with four high level Targets and Rules (two with the Effect of Permit, the others with the Effect of Deny). The fulfillment of these rules then depends on the permission stereotypes on each element. For those who have a positive permission (read or write), the elements are mapped as resources of the respective rule, and the permissions are mapped as actions. After the mapping process completes for each rule, the XACML Policy is finalized.

The enforcement process is straightforward. If a user has a role that has a no read permission (like the Nurse role), the policy enforcement point (PEP - or equivalent structure in the enforcing security architecture) filters the secured XML schema and the instance requested based on the permitted and allowed elements. For write operations, a similar enforcement takes place. These policies can also be applied to XSLT [4] or other query tools (e.g., XPath, XQuery, etc.) in order to provide filtered results to different role queries. This is an alternative to the traditional XML security approach of query rewrites, provided that the XSLT, XPath, and XQuery tools have a PEP that evaluates the XACML schema.

To summarize, Fig. 4 has the XACML policy created from the XRSD presented in Fig. 3b for the Physician role targeting the XML schema's Product element (note that because of space, not all equivalent XACML resources were included). The Physician role exhibits the special case of having all permissions allowed («read/write» on all elements). Because of this, only one Target with one Rule (with the Effect value of Permit) is needed. The Subject's AttributeValue is Physician (the role from the XRSD), and the resources are elements from the CCR schema (as also shown by the XRSD in Fig. 3b). Since the Physician role has both read and write permissions allowed for these elements, the two actions are part of the single Rule.

5   Policy Enforcement Process with Personal Health Assistant

In this section, we present the prototyping of the generated XACML policies on XML instances, transitioning from the mapping process is Sect. 4 to the enforcement process on the Personal Health Assistant (PHA) mobile application for health information management. In detail, in Sect. 5.1, we briefly review the general architecture for enforcement and its components (PHA, Microsoft HealthVault – MSHV - and our enforcement Middle-Layer Server). Section 5.2 presents the workflow utilized by the middle-layer server to enforce the permissions (read and write) set by the patient on the resulting XML instances.

5.1   General Architecture and Components

Personal Health Assistant (PHA) (Fig. 6) is a test-bed mobile application, developed in the University of Connecticut, for health information management that allows: patients to view and update their personal health record stored in their MSHV account and authorize medical providers to access certain portion of the protected health information (lower left); and, providers to obtain the permitted information from their respective patients (lower right). The patient version of PHA allows users to perform a set of actions regarding their health information (view and edit their medication list, allergies, etc.). Security settings can be set at a fine granular level, and using this information, policies are generated and stored in the patient's MSHV account (upper middle). The provider version of PHA allows the users (e.g., medical providers) to view and edit the medical information of their patients as long as they are permitted to do so as dictated by the security settings created by the patient.

   In the overall architecture in Fig. 6, MSHV acts as the main data source and stores data in a proprietary structure that can be exported as XML structures, which in turn can be converted into a CCR compliant instance. To recreate the non-normative XACML architecture, our Middle-Layer Server acts as the policy access, information,

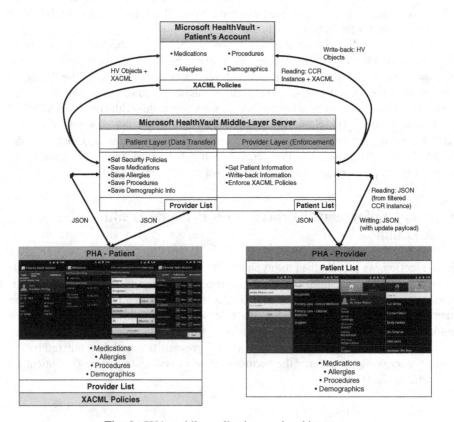

Fig. 6. PHA mobile applications and architecture.

decision, and enforcement points. To accomplish proper enforcement, we restrict all communication via our in-house developed Middle-Layer Server. With regards to data exchange, we have utilized JSON structures due to our familiarity and extensive experience with the format. Note that while we utilize JSON for transfers between PHA and the Middle-Layer Server, the security enforcement (done between the middle-layer server and MSHV) is performed on XML instances with XACML policies.

5.2   Enforcing XACML Policies on XML Instance and Segments

In this section, we describe the way that the XACML policy is enforced when handling reading and writing requests on XML instances whose schema has been secured when using the provider version of PHA. These two processes, though they utilize the same XACML policies to function, follow different workflows. We discuss the way that a medication object (StructuredProductType) from the CCR compliant instance from MSHV is secured (filtered) based on role and presented to the provider. We then explain the way that writing control is enforced with the same XACML policy.

The general process of securing the CCR instance for reading begins with a request from the provider version of PHA. When an initial request is made, the server retrieves the list of patients tied to the provider pertaining information. When a patient is selected, the server retrieves the corresponding XACML policy that targets the patient's information based on the requester's role. When a provider selects a category of health information (e.g., medications, procedures, etc.), the Middle-Layer Server, enforces the pertinent rules of the retrieved XACML policy. The process of this enforcement, as shown in Fig. 7a, involves the verification of the relevant rule (by evaluating the string representation of the users' role with the Subject role of the policy). After the relevant rule has been found (by utilizing the Resources' attributes), the reading permission is enforced by verifying it against the policy's Action elements.

If the action of the rule that is evaluated to Permit contains the read permission, then the CCR instance is not filtered. To support granular access control, recall from Sect. 4.2 that when stereotypes are not all-positive or all-negative (that is, there exists a combination of permissions over elements of the XML schema), more than one policy would match with respect to the role and resources. In this case, all policies will be evaluated and combined using the policy combination algorithm explained in Sect. 4.1. Once the CCR instance and segments have been filtered by the enforcement of the XACML policy, the resulting XML document is translated to JSON for the consumption of the provider version of the PHA application.

The process of securing the CCR schema for writing begins with a request from the provider's PHA. When a provider wants to update a patient's record (e.g., medication's StructuredProductType), the request is sent to the Middle-Layer Server tied to the update data as a JSON object, which verifies the target on which the rules of the requester's XACML Policy act upon. The server then evaluates the requester's role against the policy in order to determine if the write is allowed.

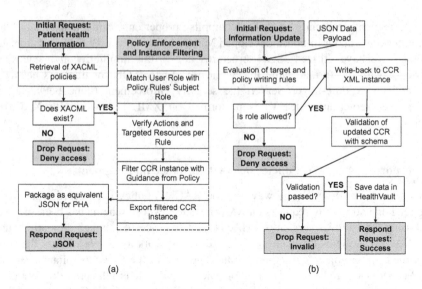

Fig. 7. Enforcing reading (a) and writing permissions (b) permissions in PHA.

The low-level enforcement of the XACML policy for writing permissions as given in Fig. 7b involves the same steps as when enforcing for reading (filtering) the document. If the user requesting an update operation has a role with a permission that allows it to occur (the write Action in the XACML Policy's Rule), the CCR instance is updated with the sent data, and validated with the CCR schema before the write-back to MSHV. If validation against the schema is successful, then the write-back occurs, and the update performed by the provider is saved in the patient's MSHV record. If the requester has a role that is not allowed to perform writing operations on the desired element, the request is dropped.

6 Conclusions and Ongoing Work

XML plays a pivotal role in the healthcare domain via the creation of standards such as CDA and CCR, which presents challenges in providing a robust security model for XML to ensure HIPAA compliance in the usage, transmission, and sharing of protected health information. To address this problem, our prior work [9] presented a security framework for XML that created UML-like artifacts for XML schemas and security, the XSCD and the XRSD. Using these as a basis, this paper has focused on the automatic generation of XACML policies from XRSDs (Sect. 4) that enforce the security defined on XML schemas against their corresponding instances. This allows the "same" instance to appear differently to specific users at a particular time. To demonstrate the feasibility and validity of our approach, Sect. 5 applied the generated XACML policies to the personal health assistant mobile application that allows patients to grant privileges to medical providers, and providers to view and update the data.

Our on-going work includes the extension of the work in this paper to support discretionary and mandatory access control, as well as applying our security framework to other platforms (e.g. Open *m*Health [11], etc.). These new approaches present many challenges; such as varied data representations (JSON, RDF, etc.), as well as the creation of more complex applications from the combination of different independent systems [7].

References

1. Baumer, D., Earp, J.B., Payton, F.C.: Privacy of medical records: IT implications of HIPAA. In: Tavani, H.T. (ed.) Ethics, Computing, and Genomics, pp. 137–152. Jones and Bartlett, Sudbury (2006)
2. Bertino, E., Carminati, B., Ferrari, E.: Access control for XML documents and data. Inf. Secur. Techn. Rep. **9**, 19–34 (2004)
3. Bertino, E., Ferrari, E.: Secure and selective dissemination of XML documents. ACM Trans. Inf. Syst. Secur. (TISSEC) **5**, 290–331 (2002)
4. Clark, J.: Xsl Transformations (Xslt). World Wide Web Consortium (W3C). http://www.w3.org/TR/xslt (1999)
5. Damiani, E., De Capitani di Vimercati, S., Paraboschi, S., et al.: Design and implementation of an access control processor for XML documents. Comput. Netw. **33**, 59–75 (2000)
6. Damiani, E., Fansi, M., Gabillon, A., et al.: A general approach to securely querying XML. Comput. Stan. Interfaces **30**, 379–389 (2008)
7. De la Rosa Algarín, A., Demurjian, S.A.: An approach to facilitate security assurance for information sharing and exchange in big data applications. In: Akhgar, B., Arabnia, H.R. (eds.) Accepted in Emerging Trends in Information and Communication Technologies Security. Elsevier, Amsterdam (2013)
8. De la Rosa Algarín, A., Demurjian, S.A., Ziminski, T.B., et al.: Securing XML with role-based access control: case study in health care. In: Ruiz Martínez, A., Pereñíguez García, F., Marín López, R. (eds.) Architectures and Protocols for Secure Information Technology, pp. 334–365. IGI Global, Hershey (2013)
9. De la Rosa Algarín, A., Demurjian, S. A., Berhe, S., et al.: A Security Framework for XML Schemas and Documents for Healthcare, pp. 782–789 (2012)
10. Dolin, R.H., Alschuler, L., Boyer, S., et al.: HL7 clinical document architecture, release 2. J. Am. Med. Inform. Assoc. **13**, 30–39 (2006)
11. Estrin, D., Sim, I.: Open mHealth architecture: an engine for health care innovation. Science **330**, 759–760 (2010). (Washington)
12. Ferraiolo, D.F., Sandhu, R., Gavrila, S., et al.: Proposed NIST standard for role-based access control. ACM Trans. Inf. Syst. Secur. (TISSEC) **4**, 224–274 (2001)
13. Kuper, G., Massacci, F., Rassadko, N.: Generalized XML security views. In: SACMAT 2005: Proceedings of the 10th ACM Symposium on Access Control Models and Technologies, pp. 77–84. ACM Press, New York (2005)
14. Leonardi, E., Bhowmick, S., Iwaihara, M.: Efficient database-driven evaluation of security clearance for federated access control of dynamic XML documents. In: Kitagawa, H., Ishikawa, Y., Li, Q., Watanabe, C. (eds.) DASFAA 2010. LNCS, vol. 5981, pp. 299–306. Springer, Heidelberg (2010)

15. Müldner, T., Leighton, G., Miziołek, J.K.: Parameterized role-based access control policies for XML documents. Inf. Secur. J. A Globa. Persp. **18**, 282–296 (2009)
16. Pavlich-Mariscal, J.A., Michel, L., Demurjian, S.A.: A formal enforcement framework for role-based access control using aspect-oriented programming. In: Briand, L.C., Williams, C. (eds.) MoDELS 2005. LNCS, vol. 3713, pp. 537–552. Springer, Heidelberg (2005)

Engineering Flexible Service-Oriented Transactions

David Paul[✉] and Frans Henskens

School of Electrical Engineering and Computer Science,
University of Newcastle, Callaghan, NSW 2308, Australia
{David.Paul,Frans.Henskens}@newcastle.edu.au

Abstract. The traditional ACID properties for transactions are not always appropriate in service-oriented environments. Instead, it is often preferable to "relax" the transactional guarantees, reducing isolation or atomicity to ensure acceptable performance at a reasonable cost. Existing standards require providers to constantly offer a fixed level of transaction support to each client that requests a particular service. We present a mechanism that allows providers to dynamically alter the level of transaction support offered on a per-service-call basis. Further, we engineer a cost-based model, based on $\pi t-$calculus, that allows clients to automatically reason about workflows consisting of service requests with various levels of transaction support. The viability of this scheme is tested with a Web Services transactions simulator, with results indicating potential benefits for both clients and service providers.

Keywords: Web Service · Transaction · Workflow

1 Introduction

In service-oriented environments, such as that offered by Web Services, clients use messages to send service requests to providers. The respective providers then respond either that the request was successful, or that the service was not performed. However, it is often the case that no single provider offers a service that completely satisfies a client's requirements. Instead, clients frequently have a need to combine multiple services, possibly from different providers, into a single workflow.

When combining multiple services into a single workflow, it is possible that some services will fail to complete successfully. However, since the client sees its workflow as a single task, the failure of one service may affect the rest of the workflow. For example, when booking a holiday, there is no point in booking a hotel in the destination city if the client is unable to book a flight to take them there.

One possible technique that can be used to ensure correct behaviour of client workflows is transactions. Transactions combine services provided by multiple, possibly completely unrelated, parties into a single action, with well-defined

© Springer-Verlag Berlin Heidelberg 2014
K.-H. Krempels and A. Stocker (Eds.): WEBIST 2013, LNBIP 189, pp. 37–52, 2014.
DOI: 10.1007/978-3-662-44300-2_3

behaviour whenever a part of the transaction fails. While traditional transactions offer strong guarantees of atomicity or isolation, the restraints these guarantees require are often considered unacceptable in service-oriented environments. Instead, weaker guarantees are often preferred [1,2].

However, different clients may have different views as to which transactional guarantees are important for a given service call. Further, since client workflows can include services from multiple unrelated providers, different levels of transaction support may need to be combined to ensure the client achieves an acceptable result. In this paper we describe a technique that allows providers to dynamically change the level of transaction support they offer for a particular service, and a means for clients to reason about such dynamic workflows. A simulator [3] is used to show the viability of this approach.

2   Motivating Example

Consider a public screen shared by multiple companies to display various pieces of information content. The screen provides a Web Service that allows clients to book time on the display. Further, consider a client that wishes to use the screen to inform the public of sporadically-changing data. The client is notified whenever new data are available, and can then use a Web Service to access the data. That data can be passed to a Web Service offered by a render farm to convert it into a visualisation suitable for the public screen. Each Web Service has a cost associated with its use.

On notification that new data are available, the client can retrieve the data, pass the data to the render farm, and display the visualisation at the time the client has the public screen booked. Since the data are updated sporadically, the client cannot book the display in advance, but can only attempt to do so when new data are released. However, since there is a fee associated with each Web Service, the client would prefer to only retrieve and render the data if it is guaranteed time on the display. Similarly, the client would not wish to retrieve the new data if ever the render farm was too busy to process the client's request.

The client can use service composition to achieve its aim of only retrieving data if the render farm is available, and only attempting either action if the screen can be booked, if each of the providers offers suitable levels of transaction support. However, different clients using the shared screen may not all have identical transactional requirements.

3   Service Composition Platforms

It is often the case that no single service in a service-oriented environment completely meets a client's needs. Thus it is often necessary for clients to combine multiple services, possibly from multiple providers, to complete the desired actions. Chakraborty and Joshi [4] identify five issues that must be provided by a comprehensive service composition platform so that such dynamic service compositions can be formed. Those requirements are:

Service Discovery. Before multiple services can be combined into a service composition, it is necessary to find a service or services that can perform the required tasks. Service discovery requires semantic information so the system can automatically determine which services (or combination of services) offer the functionality that is required by the client. This issue is beyond the scope of this paper, but efforts in the Semantic Web are making such discovery possible for Web Services.

Uniform Information Exchange Infrastructure. Different services may operate in different ways (e.g. taking different parameters, or returning information differently), but a service composition platform should abstract over these differences. With Web Services, it is possible to define an abstract service [5] that knows how to interact with each of the different services that offer similar functionality. This abstract service, when requested by a client, contacts actual providers, converting the client's request into the form that is understood by each particular provider, receiving any response(s), and returning them to the client in a uniform format.

Adaptiveness. To allow true adaptiveness, it must also be possible to dynamically compose services when necessary to provide required functionality [6]. One approach to implementing dynamic compositions is to have semantic contracts with each provider [7]. Then, by utilising a good service discovery mechanism, an abstract service that performs its own service composition could be created to provide the functionality required by the client.

Service Coordination and Management. To combine multiple services into a single composition, it is necessary to be able to communicate with each of the services in the composition to ensure their correct behaviour.

Fault Tolerance and Scalability. The system should correctly handle faults, and efficiently use the resources it has available.

Transactions allow multiple actions to be combined into a seemingly single action, can be arbitrarily nested, and each nested transaction can specify how it handles errors. Thus, it is possible to provide the service coordination and management and fault tolerance and scalability requirements of a good service composition platform by supporting transactions in the Web Services environment.

4   Web Services Transactions

Transactions typically provide the ACID properties of Atomicity, Consistency, Isolation, and Durability. However, in service-oriented environments, complete support for ACID properties is often undesirable. In these environments, transactions typically have a much longer execution time than is experienced in traditional transaction systems. The different services involved in a transaction may be offered by completely autonomous providers, and communication between these providers already increases the duration of any transaction. The independence of each provider means they will often be unwilling to reduce their autonomy to such an extent that complete ACID support is possible. Thus, certain reductions to the ACID properties are typically supported in service-oriented environments, such as replacing atomicity with semantic atomicity [1], or offering tentative holds [2].

Most Web Services transactions standards are limited in their ability to allow clients to combine services with different transactional guarantees into a single workflow [8]. Mikalsen et al. introduce a new way to ensure transactional reliability in the Web Services environment. Their technique allows providers to indicate the "transactional attitude" of the provider for each service it provides; that is, the kind of transactional support that the provider offers for the service. Clients also indicate their transactional attitude by utilising a Web Service to create and manage a pre-defined transactional pattern. Once providers and clients have specified their transactional attitudes, middleware is used to automatically manage the context and transactional interaction between a client and a set of providers.

With transactional attitudes, a provider must specify the level of transaction support it offers along with its service definition. This makes it impossible for the provider to alter the level of transaction support it offers for a particular service. In some cases, different clients may require different levels of transactional support for a particular service. Paul et al. [9,10] suggest a method that allows providers to dynamically alter the level of transaction support on offer for a particular service. In this paper, we further argue this point, and describe a formal model that allows arbitrarily complex client workflows to utilise such enhanced transactional properties.

5   Engineering Dynamic Transactions

When providers offer a service, there is a level of transactional support they offer along with that service. In the simplest case, there is no explicit transactional support offered; the service either completes successfully or fails. More advanced cases allow the provider to deliver information or guarantees to a client before the client utilises the service, or allow the client to perform the operation but later cancel it if required. This section discusses the levels of transactional support that a provider can offer.

On examining the possible reductions, it becomes apparent most can be described using a combination of five basic operations that can be requested by a client [3]:

Enquire. Allows the client to query whether a request would currently be successful, without any guarantee that a later request will succeed.

Prepare. Allows the client to query whether a request would currently be successful and, if so, guarantees that any such request sent by the client within a timeout period will succeed. On receipt of a successful reply, the client has the option to cancel the request, which relieves the provider of its responsibility to guarantee the resources to the client.

Commit. Performs the client's request. This is the only required operation for a service.

Compensate. Performs actions to undo a previously committed request, provided that the call to compensate is received within a timeout period.

Callback. Allows a provider to notify a client that has previously received a response from the provider, in the circumstance that the provider's situation has changed, that a revision of the provider's previous response is now available.

Using these five operations, a traditional ACID transaction can be described as a Prepare/Commit pattern with an infinite timeout for the Prepare stage. Similarly, semantic atomicity is provided by having the provider offer a Commit/Compensate pattern, and support for tentative holds is achieved through an Enquire/Callback/Commit pattern.

The concept of resilience [11] cannot be described using these operations. However, replacing concrete services with abstract services [5] can allow resilience in a way that is transparent to both clients and service providers. Clients use the abstract services rather than the services offered by the concrete providers, and the abstract service acts as a broker between all the providers offering alternative services. These abstract services can thus be used in transactions described by the operations defined above.

On becoming aware of the transactional pattern supported by a provider for a particular interaction, a client utilises the service by following through the states depicted in Fig. 1. The interaction begins in the *Initial* state, and a change in state occurs when the client sends a message to the provider, or the provider sends a message to the client. Before entering this state, the client receives a contract from the provider indicating the level of transaction support that will be supplied for the requested service (see Sect. 5.1).

From the *Initial* state, the client can choose to *accept* or *reject* the contract. If the client rejects the contract, then the interaction transitions to the *Failed* state. Otherwise the interaction moves into the *Active* state. From the *Active* state, either party can *cancel* the interaction, moving it to the *Failed* state. Other options from the *Active* state allow the client to request either *enquire*, *prepare*, or *commit* operations.

In the case that an *enquire* request is sent, the provider may reply that the request was successful (indicating that the provider can currently successfully complete the activity), which moves the interaction to the *EnquirySuccessful* state. If, on the other hand, the provider replies that the enquiry is unsuccessful (indicating that the provider cannot currently complete the required activity successfully), the interaction moves to the *EnquiryFailed* state. From either of these states, the client can initiate a new enquiry, though any enquiry callbacks remove the need as they transition the client between the *EnquiryFailed* and *EnquirySuccessful* states without requiring a new request. Similarly to behaviour in the *Active* state, either party can *cancel* the interaction from the *EnquiryFailed* and *EnquirySuccessful* states, or the client can request the *prepare* and *commit* operations.

When a *prepare* request is sent, the provider can either send a *cannotComplete* reply to indicate that the prepare has not occurred, or a *prepared* message

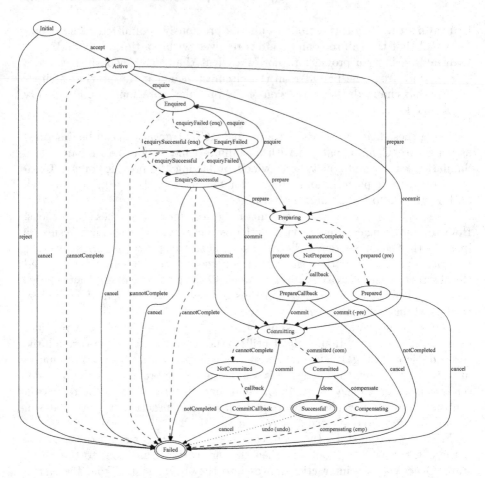

Fig. 1. State transition diagram for a client's processing of an activity. Solid lines represent messages sent by the client. Dashed lines represent messages sent by the service provider. Dotted lines indicate client-side only transitions. Values in parentheses represent the associated cost to the client.

to indicate that the prepare has been performed successfully. On receipt of a *cannotComplete* message, the client can either acknowledge the failure, moving to the *Failed* state, or, if applicable, wait for a call back from the provider and then send another *prepare* request. If the prepare is completed successfully, the client can choose to either *cancel* the activity, or request to *commit*.

After a request to *commit*, the provider can either perform the requested service successfully, or indicate that it cannot be completed at the current time. If the *commit* request was sent from the *Prepared* state then the second option should not be possible, as the *prepare* operation guarantees that a later call to *commit* will succeed. On receipt of a *committed* message, the interaction moves to the *Committed* state. With compensation support, the client can choose to either *close* the interaction, moving it to the *Successful* state, or *compensate* the activity, moving to the *Failed* state. If the provider indicated that it could not complete the commit operation, the interaction moves to the *Failed* state unless the provider sends a callback to the client to indicate that the commit operation would now succeed.

Finally, from the *Successful* state, the client may choose to take some action to undo the operation performed by the provider, without the provider's knowledge. In this case, the provider would believe that the interaction completed successfully, while the client would see it as a failure. This allows the client to compensate the action performed by the provider even when the provider does not support compensation. For example, if the client is requesting an item from the provider that has already shipped to the client, the client could immediately dispose of the item to effectively have it appear as though the operation failed.

5.1 Provider Contracts

When a provider receives a request from a client, it must decide on the level of transactional support it wishes to provide to the client. The provider may be willing to support more than one possible level of transaction support, but at this stage will not know which level would be preferable for any particular client.

Once the provider has decided on the level of transaction support it is willing to provide, it must notify the client of the decision. This can be achieved by having the client first request the level of transactional support that the provider is willing to offer for a given service request [10]. The provider must then inform the client of any transactional interaction patterns it is willing to provide for that service request, by sending contract offers describing the level(s) of support the provider is willing to support. The client must then agree to one of these contracts before the service request can be handled in the required transactional manner. If the client does not agree with the initial patterns offered by the provider, it may wish to renegotiate with the provider until both sides have found a level of transactional support they are willing to accept [10]. Once the client has accepted one of the offers from the provider, the interaction continues following the pattern specified in the agreed-upon contract.

5.2 Combining Contracts

Once the client begins accepting agreements from various service providers, it must choose how to proceed. The client can achieve this by prioritising those yet-to-be-completed activities in its workflow, and determining whether the risk of performing the next stage of the first activity in the prioritised list is acceptable. If the risk is acceptable, then the client performs the next stage of the first activity.

When the client deems the risk of performing the next stage of the first activity to be too great, behaviour depends on the activity being performed. If the client thinks it likely that waiting will reduce the risk, the client may choose to wait. Otherwise, if there is an alternate activity that can replace the current activity, the client may choose to cancel the current activity and replace it with the alternative. If the risky activity is optional for the success of the workflow, then the client may choose to cancel the activity. If, however, the activity is necessary and none of the previous options are available, the client must cancel its workflow.

In order to allow a client to calculate risk, it is assumed that the client has knowledge of a price for each action it performs. This could be prescribed by a provider, for example as part of the contract, by specifying a particular price for each of the five supported basic transaction operations (enquire, prepare, commit, compensate, callback) [10].

To allow the client to make decisions based on these costs, it is assumed the client has a maximum budget it is willing to spend to have its workflow complete successfully, and a maximum budget it does not want to exceed should the workflow fail. It is possible that a cost to the client could be multidimensional. For example, if a client orders a physical item from a provider, it will have to pay the provider as well as have storage space for the item. The model presented here assumes a single-dimensional cost, though this could be extended to more dimensions by specifying a cost for each action in each dimension.

A contract identifying the level of transaction support that a provider will offer to a client for a particular service call, and the cost for this support, can be defined as a tuple $(enq, ecb, eth, pre, pcb, com, ccb, cmp)$, where:

$enq \in \mathbb{R}$ is the cost of an enquiry operation.

$ecb \in \{0, 1\}$ specifies whether the provider may call back after an unsuccessful enquire operation if the enquiry would now be successful.

$eth \in \{0, 1\}$ specifies whether the provider may call back if a tentative hold on an item is revoked.

$pre \in \mathbb{R}$ is the cost of a successful prepare operation.

$pcb \in \{0, 1\}$ specifies whether the provider may call back after an unsuccessful prepare request if the prepare would now be successful.

$com \in \mathbb{R}$ is the cost of a successful commit operation.

$ccb \in \{0, 1\}$ specifies whether the provider may call back after an unsuccessful commit request if the commit would now be successful.

$cmp \in \mathbb{R}$ is the cost of a successful compensate operation.

To support the client's undoing of a successfully completed interaction without the provider's knowledge, it is also necessary for the client to specify a cost $undo \in \mathbb{R}$ to indicate the cost to compensate a completed interaction on the client's side. For each cost, a value of ∞ indicates that the associated operation is not supported by the interaction. It is also possible to use a contract to specify time out behaviour for an interaction. However such details are beyond the scope of this paper, in which it is assumed that time outs never occur.

Figure 1 indicates which transitions trigger a cost to the client. Using this information, a client can determine the minimal cost required for an interaction to complete in the *Successful* state, and the maximum cost required to move the interaction into the *Failed* state. Table 1 displays the *success* and *fail* costs for each state.

Table 1. Costs required for a client to guarantee the completion of an interaction. *success* defines the minimal cost required to transition to the *Successful* state, and *fail* defines the maximum cost necessary to transition to the *Failed* state.

State	*success*	*fail*
Initial	*com*	0
Active	*com*	0
Enquired	*enq* + *com*	*enq*
EnquiryFailed	*com*	0
EnquirySuccessful	*com*	0
Preparing	*com*	max $\{0, pre\}$
NotPrepared	*com*	0
PrepareCallback	*com*	0
Prepared	−*pre* + *com*	0
Committing	*com*	max $\{com + \min\{undo, cmp\}, 0\}$
NotCommitted	*com*	0
CommitCallback	*com*	0
Committed	0	min $\{undo, cmp\}$
Compensating	∞	*cmp*
Successful	0	*undo*
Failed	∞	0

Client workflows typically combine multiple interactions with multiple providers. Using a system inspired by πt-calculus [12], we describe a workflow W as:

$$
\begin{aligned}
W \triangleq \quad & done && \text{(success)} \\
\mid \quad & abort && \text{(failure)} \\
\mid \quad & W \mid W && \text{(parallel)} \\
\mid \quad & W; W && \text{(sequence)} \\
\mid \quad & W, W && \text{(alternative)} \\
\mid \quad & (p)(s, c, u) && \text{(client interaction)}
\end{aligned}
$$

where *done* and *abort* are activities that respectively indicate the successful or unsuccessful completion of a workflow. The parallel operation $W \mid W$ executes two workflows in parallel, with no guarantee as to which will complete first. In contrast, the sequence operator $W; W$ guarantees that the workflow on the right will only succeed if the workflow on the left succeeds first. The alternative operator W, W means that the workflow succeeds if either the workflow on the left succeeds and the one on the right fails, or, given the first workflow's failure, the second workflow succeeds (i.e. only one of the two ever succeeds).

The final operation is a client interaction, $(p)(s, c, u)$. p is a unique identifier for a client's interaction with a provider; s is the current state of the interaction, which can be any of the states in Fig. 1; c is a contract as defined above; and u

$$success((p)(s,c,u)) = success(s) \qquad\qquad fail((p)(s,c,u)) = fail(s)$$
$$success(done) = 0 \qquad\qquad\qquad fail(done) = \infty$$
$$success(abort) = \infty \qquad\qquad\qquad fail(abort) = 0$$
$$success(V|W) = success(V) + success(W) \qquad fail(V|W) = fail(V) + fail(W)$$
$$success(V;W) = success(V) + success(W) \qquad fail(V;W) = fail(V) + fail(W)$$
$$success(V,W) = \min\{success(V) + fail(W), \qquad fail(V,W) = fail(V) + fail(W)$$
$$fail(V) + success(W)\}$$

Fig. 2. The minimal success and maximal failure cost of a workflow.

is the undo cost to the client to move the interaction from the *Successful* state to the *Failed* state.

Given the above definition, and workflows V, W, X, the following structural congruences hold:

$$V|W \equiv W|V \qquad\qquad V,(W,X) \equiv (V,W),X$$
$$V|(W|X) \equiv (V|W)|X \qquad\qquad V;(W;X) \equiv (V;W);X$$
$$done|W \equiv W \qquad\qquad done;W \equiv W$$
$$abort|abort \equiv abort \qquad\qquad abort;abort \equiv abort$$
$$abort,W \equiv W \qquad\qquad W,abort \equiv W$$

Seven of these congruences are directly analogous to those in $\pi t-$calculus [12]. The remaining three specify that $\_,\_$ is associative and that *abort* is an identity to the operation.

Using this definition of workflows, it is possible to calculate the minimal success cost, *success*, and maximal failure cost, *fail* of a workflow as specified in Fig. 2.

The success or failure cost of an interaction with a particular provider is the success or failure cost of the interaction as defined in Table 1. *done* represents the successful completion of a workflow interaction, and thus has a success cost of 0 and a failure cost of ∞ (as it is not undoable). Similarly, *abort* represents a failure of the workflow, so its failure cost is 0 and its success cost is ∞. Both the success and failure costs of workflows performed in parallel $(V|W)$ or in sequence $(V;W)$ are simply the sums of associated costs of each component included in the workflow. Alternatives such as (V,W) are successful whenever exactly one of the alternatives succeeds, making the minimum success cost the minimum cost required to have one of the alternatives fail and the other succeed. The failure cost of alternatives is the sum of the failure cost of each component, as both must fail for the alternatives to fail.

By combining the client's success and fail budgets with the costs calculated by the above *success* and *fail* functions, a client is able to determine whether its workflow can succeed. Each workflow begins with the client having not accepted any of the provider-offered contracts and, since the *fail* cost of an interaction from the *Initial* state is always 0, it is guaranteed that the client can initially cancel the workflow without exceeding its failure budget. The client then chooses the next action to perform by ensuring that the action will not cause the cost of the workflow to exceed the client's success or failure budgets.

For a single client interaction, the set of possible next steps is specified by the transitions in Fig. 1 (with some transitions being removed if the contract does not support them. For example, if $pcb = 0$ then the transition from *NotPrepared* to *PrepareCallback* is removed). The next step progresses the workflow by changing the state of the interaction, while keeping the contract and *undo* cost constant. If the next step requires a provider-generated message, the client's action is to wait for that message to arrive. When a number of client interactions are combined in a workflow, the possible next steps are the union of the possible next steps for each interaction in the workflow.

The client begins by considering all of the possible actions that can be performed from its current state. Each of these actions has a possible cost (as displayed in Fig. 1) and moves one of the client interactions in the workflow to a new state. If the cost of a potential action, plus the *success* or *fail* cost of the resultant workflow, exceeds the success or failure budget (respectively), that action is removed from the set of possible actions. In this way, the client creates a set of possible actions it can perform, given the current state of its workflow, which will not exceed the client's budgets.

The aim of the client is firstly to complete the workflow successfully, by reducing it to *done*. If that becomes impossible then the aim shifts to completing the transaction by reducing it to *abort*. The client thus chooses an action, from its set of possible actions, to bring it closer to one of these outcomes. Once an action has been performed, the client uses structural congruences to simplify the workflow as much as possible. The client also uses the following reduction rules:

- Any client interaction that is in the *Failed* state is replaced with *abort*.
- Any workflow that has no alternatives, and all client interactions in the *Successful* state, is replaced with *done*.

The first rule indicates that a failed interaction is equivalent to *abort*, since they are both failures. The second rule ensures that any sequence or set of workflows running in parallel succeeds if each client interaction in the workflow succeeds. Further, since the structural congruence rules only remove an alternative if it is *abort*, the restriction on alternatives ensures that, for each set of alternatives, exactly one alternative succeeds.

By following this strategy, the client is assured that it will only ever perform an action that will not exceed its budgets. However, the client can still optimise the strategy for its own purposes. Once the client has determined the set of possible actions for its current state, the client can choose which action to perform based on other criteria. For example, the client may choose the next action that minimises either the *success* or *fail* cost of the workflow. Regardless of how the action is chosen, the client performs the action, which moves the workflow to a new state. The client then repeats the process for the new workflow state, until the workflow is complete.

Note that, while this work borrows from the algebraic laws of πt−calculus [12], this system augments these laws with client reasoning about the individual inter- actions included in its combined workflow. Thus the presented system is not a process calculus, but instead a tool to allow client reasoning. In particular, a client only requires a model of its own workflow and a knowledge of the required trans- actional behaviour of the providers it is using to allow its reasoning, whereas most process calculi require a complete description of not only all service providers that may be used by the client, but also of any other clients that may utilise those provider's services while the first client's workflow is still processing [13]. By thus reducing the complexity of the model, it is possible for a client to guarantee its correct behaviour, rather than having the system grow to a size that such analy- sis become intractable (as in [14]).

6   Simulation

Web Services transactions have been shown to be very different from traditional transactions. Multiple parties work together to achieve a client's aims, but still wish to remain autonomous. Further, the different service providers may have different levels of transactional support, making verification and testing of dif- ferent transaction schemes very complex. While theoretical analysis is essential to ensure that transaction schemes work correctly, these models (e.g. [14,15]) do not easily allow comparison between different transaction techniques. In partic- ular, these models make it difficult to determine which transaction schemes are best suited for certain conditions, applications, or environments.

Instead, simulation can be used to provide an indication of practical results. In simulation, some or all of a system is abstracted so that only the features important to the current investigation are tested. When simulating Web Ser- vices transactions, details such as the networking topology, the timing of events, and the actual services being used can be abstracted. This can allow intricate comparison of various transaction strategies, by allowing the parameters of inter- est to be studied while ensuring that all other factors are kept constant.

Most available Web Services simulation environments replace a Web Service with a simple, usually local, program that sends and responds to messages in a way that is appropriate to the service being simulated [3]. However, when examining Web Services transactions, further abstraction can occur [3]. Messages are not required to be sent in the exact same format as with real services; it is only the transaction interaction patterns that need to be simulated. A simulator, based on the model introduced in Sect. 6, that models transaction flow rather than message flow, has been described previously [3,10].

The simulator accepts a description of the scenario to process, which includes details of the providers and clients to simulate. Provider information describes the number of resources available from each provider, cost information for accessing those resources, and the availability of abstract providers that provide resilience for the simulation. Client definitions contain a description of a workflow, which consists of a sequence of activities to be performed, and specifies whether success- ful completion of each activity is required, or if the workflow is successful when at least one of the included activities succeeds. An activity can either be a work-flow or a service call. Finally, the scenario description contains timing information to specify the length of time that messages take to be sent between the different participants in the system being modelled.

The simulator also accepts various parameters to specify the level of trans-action support offered by the various service providers, and the risk-taking behaviour of the clients. These parameters can be changed independently of the scenario description, and any changes to results can be directly attributed to these changed values. The level of transaction support offered by providers is specified based on the five operations described in Sect. 5 and, when combined with abstract services, this allows providers to utilise all of the reductions to the standard ACID properties. Client risk-taking behaviour is specified using budgets, as described in Sect. 5.2.

The simulator models the passing of messages between the various partici-pants in the simulated scenario. Each provider tracks the state of its resources to ensure the provider can support any transactional contract it offers to a client. Clients similarly monitor their interactions with providers to track the progress through their workflows, and to determine the next action the client should take. By tracking all messages sent through the simulator it is possible to extract details such as whether a particular client's workflow succeeded or failed, and the cost for that outcome, or the number of a provider's resources that were utilised, and the amount it was paid.

Thus, by defining appropriate scenarios, it is possible to use the simulator to measure the way different transactional support from providers, or different risk-taking behaviour of clients, affects the outcome of the simulation. The following section will describe a scenario, based on the preceding motivating example, to demonstrate the effects of using a dynamic transaction scheme rather than a scheme in which the transaction support offered by each provider remains fixed.

7   Results

The Web Services transactions simulator described in Sect. 6 was used to validate the dynamic transaction model introduced in Sect. 5. The validation experiment was based on the motivating example described in Sect. 2.

According to the scenario, the display system offered either 100 or 1000 time units for clients to book. A total of 500 clients, each requiring between 1 and 5 time units, were included in the simulation. Each client had a success budget that allowed for successful completion of both the display booking and the other required services. 100 of the clients were given a fail budget of 0, meaning that they would only perform an action that required payment if success was guaranteed. The remaining clients had a budget that allowed either the booking of the display to fail while the other actions succeeded, or for the other actions to succeed and the booking of the display to fail. The other services were modelled as a service that was successful 80 % of the time, with no special transaction support, giving a sufficient error rate to allow comparison of different transactional support levels.

Three different levels of transactional support offered by the display booking service were simulated. The first level provided semantic atomicity, allowing clients to book a time unit and then later cancel that booking without charge. The second level offered tentative holds. When granted a tentative hold, 50 % of the clients immediately converted that tentative hold into a booking, and then attempted the other services. The remaining 50 % retained the hold and attempted the other services, only confirming the booking if the other services completed successfully. The final level of transaction support was a variable scheme which offered semantic atomicity until 50 % of the time units had been booked, and then offered tentative holds instead. This final level was only possible with dynamic transaction support.

Assuming the data service is *data*, the rendering service *render*, and the visualisation service *display*, and each has a cost per service call of 1, the system can be modelled as follows. Each client has a success budget of 4, a fail budget of 0 or 2 (as specified above), and the following workflow:

$$(data)(\text{Initial}, c_1, \infty); ((render)(\text{Initial}, c_2, \infty) | (display)(\text{Initial}, c_3, \infty))$$

where c_1, the contract for the data service, is $(\infty, 0, 0, \infty, 0, 1, 0, \infty)$, c_2, the contract for the render service is similarly $(\infty, 0, 0, \infty, 0, 1, 0, \infty)$, and c_3, the contract for the display service, is $(\infty, 0, 0, 0, 0, 2, 0, \infty)$ if semantic atomicity is offered, or $(0, 0, 0, \infty, 0, 2, 0, \infty)$ if tentative hold is offered.

The results for these simulations can be seen in Table 2. The first column indicates the level of transaction support that was offered by the display-booking service. The "Offered" and "Booked" columns give, respectively: the number of time units that the provider offered to clients; and the number of time units that were actually booked. The "Succeeded", "Failed", and "Penalised" columns indicate, respectively: the number of client workflows that completed successfully; the number of client workflows that failed with neither the display booking nor the other services requiring payment; and the number of client workflows that failed with either the display booking service or the other services completing successfully (and thus requiring payment). The "Reserved Time" column indicates the total length of time during which the provider held resources for a client that later cancelled its request (i.e. the time resources were withheld from other clients, ultimately unnecessarily).

Table 2. Results of simulation based on motivating example.

Transactionality	Offered	Booked	Succeeded	Failed	Penalised	Reserved Time
Semantic atomicity	100	100	42	458	0	119
Tentative hold	100	100	48	420	32	0
Variable	100	100	44	444	12	76
Semantic atomicity	1000	963	393	107	0	1350
Tentative hold	1000	805	330	130	40	0
Variable	1000	914	367	112	21	588

When only 100 time units were offered, each time unit was booked by a client. This is unsurprising, as the large number of clients compared to the available resources meant that each time unit was highly contended. In contrast, when 1000 time units were offered, more time units were booked when semantic atomicity was offered. This is because the clients with a 0 fail budget would only attempt their workflow if such a level of transactional support was offered. However, as can be seen from the "Reserved Time" column, semantic atomicity places a higher burden on the service provider, as the provider must ensure that a completed action can be undone until the client determines whether or not it will compensate the booking, whereas tentative holds have no such restrictions. Using the variable scheme, the provider obtained results that were a compromise between only offering tentative holds and only offering semantic atomicity.

From the point of view of clients, the benefits of better transactional support can be seen in the "Penalised" column of Table 2. Tentative holds give no future guarantee about the state of resources, so a client may commit one part of its workflow, but have the tentative hold expire before completing the booking. In contrast, when semantic atomicity is offered, the client can perform the action before attempting the rest of its workflow. If any part of the workflow later fails, the performed action can be compensated to allow completion without penalty. Thus, no clients failed with a penalty when the display provider offered semantic atomicity, though, as can be seen by the "Reserved Time" column, transactions did take longer to be processed. The use of the variable scheme reduced the number of clients that were forced to pay for an incomplete workflow compared to when only tentative holds were used, and the average transaction length was shorter than when only semantic atomicity was offered.

8 Conclusions

Service-oriented environments have different transactional requirements to traditional transaction systems. Reductions to the ACID properties are often used to help retain autonomy for service providers while still offering an acceptable level of service for clients. In some cases, it is desirable to dynamically alter the level of transaction support offered for a particular service as the provider's environment changes, but the level of transaction support is typically specified along with the definition of the service.

This paper describes a technique whereby providers offer transactional contracts to clients on a per-service-call basis. Once a provider and client agree upon a level of transaction support, the client can include that service call in its workflow. A formal model, inspired by πt-calculus, was presented to allow automated reasoning about arbitrarily complex client workflows. This model allows a client to ensure its workflow has an acceptable outcome.

A Web Services transactions simulator was developed to allow the investigation of different transactional strategies. By varying the offered level of transaction support, the provider was able to better balance the strength of the transactional guarantees it supported and the number of clients that completed successfully, offering benefits to both clients and service providers.

References

1. Garcia-Molina, H.: Using semantic knowledge for transaction processing in a distributed database. ACM Trans. Database Syst. **8**, 186–213 (1983)
2. Fauvet, M.-C., Duarte, H., Dumas, M., Benatallah, B.: Handling transactional properties in web service composition. In: Ngu, A.H.H., Kitsuregawa, M., Neuhold, E.J., Chung, J.-Y., Sheng, Q.Z. (eds.) WISE 2005. LNCS, vol. 3806, pp. 273–289. Springer, Heidelberg (2005)
3. Paul, D., Henskens, F. A., Hannaford, M.: Simulating web services transactions. In: Special Session on Web Services Principles and Applications (WSPA 2011) at the 7th International Conference on Web Information Systems and Technologies (WEBIST-2011), Noordwijkerhout, The Netherlands (2011)
4. Chakraborty, D., Joshi, A.: Dynamic service composition: State-of-the-art and research directions. Technical report, University of Maryland (2001)
5. Schäfer, M., Dolog, P., Nejdl, W.: Engineering compensations in web service environment. In: Baresi, L., Fraternali, P., Houben, G.-J. (eds.) ICWE 2007. LNCS, vol. 4607, pp. 32–46. Springer, Heidelberg (2007)
6. Milanovic, N., Stantchev, V., Richling, J., Malek, M.: Towards adaptive and composable services. In: International Conference on Internet, Processing, Systems, Interdisciplinaries (IPSI2003) (2003)
7. Milanovic, N.: Contract-based web service composition. Ph.D. thesis, Humboldt-Universität zu Berlin (2006)
8. Mikalsen, T., Tai, S., Rouvellou, I.: Transactional attitudes: reliable composition of autonomous web services. In: Workshop on Dependable Middleware-based Systems (WDMS'02) at the Dependable Systems and Network Conference (DSN'02), Bethesda, MD, USA (2002)
9. Paul, D., Henskens, F.A., Hannaford, M.: Per-request contracts for web services transactions. In: 6th International Conference on Web Information Systems and Technologies (WEBIST-2010), Valencia, Spain, INSTICC (2010)
10. Paul, D.: Deliberate cooperation in service-oriented environments: dynamic transactional workflows for web services. Ph.D. thesis, University of Newcastle (2012). http://hdl.handle.net/1959.13/932268
11. Younas, M., Eagelstone, B., Holton, R.: A formal treatment of a SACReD protocol for multidatabase web transactions. In: Ibrahim, M., Küng, J., Revell, N. (eds.) DEXA 2000. LNCS, vol. 1873, pp. 899–908. Springer, Heidelberg (2000)
12. Bocchi, L., Laneve, C., Zavattaro, G.: A calculus for long-running transactions. In: Najm, E., Nestmann, U., Stevens, P. (eds.) FMOODS 2003. LNCS, vol. 2884, pp. 124–138. Springer, Heidelberg (2003)
13. Laneve, C., Zavattaro, G.: Foundations of web transactions. In: Sassone, V. (ed.) FOSSACS 2005. LNCS, vol. 3441, pp. 282–298. Springer, Heidelberg (2005)
14. Fantechi, A., Gnesi, S., Lapadula, A., Mazzanti, F., Pugliese, R., Tiezzi, F.: A logical verification methodology for service-oriented computing. Technical report, Universita' degli Studi di Firenze (2009)
15. Casado, R., Tuya, J., Younas, M.: A framework to test advanced web services transactions. In: IEEE 4th International Conference on Software Testing, Verification and Validation (ICST'11), Berlin, Germany (2011)

HTML5 Agents: Mobile Agents for the Web

Kari Systä[✉], Tommi Mikkonen, and Laura Järvenpää

Department of Pervasive Computing, Tampere University of Technology,
P.O. Box 553 33101 Tampere, Finland
{kari.systa, tommi.mikkonen}@tut.fi,
laura.jarvenpaa@gmail.com

Abstract. We argue that the modern Web infrastructure with HTML5 as such can be an agent platform and mobile agents could be developed in similar way as Web applications. For us the agents can also be end-user applications that the user can send to a server so that the state is preserved and the execution can continue. The user can later fetch the agent to the same client device or to another device. In addition to the mobile agent use cases, the concept also allows users to continue their work later on another device or even allows other users to continue execution in their own devices. The paper presents the overall concept and architecture of HTML5 agents, a number of use cases, the proof-of-concept implementation, and a list of example applications.

Keywords: HTML5 · Mobile agents · Web applications

1 Introduction

HTML5, the latest version of standards in the HTML family, extends the applicability of the technology towards client-side applications. Traditionally, Web applications have more or less been acting as user interfaces for applications running in a server, but the goal of HTML5 is to allow the development of complete client-side applications. Consequently the emergence of HTML5 allows more applications to be run in browser, and these applications can be deployed over network by using the standard Web technologies. Moreover, although most of these applications are often network connected, they can also run in off-line mode and especially after deployment they are not necessarily dependent on any server. For us the overall goal of HTML5 to support rich applications is important, and in this paper we do not refer to any specific new technology introduced by HTML5.

The capabilities of HTML5 described above, together with other recent developments, such as increasing pervasiveness of the Web and improving performance of JavaScript virtual machines inside browsers, enable the introduction of Web-based application platforms and operating systems – something that can be called Web operating systems. In these systems applications can be stored in a cache so that downloading is not necessary at the subsequent invocations of the application. For the user this means that the applications do not differ from using traditional installed applications. Examples of such systems include Cloudberry [1], Google Chromium OS [2] and Firefox OS of Mozilla [3]. Of these systems, Chromium OS is almost a generic

© Springer-Verlag Berlin Heidelberg 2014
K.-H. Krempels and A. Stocker (Eds.): WEBIST 2013, LNBIP 189, pp. 53–67, 2014.
DOI: 10.1007/978-3-662-44300-2_4

operating system for web-enabled devices, whereas Firefox OS and Cloudberry are systems where all user-visible functionality of a smart phone is implemented as HTML5 applications. The listed systems also prove the above claim that HTML5 technology can be used to build complete and advanced applications which in many ways are indistinguishable from traditional, installable binary applications.

From the technological perspective, however, Web operating systems differ from traditional application platforms, because they build on principles of the Web instead of more traditional concepts associated with operating systems and binary applications. Although applications are often cached, they are not necessarily explicitly "installed" and updates can be delivered automatically and without bothering the end user.

The development of Web operating systems and especially Cloudberry [1] have inspired an idea of Cloud browser [4]. In Cloud browser the browser session – in essence a set of active "pages" and HTML5 applications, both of which are identified by associated URLs – constitutes the user session. This user session – the URLs of applications and information on the state of the applications – is stored in the Web. Support for multiple devices is a key driver of these concepts. The idea is that the users can stop their work on one device and continue it on another. In fact we want 'cloudify' the browsing experience to the Internet, and we call these destinations in the Internet as *Cloud Spaces*.

The Web is based on mobile code. Four paradigms of mobile code have been presented in [5]:

- *Client-Server* where client uses code that is located in another node.
- *Remote Evaluation* where client sends execution instructions, for example SQL queries, to another node.
- *Code On Demand* where code is downloaded to the client for execution. HTML5 applications are widely used examples of code-on-demand.
- *Mobile Agent* where code together with internal state of the application is moved to other node for execution.

The first three paradigms are regularly used in Web applications and [4] presented the Cloud Browser concept where the whole browsing context, including the internal state of HTML5 applications, were stored in server in the cloud.

This paper builds on the above ideas, where the browser is increasingly acting as the application platform, and where applications can store their internal state in the server for future use. In addition, we propose moving the executable code with the internal state of the application. As a concrete contribution, we propose a system where the applications can also continue their execution while being stored in the server, and the running applications can later be retrieved back to a browser. We consider these applications as *mobile agents* since they comply with commonly used definitions of mobile agents, like the ones presented in [6] and [7]. Although our current applications do not include autonomous migration, the proposed approach supports it at the conceptual level. Our agents are implemented as HTML5 applications and thus we call them HTML5 agents in this paper.

A reference model for mobile agents has been presented in [8]. Our HTML5 agents match this reference model as follows. The **agent model** defines the intelligent and self-directed part of the agent. In our case the agent model mostly depends on the application and our current agents do not have much self-direction, yet. The **life-cycle model** defines the execution states of the agent as start, running, frozen and death. HTML5 agents follow these states defined in [8] directly. We have two variants of running state: with UI and headless. At the moment our frozen state is only transient and active only when the agent moves, but there is no technical reason why frozen state could not be stored for later use. **Computation model** defines the execution in the running state. We implement all computation in JavaScript and the framework is based on event handlers as described in SubSect. 2.1. **Navigation model** includes possible hosts for mobile agents and the ways of transmitting the mobile agents between the hosts. The navigation model of HTML5 agent consists of the configuration file that is downloaded with the agent. **Communication model** defines means to communicate with the environment and other agents. Communication with the user is done through the browser, with web resources the agents communicate by using standard XMLHttpRequest primitive [9], and an agent-to-agent communication framework has been implemented and presented in [10]. Security model defines how system is protected against malicious agents and how agents are protected against malicious hosts. In the current implementation security model rely on standard security mechanisms of HTML5 applications in browser.

We claim that HTML5 technology provides important benefits in implementation and use of mobile agent for two main reasons:

1. HTML5 technologies are widely used and have a strong ecosystem. This means that platforms are widely available and there are de facto standards and tools.
2. A new class of use cases for mobile agents becomes available since the users can run the same application as a normal application and transfer it to an agent server, and pull it back in another context. This puts the users in control and makes the agent platform more user-oriented.

Many applications can also be implemented with other paradigms of moving code presented in [5]. Especially, some of our use cases could be implemented with Client-Server paradigm so that most of the logic is moved to server and only the user interface is in browser. We believe that our approach is more suitable for cases where:

- local execution gives additional value because of access to local resources, responsiveness requirements or cost or quality issues in network quality, and
- the original source location of application cannot be used as a host for execution, e.g., for commercial or privacy reasons.

In addition, the agents can visit several servers and browser clients during its execution. This enables the use cases that typically require specialized agent platform.

The rest of this paper has been organized as follows. Section 2 describes the proposed architecture, and a number of use cases that can be associated with our approach. Section 3 introduces our proof-of-concept implementation of the framework, and Sect. 4 discusses some example applications. Section 5 discusses related work, and pinpoints unique features of our approach. Section 6 provides a discussion on the lessons we have learned in the development process and potential ideas for future work. Towards the end of the paper, Sect. 7 draws some final conclusions.

2 Architecture and Use Cases

In the following, we address two principal elements of our work. First, we discuss how we have realized the system at the level of principal design, and then, we provide some use cases that can be implemented with our system. We place the focus on conceptual level, and do not yet go to concrete technical details of the system, which will be addressed later on in the paper.

2.1 Architecture

In the proposed system, an HTML5 agent can run in two modes:

1. With a user interface inside a client runtime engine, i.e. the browser.
2. In a headless mode, i.e. without a user interface, in an application server that we call agent server in this paper.

The agent can move between these modes and locations when the browser pulls the agent from a server and when the browser pushes the agent back to a server. Furthermore, we support multi-device usage – the browser instance that pulls an executing agent can be different from the browser instance that had originally pushed the agent to the server. Therefore, during its life-cycle the agent may visit several browsers and several agent servers. An example life cycle is presented in Fig. 1.

In Fig. 1, agent is started by Browser1, when the agent is downloaded from its origin server (Step 1). In this phase the agent is initialized and the execution begins. Since the agent executes in a browser it has a user interface. In Step 2, the agent is pushed to an agent server. This means that the agent server gets the internal execution state of the agent and the application code (actually a URL to the code). The agent can continue the execution in the server. In Steps 3-5, the agent moves from one environment to other but preserves its internal state and continues execution. Finally, the execution is terminated in Step 6. Note that in life cycle shown in Fig. 1, as well as in our experimental implementation, too, the agent always moves between server and client. However, it would be technically trivial to make the agent to move at least between servers.

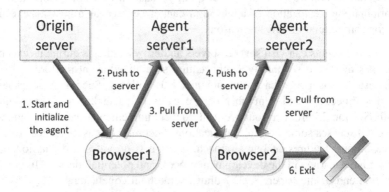

Fig. 1. Life-cycle of HTML5 agent.

It should also be noted that not all applications need to execute in the server, but execution resumes when the agent migrates to (some) browser again. For example, in the media player scenario presented in [7] playing should be resumed when agent is in the browser again. However, for some systems, headless mode may provide important functions that are essential for satisfying certain types of requirements. In case of monitoring applications, for instance, certain events might trigger moving the application back to the client so that the user can take appropriate actions. Naturally, this would require presence of some push notification technology.

Internal state of the application is an important part of a mobile agent. The state needs to be serialized, transferred and de-serialized in the new location. It is obvious that without modifying the implementations of the browser the complete state of the application cannot be serialized, and the agent needs to be written so that serialization of the relevant components of the state is possible. Our design provides support for such serialization of the important parts of the state.

In our current implementation a single agent instance moves from host to host, but it would be trivial to change the behavior so that a new copy is created when needed. For instance when a browser fetches the agent from the agent server, a new copy could be created and the original application could also continue its execution in the agent server. We believe that this can be performed with configuration options included in the framework, but this remains a piece of future work as discussed towards the end of the paper.

Since the agent can run both with and without UI, the architecture has to be designed to separate UI from execution. HTML5 provides a good ground for this separation. Similarly to most HTML5 applications, HTML5 agents are composed of two major parts:

1. Declarative description of the user interface in a form of HTML, CSS and image files.
2. JavaScript-files describing the executable code.

As is common in today's web applications, the HTML-file includes references to Cascading Style Sheets (CSS), images and other resources, and JavaScript files.

When the HTML5 agent is running in the agent server, it runs in the headless mode and the HTML and CSS files are not needed. Only the virtual machine executing JavaScript is needed for the execution of the agent. Naturally, whenever the agent moves to a browser HTML and CSS files need to be available again. Therefore, the agents need to preserve at least URLs of the UI components of the agent. Also the JavaScript code of the agents has to be written in such a way that it can be executed without presence of the Document Object Model (DOM) [11] tree, the data structure that is used as an internal presentation of a web page inside the browser. In our current implementation we provide a simple browser emulation system that supports running of browser-based applications in a server, but certain coding rules need to be followed.

The execution model of the application also needs to be suitable for our approach. First of all it needs to be suitable for running in the browser, for instance it should not block the event loop of the browser run-time. On the other hand it needs to execute without UI events delivered by the browser. Furthermore, the agent needs to have safe points in execution in which the internal state can be serialized in consistent state. In practice this means that all the application logic has to be embedded in the event handlers and in addition to handlers for UI events there is a handler for timer events that are generated by our framework.

If the only requirement is that the application and its internal state are stored to an agent server but the application does not need to execute there, there are fewer constraints for the design. The application state must be serialized, but support for the agent execution model – timer-based events – is not needed.

2.2   Use Cases

Our system targets two kinds of use cases: traditional use cases of mobile agents and long-lasting sessions in web applications that are used in multi-device environment.

We fundamentally agree with [12] and assume no single killer application for mobile agents, but several applications can benefit from mobile agent technology. From the example application areas presented in [12] the following would at least benefit from our solution:

- *E-commerce*. If the product a user wants is not immediately available, or if the pricing is not satisfactory, the user can set her constraints and then send the e-commerce application to the agent server for execution.
- *Personal assistance*. The example given in [12] "to schedule a meeting with several other people, a user can send a mobile agent to interact with the agents representing each of the people invited to the meeting. The agents negotiate and establish a meeting time." would be good use case for us, too.
- *Secure brokering*. The agent server could be a mutually trusted host that enables collaboration between the agents.
- *Workflow applications*. The workflow application can be a web application that is executed both in a server and in browsers of several users.

Among web applications all applications that should execute continuously but the user would still like to have a break or just switch to another device are potential use cases of our HTML5 agents. With normal web applications the application state is lost when user switches from one device to another.

Our solution allows users to continue their work in another device. The novel idea presented in this paper is that the execution of the application can also continue while user is not using it through any device. This is beneficial for instance, in the following cases:

- monitoring applications that collect data about events or values of various sensors,
- strategy games that should continue execution of users instructions as robots when user is not present, and
- applications whose execution takes a lot of time or need to access big server-side resources are better executed in the agent server.

Many of these applications can also be implemented as server-side applications that users access with a browser. However, the server-side applications are typically bound to a specific service and configurability for individual users is limited. Some applications would also like to access resources in the client device and thus the execution should take place in the client device. Finally, the ability to move computational agents between clients and servers adds an extra layer of flexibility.

3 Proof-of-Concept Implementation

To test and validate our idea we have created an experimental implementation of the agent architecture. The server side of the implementation is based on Node.js technology [13], which is a platform for the development of scalable network applications using JavaScript. Thanks to Node.js we can execute the same JavaScript code both in server and in browser.

The implementation consists of three main components: (1) *agent framework* that acts as a superclass for the agent applications, (2) *execution context* in the server-side including an emulation of the browser environment, (3) *serialization format and transfer protocol* for application state and information. More detailed explanations of these components are given in the following.

3.1 The Agent Framework

The execution model is event-based which is normal in browsers and Node.js server. To support execution of possible computing tasks of the agent, a periodic timer calls an application-specific work-function on regular intervals.

As explained earlier, the complete internal state cannot be stored and migrated by the system and also in this experimental system the application need to explicitly define state information that should be serialized and delivered when the agent moves from a location to another. In practice, the agents have variable list that contains the state that has been saved and transferred.

In our proof of concept a superclass Agent is defined by using the functional inheritance pattern presented in [14]. It should be noted that the concept does not require use of this pattern, and we have also tried use of prototype-based approach. In this inheritance pattern the super class defines the set of methods as follows:

```
function Agent(src,html) {
    var that = {};
    that.method1 = function(args) {…}
    that.method2 = function(args) {…}
    return that;
}
```

This Agent class is not to be instantiated, but each concrete agent *gmonitor* application inherits from Agent as follows:

```
function GMonitor(src,html) {
  var that = Agent(src,html);
  that.high = 0;
  /* definitions other variables in state */
  that.registerVar('high'); /* 'high' is now part of state */
  /* new and overridden methods */
}
```

Interesting sections of the HTML file of our example agent are:

```
<head>
  <meta name="viewport" content="width=device-width">
  <script        src="http://xx.xx.xx.fi:pppp/configuration.js">

  </script>
  <script>
    configuration.downloadAgent("gmonitor.js")
  </script>
</head>

<body onload="initExecution()">
  <input type='button'
         onclick="agent.upload()"
         value="UPLOAD">
</body>
```

In this example the configuration file includes the first parts of the agent framework and the rest of the framework and actual agent is downloaded with downloadAgent(). The example also shows how agent is started with initExecution() and uploaded with upload().

In our design, the class Agent offers the following utility methods:

- createVar(name,value) creates a new variable to the variable list, i.e. extends the state of the agent.
- setVal(name,value) sets a value of a variable in the state of the agent.
- getVal(name) – gets value of a variable in the state of the agent.
- registerVar(name) – alternative approach to createVar(), setVal() and getVal(). With registerVar() application can state that the defined variable will be automatically serialized.
- setWork(function, interval) – sets the work function that is periodically executed with the given interval. The framework assumes that the work function returns reasonable quickly.
- setRunInterval(interval) – changes the interval between executions.
- start() and stop() – starts/resumes and stops execution of the agent. In practice, the timer is started and stopped.
- serialize() – returns a JSON-string that includes all necessary information to preserve the state and continue execution of the agent in a new location. This method is for the framework and is not usually called from application code.
- upload(url) – uploads the agent to an agent server specified by parameter url. Default value for the url is defined in the configuration file. This function first stops execution, then serializes the state and finally sends the serialized agent to the agent server.

The application-specific sub-class of the Agent can override the following methods:

- Method `getRunningStatus()` – should return a string that the management interface of the agent server context can show.
- Method `preupload()` is called by `upload()` just before serialization as the first the uploading. By overriding this method the agent can implement application specific preparations for the uploading.
- Function `continueWork()` – re-initializes the execution when the agent has arrived and de-serialized in a new location and the execution should be resumed. This function initializes the state of the agent by recreating the variables.

In addition, the agent has to provide a function that creates and initializes the agent object.

3.2 Managing Execution Context in the Server Side

As hinted earlier we have implemented a simple HTTP server with Node.js. This server receives description of the agent, i.e., the location of executable JavaScript file(s) and state information, in an HTTP-POST request. Then, the following steps are performed:

- The executable JavaScript file is downloaded from the origin server.
- The required run-time structures are created.
- The function `continueWork()` of the downloaded agent is called.
- A timer to periodically fire the work-function is initialized.

The application code of web applications typically assumes existence of a DOM tree created from the HTML. For the headless mode we have a minimal browser emulation layer for applications that refer to HTML document. The design principle is to provide as minimal emulation as possible and require applications to adapt, too.

Web applications typically use `getElementbyId()` and similar methods in JavaScript to access the rendered document tree. We assume that providing a dummy document object the UI part of the agent can silently fail in server. Also, some of our example applications draw graphics through Canvas API [15]. The application code should check if Canvas API is available, in accordance to the following snippet of code:

```
var ctx = comp.getContext("2d");
if (ctx != null) {
    that.draw(…);
}
```

This would actually be a good coding practice for all web applications since `getContext()` could return null in browsers, too, if Canvas API is not available. For the dummy object and Canvas API simulation of browser in the Agent server in Node.js environment is simply:

```
function document () {
  this.getElementById = function(str) {
    this.id = str;
    return new document();
  }
  this.toString = function () {
    return "<element id='" + this.id + "'>";
  }
  this.getContext = function () {
    return null;
  }
}
module.exports.document = new document();
```

In addition, our browser emulation framework includes implementation of standard JavaScript function `getElementById(id)` that always returns a new object that carries the given id and implements our emulation interface. We also have `toString()` that is mainly used for debugging purposes.

In order to use the same API for network configuration, we have installed an implementation of XMLHttpRequest [9] module to our Node.js server.

3.3 Serialization Format and Transfer Protocol

In our design, the browser can receive the agent in two alternative ways 1) by fetching the HTML-files of the application from the origin server, or 2) by fetching an agent description from agent server. In contrast, the agent server gets the agent by 3) receiving an agent description in a HTTP POST message.

In cases 2 and 3 information about the agent and its internal state is encapsulated in an *agent description* that is a JSON document containing the following information:

- *auri*: a URL that points to the JavaScript file of the application. The agent runtime, in the new execution location, needs to download the JavaScript file from this URL.
- *huri*: a URL pointing to HTML file, i.e., UI of the application. The HTML file then refers to required CSS and image files.
- *id*: unique ID of the agent instance
- *variables/memory*: local state in terms of names and values of local variables.

An example of serialized agent description is shown below. The state of this agent includes four variables *low*, *high*, *count* and *history*.

```
{"auri": "http://xx.xx.xx.fi:pppp/gmonitor.js",
 "huri": "http://xx.xx.xx.fi:pppp/gmonitor.html",
 "id"   : "526636" ,
 "variables": {},
 "memory": {
    "high"    : 0.025390625 ,
    "low"     : 0.021484375 ,
    "count"   : 3,
    "history": [0.025390625, 0.0234375 ,0.021484375]}
 }
}
```

The utility method `serialize()` of class Agent creates this agent description. When the agent server receives a request to pull an agent (Step 3 in Fig. 1) the agent server calls method `serialize()` of running agent and includes the result in the response. When client browser wants to push agent to the agent server, it also calls this method and embeds the result to the HTTP POST request that send the agent to the server.

For optimization reasons, when the application is fetched from agent server, the content of the HTML file is attached to the agent description.

The implementation of our agent system requires the browser to fetch content from several origins. To enable this we have used the Cross-Origin Resource Sharing (CORS) [16] technology to allow use of several origins.

4 Example Applications

We have experimented and tested the framework with some test applications. The example applications have been used to further develop and validate different aspects of our agent framework.

Monitoring. Our first example application was a simple monitoring application that tracks the CPU load of a server machine. While implementing this application we also made most of our current design decisions. When this agent is run in a browser, the application shows current load level, minimum and maximum values, and latest history graphically. When this application is run in a server, the information is still collected so that a non-interrupted sequence of data can be shown when the agent has migrated back to a browser. This application was tested both on PC browsers and on a smartphone.

Image Analysis. We also wanted to test the framework with an application that contains long-lasting computation and user would like to push the computation to the server after seeing that it has been started correctly. As a concrete example we selected an image analysis application that can compute characteristics of images both in browser and server. With this application we investigated issues with large amounts of data, and the main learning is that the future agents should have pointers in the resources in the Internet instead of carrying the data in the state of the agent.

On-line Query Applications. We assume that many applications of our HTML5 agents collect information for the user. The motivation could be e-commerce or just to get information when it becomes available. To experiment with this application area we have implemented an agent that lets users to follow an on-line artist community - in our case DeviantArt [17] for new content from favorite artists or by selected keywords. With this application we also experimented with a computation that had behaves slightly differently in browser and server because the source of RSS feed provides different format and content for different clients.

3D Virtual World. We wanted to test how we can use the 3D widget library [18] as the user interface for our agents. This example gave us input on how the DOM-emulation should be done in the future.

Reading of Sensor Data. In an experiment reported in [19] we implemented the agent server in Raspberry PI minicomputer [20] and connected a temperature sensor to it. The application then measured and tracked the temperature. While in mobile phone with accelerator sensor the agent tracks movements of the device. With this application we showed how agent can pre-process that data and only store limited amount of relevant information. With this we application we also, for the first time, implemented an agent that is designed to execute on several agent servers.

While the above applications demonstrate the main capabilities of the present implementation, we will continue development of new applications when new and improved capabilities are introduced. Some of these ideas are discussed in Sect. 6 of this paper.

5 Related Work

As already pointed out, our agents comply with commonly used definitions such as "*Mobile* agents are programs that can migrate from host to host in a network, at times and to places of their own choosing. The state of the running program is saved, transported to the new host, and re stored, allowing the program to continue where it left off" [6] or "Mobile agents are self-contained and identifiable computer programs that can move *autonomously within the network and act on behalf of the user or other entities. A mobile agent can execute at a host for a while, halt execution, dispatch itself to another host, and resume execution there*". [7] A survey of mobile agent technologies has been given in [21], but the discussion is limited to traditional mobile agents. In this paper we propose a new approach in which HTML5 - a standard feature of a browser - and the emulation in application server constitute the agent platform.

Benefits and application areas of mobile agents have been discussed in [12]. From the motivations presented in [12], at least reduction of network load and latency, asynchronous and anonymous execution are valid for HTML5 agents, too. Also many of the presented application areas are common to HTML5 agents.

An agent platform hosted in browsers has been presented in [22]. This work has common targets with ours; it allows agents to be executed both in server and browser. In [22] mobile agent platform is based on concepts of *Pneuna* that is relatively close to our agent description and *Soma* that is the execution environment. In this approach Soma hides the differences of browser and server environment and creates a completely new application platform for mobile agents. In our approach standard and well-known HTML5 is the agent/application platform. In addition, the approach presented in [22] has not been designed for pushing agents to agent server when user or browser is not active or when the agent should find a new browser to run on.

The basic idea presented in [7] is somewhat similar to our approach, but they do not use HTML5 as the application platform. For example, their media player example would fit nicely to our approach, too, especially if HTML5 media API would be used to implement the player. A particularly interesting aspect in [7] is self-adaptation and context awareness – in practice different UI to different devices. It would be interesting to implement similar behavior using web technologies.

The relation between trends in the Internet and in mobile agents has also been discussed in [6]. The paper discusses these trends and forecasts that "within a few years, nearly all major Internet sites will be capable of hosting and willing to host some form of mobile code or mobile agents." This paper has also interesting discussions about technical and non-technical hurdles of mobile agents. From the presented technical hurdles using HTML5 overcomes "standardization and portability" and to limited extent also "security". From the non-technical hurdles our approach solves "Getting ahead of the evolutionary path" because we use the de facto HTML5 technology, and "Revenue and image" has effectively been eliminated by the evolution of the Internet and its business models.

6 Future Work

We are still in initial phase of our work and have only tested our approach with a limited number of applications. Although we have proven that the approach works with these applications, we anticipate a need to improve the architecture so that development of new agents becomes easier. We need to develop new applications and collect feedback from other developers. For example, our browser emulation interface for the server side is still incomplete, and it has only been tested with very a limited set of test applications. Therefore new features must and have been added to the system as new applications are implemented.

During development of our example applications we have experimented with various development ideas for the programming framework of HTML5 Agents. In the future we should analyze the learnings and redesign some aspects of the programming APIs before we introduce framework to wider developer community. This also includes consideration of well-known JavaScript libraries such as JQuery [23].

We should also consider use of more complete approaches to DOM-emulation. That would support reuse of existing libraries and applications in development of HTML5 Agents.

Context awareness, as in [7] should also be added, and we should work more with different types of devices. In particular context awareness should be complemented with mechanisms for self-adaptation, which would provide extra flexibility in some use cases.

Security is an obvious concern for all dynamically moving code. In the current system we rely on standard security mechanisms of HTML5 applications in browser. However, if the agents need to execute sensitive tasks in the server or agents of several users should collaborate in the server, we need to develop additional security mechanisms that are missing from today's Web.

In our current example a single instance of an agent migrates between hosts. Extensions to multiplying agents should be experimented with and we should develop configuration techniques for when to move applications and when to multiply them.

Finally, exploring agents that are able to autonomously extend their behavior in accordance to the needs of the application is one of the directions we have been considering. Building on the immense flexibility of the Web and web applications, this would be a step towards mashware where components offered as a service form the basis for constructing applications [24].

7 Conclusions

Recent development of web technologies is rapidly gearing the Web towards a role where it offers more and more facilities that have been commonly associated with traditional operating systems and binary applications.

In this paper, we have shown that HTML5 technology can be used to implement mobile agents and that use of agent approach can improve the user experience especially in multi-device scenario. In addition, we introduced a proof-of-concept implementation that is able to run simple applications. While as future work, we list a number of ideas that will improve the capabilities of the system; we believe that the present implementation validates the feasibility of the fundamental design.

References

1. Taivalsaari, A., Systä, K.: Cloudberry: HTML5 cloud phone platform for mobile devices. In: IEEE Software, July/August 2012, pp. 30–35 (2012)
2. Google, Chromium OS Web page. http://www.chromium.org/chromium-os. Accessed 2 Sept 2013
3. Mozilla, Firefox OS web page. http://www.mozilla.org/en-US/firefoxos. Accessed 2 Sept 2013
4. Taivalsaari, A., Mikkonen, T., Systä, K.: Cloud browser: enhancing the web browser with cloud sessions and downloadable user interface. In: Park, J.J.H., Arabnia, H.R., Kim, C., Shi, W., Gil, J.-M. (eds.) GPC 2013. LNCS, vol. 7861, pp. 224–233. Springer, Heidelberg (2013)
5. Carzaniga, A., Picco, G.P., Vigna, G.: Designing distributed applications with mobile code paradigms. In: Proceeding of the 19th International Conference on Software Engineering (ICSE'97), 17–23 May 1997, Boston, Massachusetts, USA, pp. 22–32 (1997)
6. Kotz, K., Gray, R.S.: Mobile agents and the future of the internet. SIGOPS Oper. Syst. Rev. 33(3), 7–13 (1999)
7. Yu, P., Cao, J., Wen, W., Lu, J.: Mobile agent enabled application mobility for pervasive computing. In: Ma, J., Jin, H., Yang, L.T., Tsai, J.J.-P. (eds.) UIC 2006. LNCS, vol. 4159, pp. 648–657. Springer, Heidelberg (2006)
8. Green, S., Somers, F.: Software agents: a review. Technical report TCD-CS-1997-06, Technical Report of Trinity College, University of Dublin, pp. 26–39 (1997)
9. W3C: XMLHttpRequest, W3C working draft 6 December 2012. http://www.w3.org/TR/XMLHttpRequest/. Accessed 2 Sept 2013
10. Järvenpää, L.: Development and evaluation of HTML agent framework. Master of Science thesis, Tampere University of Technology (2013)
11. W3C: Document Object Model (DOM). http://www.w3.org/DOM/. Accessed 04 Feb 2013
12. Lange, D.B., Oshima, M.: Seven good reasons for mobile agents. Commun. ACM 42(3), 88–89 (1999)
13. Nodejs, n.d.: Web page for document and download of nodejs technology. http://nodejs.org/. Accessed 03 Feb 2013
14. Crockford, D.: JavaScript: the Good Parts, O'Reilly Media Inc. (2008)
15. W3C: The Canvas 2D API 1.0 specification. W3C Editor's Draft. http://dev.w3.org/2006/canvas-api/canvas-2d-api.html. Accessed 04 Feb 2013

16. W3C: Cross-origin resource sharing. W3C Candidate Recommendation 29 January 2013. http://www.w3.org/TR/cors/. Accessed 03 Feb 2013. (2013)
17. DeviantArt n.d.: home page. http://www.deviantart.com/. Accessed 3 Feb 2013
18. Mattila, A.-L., Mikkonen, T.: Designing a 3D widget library for WebGL enabled browsers. In: Proceedings of the 28th Annual ACM Symposium on Applied Computing, SAC '13, Coimbra, Portugal, 18–22 March 2013
19. Järvenpää, L., Lintinen, M., Mattila, A.-L., Mikkonen, T., Systä K., Voutilainen, J.-P.: Mobile agents for the internet of things. In: 3rd Workshop on Applications of Software Agents, WASA2013, Sinaia, Romania, 11–13 October (2013)
20. Raspberry PI web page. http://www.raspberrypi.org. Accessed 28 June 2013
21. Gupta, R., Kansal, G.: A survey on comparative study of mobile agent platforms. Int. J. Eng. Sci. Technol. (IJEST) 3(3), 1943–1948 (2011)
22. Feldman, M.: An approach for using the web as a mobile agent infrastructure. In: Proceedings of the International Multiconference on Computer Science and Information Technology, pp. 39–45. (2007)
23. JQuery Web page. http://jquery.com/. Accessed 2 Sept 2013
24. Mikkonen, T., Salminen, A.: Implementing mobile mashware architecture: downloadable components as on-demand services. Procedia Comput. Sci. 10, 553–560 (2012)

Watermarking Digital Images in the Frequency Domain: Performance and Attack Issues

Maria Chroni$^{(\boxtimes)}$, Angelos Fylakis, and Stavros D. Nikolopoulos

Department of Computer Science and Engineering, University of Ioannina,
45110 Ioannina, Greece
{mchroni,afylakis,stavros}@cs.uoi.gr

Abstract. In this work we propose an efficient model for watermarking images that are intended for uploading on the web under intellectual property protection. Headed to this direction, we recently suggested a way in which an integer number w which being transformed into a self-inverting permutation, can be represented in a two dimensional (2D) object and thus, since images are 2D structures, we propose a watermarking algorithm that embeds marks on them using the 2D representation of w in the frequency domain. In particular, we propose a watermarking technique that uses the 2D representation of self-inverting permutations and utilizes marking at specific areas thanks to partial modifications of the image's Discrete Fourier Transform (DFT). Those modifications are made on the magnitude of specific frequency bands and they are the least possible additive information ensuring robustness and imperceptiveness. We have experimentally evaluated our algorithms using various images of different characteristics under JPEG compression, Gaussian noise addition, and geometric transformations. The experimental results show an improvement in comparison to the previously obtained results and they also depict the validity of our proposed codec algorithms.

Keywords: Watermarking techniques · Image watermarking algorithms · Self-inverting permutations · 2D representations of permutations · Encoding · Decoding · Frequency domain · Experimental evaluation

1 Introduction

Internet technology, in modern communities, becomes day by day an indispensable tool for everyday life since most people use it on a regular basis and do many daily activities online [1]. This frequent use of the internet means that measures taken for internet security are indispensable since the web is not risk-free [2,3]. One of those risks is the fact that the web is an environment where intellectual property is under threat since a huge amount of public personal data is continuously transferred, and thus such data may end up on a user who falsely claims ownership.

It is without any doubt that images, apart from text, are the most frequent type of data that can be found on the internet. As digital images are a characteristic kind of intellectual material, people hesitate to upload and transfer them

© Springer-Verlag Berlin Heidelberg 2014
K.-H. Krempels and A. Stocker (Eds.): WEBIST 2013, LNBIP 189, pp. 68–84, 2014.
DOI: 10.1007/978-3-662-44300-2_5

via the internet because of the ease of intercepting, copying and redistributing in their exact original form [4]. Encryption is not the problem's solution in most cases, as most people that upload images in a website want them to be visible by everyone, but safe and theft protected as well. Watermarks are a solution to this problem, since thanks to them someone can claim the property of an image if he previously inserted one in it.

Watermarking. Digital watermarking (or, hereafter, watermarking) is a technique for protecting the intellectual property of a digital object; the idea is simple: a unique marker, which is called *watermark*, is embedded into a digital object which may be used to verify its authenticity or the identity of its owners [6,7]. More precisely, watermarking can be described as the problem of embedding a watermark w into an object $\mathcal{O}$ and, thus, producing a new object I_w, such that w can be reliably located and extracted from $\mathcal{O}_w$ even after $\mathcal{O}_w$ has been subjected to transformations [7]; for example, compression, scaling or rotation in case where the object is an image.

In the image watermarking process the digital information, i.e., the watermark, is hidden in image data. The watermark is embedded into image's data through the introduction of errors not detectable by human perception [8]; note that, if the image is copied or transferred through the internet then the watermark is also carried with the copy into the image's new location.

Motivation. Intellectual property protection is one of the greatest concerns of internet users today. Digital images are considered a representative part of such properties so we consider important, the development of methods that deter malicious users from claiming others' ownership, motivating internet users to feel more safe to publish their work online.

Image Watermarking, is a technique that serves the purpose of image intellectual property protection ideally as in contrast with other techniques it allows images to be available to third internet users but simultaneously carry an "identity" that is actually the proof of ownership with them. This way image watermarking achieves its target of deterring copy and usage without permission of the owner. What is more by saying watermarking we don't necessarily mean that we put a logo or a sign on the image as research is also done towards watermarks that are both invisible and robust.

Our work suggests a method of embedding a numerical watermark into the image's structure in an invisible and robust way to specific transformations, such as JPEG compression, Gaussian noise addition, and geometric transformation.

Contribution. In this work we present an efficient and easily implemented technique for watermarking images that we are interested in uploading in the web and making them public online; this way web users are enabled to claim the ownership of their images.

What is important for our idea is the fact that it suggests a way in which an integer number can be represented with a two dimensional representation (or, for short, 2D representation). Thus, since images are two dimensional objects that representation can be efficiently marked on them resulting the watermarked images. In a similar way, such a 2D representation can be extracted for a water-marked image and converted back to the integer w.

Having designed an efficient method for encoding integers as self-inverting permutations, we propose an efficient algorithm for encoding a self-inverting permutation π^* into an image I by first mapping the elements of π^* into an $n^* \times n^*$ matrix A^* and then using the information stored in A^* to mark specific areas of image I in the frequency domain resulting the watermarked image I_w. We also propose an efficient algorithm for extracting the embedded self-inverting permutation π^* from the watermarked image I_w by locating the positions of the marks in I_w; it enables us to recontract the 2D representation of the self-inverting permutation π^*.

It is worth noting that although digital watermarking has made considerable progress and became a popular technique for copyright protection of multimedia information [8], our work proposes something new. We first point out that our watermarking method incorporates such properties which allow us to success-fully extract the watermark w from the image I_w even if the input image has been compressed with a lossy method, scaled and/or rotated. In addition, our embedding method can transform a watermark from a numerical form into a two dimensional (2D) representation and, since images are 2D structures, it can efficiently embed the 2D representation of the watermark by marking the high frequency bands of specific areas of an image. The key idea behind our extracting method is that it does not actually extract the embedded information instead it locates the marked areas reconstructing the watermark's numerical value.

We have evaluated the embedding and extracting algorithms by testing them on various and different in characteristics images that were initially in JPEG format and we had positive results as the watermark was successfully extracted even if the image was converted back into JPEG format with various JPEG compression ratios. We had also positive results on Gaussian noise addition and geometric transformation attacks. All the algorithms have been developed and tested in MATLAB environment [9].

2   Theoretical Framework

In this section we first describe discrete structures, namely, permutations and self-inverting permutations, and briefly discuss a codec system which encodes an integer number w into a self-inverting permutation π. Then, we present a transformation of a watermark from a numerical form to a 2D form (i.e., 2D representation) through the exploitation of self-inverting permutation properties.

2.1   Self-Inverting Permutations

Permutations may be represented in many ways [10]. The most straightforward is simply a rearrangement of the elements of the set $N_n = \{1, 2, \ldots, n\}$; in this way we think of the permutation $\pi = (5, 6, 9, 8, 1, 2, 7, 4, 3)$ as a rearrangement of the elements of the set N_9 such that "1 goes to 5", "2 goes to 6", and so on [10,11]. Hereafter, we shall say that π is a permutation over the set N_9.

Definition 2.1.1. Let $\pi = (\pi_1, \pi_2, \ldots, \pi_n)$ be a permutation over the set N_n, $n > 1$. The inverse of the permutation π is the permutation $q = (q_1, q_2, \ldots, q_n)$ with $q_{\pi_i} = \pi_{q_i} = i$. A *self-inverting permutation* (or, for short, SiP) is a permutation that is its own inverse: $\pi_{\pi_i} = i$.

By definition, a permutation is a SiP (self-inverting permutation) if and only if all its cycles are of length 1 or 2; for example, the permutation $\pi = (5, 6, 9, 8, 1, 2, 7, 4, 3)$ is a SiP with cycles: $(1, 5)$, $(2, 6)$, $(3, 9)$, $(4, 8)$, and (7).

2.2 Encoding Numbers as SiPs

There are several systems that correspond integer numbers into permutations or self-inverting permutation [10]. Recently, we have proposed algorithms for such a system which efficiently encodes an integer w into a self-inverting permutations π and efficiently decodes it. The algorithms of our codec system run in $O(n)$ time, where n is the length of the binary representation of the integer w. The key-idea behind our algorithms is mainly based on mathematical objects, namely, bitonic permutations [12,13].

2.3 2D and 2DM Representations

In the 2D representation, the elements of the permutation $\pi = (\pi_1, \pi_2, \ldots, \pi_n)$ are mapped in specific cells of an $n \times n$ matrix A as follows:

- number $\pi_i \longrightarrow$ entry $A(\pi_i^{-1}, \pi_i)$

or, equivalently, the cell at row i and column π_i is labeled by the number π_i, for each $i = 1, 2, \ldots, n$. Figure 1(a) shows the 2D representation of the self-inverting permutation $\pi = (6, 3, 2, 4, 5, 1)$.

Based on the previously defined 2D representation of a permutation π, we next propose a two-dimensional marked representation (2DM representation) of π, which is an efficient tool for watermarking images. In our 2DM representation, a permutation π over the set N_n is represented by an $n \times n$ matrix A^* as follows:

- the cell at row i and column π_i of matrix A^* is marked by a specific symbol (in our implementation we use the asterisk "*"), for each $i = 1, 2, \ldots, n$.

Figure 1(b) shows the 2DM representation of the permutation π. It is easy to see that, since the 2DM representation of π is constructed from the corresponding 2D representation, there is one symbol in each row and in each column of the matrix A^*. It is also easy to see that we can extract π from A^* in linear time (i.e., linear in the size of matrix A^*); we call Extract_π_from_2DM the extraction algorithm.

Remark 2.3.1. Since the permutation π is a self-inverting permutation, its 2D matrix A has the following property: $A(i, j) = j$ if $\pi_i = j$ and $A(i, j) = 0$ otherwise, $1 \le i, j \le n$. Thus, the corresponding matrix A^* is symmetric. Hereafter, we shall denote by π^* a SiP and by n^* the number of elements of π^*.

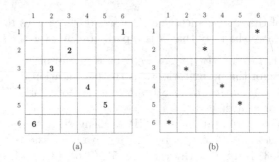

Fig. 1. The 2D and 2DM representations of the self-inverting permutation $\pi = (6, 3, 2, 4, 5, 1)$.

2.4   The Discrete Fourier Transform

The Discrete Fourier Transform (DFT) is used to decompose an image into its sine and cosine components. The output of the transformation represents the image in the frequency domain, while the input image is the spatial domain equivalent. In the image's fourier representation, each point represents a particular frequency contained in the image's spatial domain.

Typically, in our method, we are interested in the magnitudes of DFT coefficients. The magnitude $|F(u, v)|$ of the Fourier transform at a point is how much frequency content there is [14].

3   The Frequency Domain Approach

Having described an efficient method for encoding integers as self-inverting permutations using the 2DM representation of self-inverting permutations, we next describe codec algorithms that efficiently encode and decode a watermark into the image's frequency domain [14–16].

3.1   Embed Watermark into Image

We next describe the embedding algorithm of our proposed technique which encodes a self-inverting permutation (SiP) π^* into a digital image I. Recall that, the permutation π^* is obtained over the set N_{n^*}, where $n^* = 2n + 1$ and n is the length of the binary representation of an integer w which actually is the image's watermark [12].

The watermark w, or equivalently the self-inverting permutation π^*, is inserted in the frequency domain of specific areas of the image I. More precisely, we mark the DFT's magnitude of an image's area using two ellipsoidal annuli, denoted hereafter as "Red" and "Blue" (see, Fig. 2). The ellipsoidal annuli are specified by the following parameters:

- P_r, the width of the "Red" ellipsoidal annulus,
- P_b, the width of the "Blue" ellipsoidal annulus,
- R_1 and R_2, the radiuses of the "Red" ellipsoidal annulus on y-axis and x-axis, respectively.

The algorithm takes as input a SiP π^* and an image I, and returns the watermarked image I_w; it consists of the following steps.

Algorithm. Embed_SiP-to-Image

Input: the watermark $\pi^* \equiv w$ and the host image I;
Output: the watermarked image I_w;

Step 1: Compute first the 2DM representation of the permutation π^*, i.e., construct an array A^* of size $n^* \times n^*$ such that the entry $A^*(i, \pi_i^*)$ contains the symbol "*", $1 \leq i \leq n^*$.

Step 2: Next, compute the size of the input image I, say, $N \times M$, and cover the image I with an imaginary grid C with $n^* \times n^*$ grid-cells C_{ij} of size $\lfloor \frac{N}{n^*} \rfloor \times \lfloor \frac{M}{n^*} \rfloor$, $1 \leq i, j \leq n^*$.

Step 3: For each grid-cell C_{ij}, compute the Discrete Fourier Transform (DFT) using the Fast Fourier Transform (FFT) algorithm, resulting in a $n^* \times n^*$ grid of DFT cells F_{ij}, $1 \leq i, j \leq n^*$.

Step 4: For each DFT cell F_{ij}, compute its magnitude M_{ij} and phase P_{ij} matrices which are both of size $\lfloor \frac{N}{n^*} \rfloor \times \lfloor \frac{M}{n^*} \rfloor$, $1 \leq i, j \leq n^*$.

Step 5: Then, the algorithm takes each of the $n^* \times n^*$ magnitude matrices M_{ij}, $1 \leq i, j \leq n^*$, and places two imaginary ellipsoidal annuli, denoted as "Red" and "Blue", in the matrix M_{ij} (see, Fig. 2). In our implementation,

- the "Red" is the outer ellipsoidal annulus while the "Blue" is the inner one. Both are concentric at the center of the M_{ij} magnitude matrix and have widths P_r and P_b, respectively;
- the radiuses of the "Red" ellipsoidal annulus are R_1 (y-axis) and R_2 (x-axis), while the "Blue" ellipsoidal annulus radiuses are computed in accordance to the "Red" ellipsoidal annulus and have values $(R_1 - P_r)$ and $(R_2 - P_r)$, respectively;
- the inner perimeter of the "Red" ellipsoidal annulus coincides to the outer perimeter of the "Blue" ellipsoidal annulus;
- the values of the widths of the two ellipsoidal annuli are $P_r = 2$ and $P_b = 2$, while the values of their radiuses are $R_1 = \lfloor \frac{N}{2n^*} \rfloor$ and $R_2 = \lfloor \frac{M}{2n^*} \rfloor$.

The areas covered by the "Red" and the "Blue" ellipsoidal annuli determine two groups of magnitude values on M_{ij} (see, Fig. 2).

Step 6: For each magnitude matrix M_{ij}, $1 \leq i, j \leq n^*$, compute the average of the values that are in the areas covered by the "Red" and the "Blue" ellipsoidal

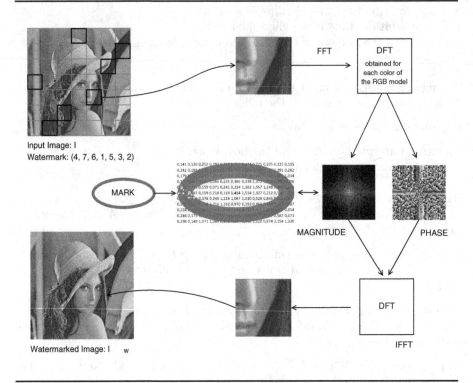

Input Image: I
Watermark: (4, 7, 6, 1, 5, 3, 2)

MARK

MAGNITUDE   PHASE

Watermarked Image: I $_w$

FFT

DFT
obtained for
each color of
the RGB model

DFT

IFFT

Fig. 2. The embedding process (Colour figure online).

annuli; let $AvgR_{ij}$ be the average of the magnitude values belonging to the "Red" ellipsoidal annulus and $AvgB_{ij}$ be the one of the "Blue" ellipsoidal annulus.

Step 7: For each magnitude matrix M_{ij}, $1 \leq i,j \leq n^*$, compute first the variable D_{ij} as follows:

- $D_{ij} = |AvgB_{ij} - AvgR_{ij}|$, if $AvgB_{ij} \leq AvgR_{ij}$
- $D_{ij} = 0$, otherwise.

Then, for each row i of the matrix M_{ij}, $1 \leq i,j \leq n^*$, compute the maximum value of the variables $D_{i1}, D_{i2}, \ldots, D_{in^*}$ in row i; let $MaxD_i$ be the max value.

Step 8: For each cell (i,j) of the 2DM representation matrix A^* of the permutation π^* such that $A^*_{ij} = $ "*" (i.e., marked cell), mark the corresponding grid-cell C_{ij}, $1 \leq i,j \leq n^*$; the marking is performed by increasing all the values in magnitude matrix M_{ij} covered by the "Red" ellipsoidal annulus by the value

$$AvgB_{ij} - AvgR_{ij} + MaxD_i + c, \tag{1}$$

where $c = c_{opt}$. The additive value of c_{opt} is calculated by the function f (see, Subsect. 3.3) which returns the minimum possible value of c that enables successful extracting.

Step 9: Reconstruct the DFT of the corresponding modified magnitude matrices M_{ij}, using the trigonometric form formula [14], and then perform the Inverse Fast Fourier Transform (IFFT) for each marked cell C_{ij}, $1 \leq i, j \leq n^*$, in order to obtain the image I_w.

Step 10: Return the watermarked image I_w.

In Fig. 2 we demonstrate the main operations performed by our embedding algorithm. In particular, we show the marking process of the grid-cell C_{44} of the Lena image; in this example, we embed in the Lena image the watermark number w which corresponds to SiP $(6, 3, 2, 4, 5, 1)$.

3.2 Extract Watermark from Image

In this section we describe the decoding algorithm of our proposed technique. The algorithm extracts a self-inverting permutation (SiP) π^* from a watermarked digital image I_w, which can be later represented as an integer w.

The self-inverting permutation π^* is obtained from the frequency domain of specific areas of the watermarked image I_w. More precisely, using the same two "Red" and "Blue" ellipsoidal annuli, we detect certain areas of the watermarked image I_w that are marked by our embedding algorithm and these marked areas enable us to obtain the 2D representation of the permutation π^*. The extracting algorithm works as follows:

Algorithm. Extract_SiP-from-Image
Input: the watermarked image I_w marked with π^*;
Output: the watermark $\pi^* = w$;

Step 1: Take the input watermarked image I_w and compute its $N \times M$ size. Then, cover I_w with the same imaginary grid C, as described in the embedding method, having $n^* \times n^*$ grid-cells C_{ij} of size $\lfloor \frac{N}{n^*} \rfloor \times \lfloor \frac{M}{n^*} \rfloor$.

Step 2: Then, again for each grid-cell C_{ij}, $1 \leq i, j \leq n^*$, using the Fast Fourier Transform (FFT) get the Discrete Fourier Transform (DFT) resulting a $n^* \times n^*$ grid of DFT cells.

Step 3: For each DFT cell, compute its magnitude matrix M_{ij} and phase matrix P_{ij} which are both of size $\lfloor \frac{N}{n^*} \rfloor \times \lfloor \frac{M}{n^*} \rfloor$.

Step 4: For each magnitude matrix M_{ij}, place the same imaginary "Red" and "Blue" ellipsoidal annuli, as described in the embedding method, and compute as before the average values that coincide in the area covered by the "Red" and the "Blue" ellipsoidal annuli; let $AvgR_{ij}$ and $AvgB_{ij}$ be these values.

Step 5: For each row i of C_{ij}, $1 \leq i \leq n^*$, search for the j_{th} column where $AvgB_{ij} - AvgR_{ij}$ is minimized and set $\pi_i^* = j$, $1 \leq j \leq n^*$.

Step 6: Return the self-inverting permutation π^*.

Having presented the embedding and extracting algorithms, let us next comment on the function f which returns the additive value $c = c_{opt}$ (see, Step 8 of the embedding algorithm).

3.3 Function f

In our watermarking model, the embedding algorithm amplifies the marks in the "Red" ellipsoidal annulus by adding the output of the function f. What exactly f does is returning the optimal value that allows the extracting algorithm under the current requirements, such as JPEG compression, noise addition, to still be able to extract the watermark from the image.

The function f takes as an input the characteristics of the image and the parameters R_1, R_2, P_b, and P_r of our proposed watermark model (see, Step 5 of embedding algorithm and Fig. 2), and returns the minimum possible c_{opt} that added as c to the values of the "Red" ellipsoidal annulus enables extracting (see, Step 8 of the embedding algorithm). More precisely, the function f initially takes the interval $[0, c_{max}]$, where c_{max} is a relatively great value such that if c_{max} is taken as c for marking the "Red" ellipsoidal annulus it allows extracting, and computes the c_{opt} in $[0, c_{max}]$.

Note that, c_{max} allows extracting but because of being great damages the quality of the image (see, Fig. 3). We mentioned relatively great because it depends on the characteristics of each image. For a specific image it is useless to use a c_{max} greater than a specific value, we only need a value that definitely enables the extracting algorithm to successfully extract the watermark.

We next describe the computation of the value c_{opt} returned by f; note that, the parameters P_b and P_r of our implementation are fixed with the values 2 and 2, respectively. The main steps of this computation are the following:

original $c = c_{max}$ $c = c_{opt}$

Fig. 3. The original image of Lena and its two watermarked images with $c = c_{max}$ and $c = c_{opt}$; the watermark corresponds to SiP (6,3,2,4,5,1).

(i) Check if the extracting algorithm for $c = 0$ validly obtains the watermark $\pi^* = w$ from the image I_w; if yes, then the function f returns $c_{opt} = 0$;

(ii) If not, that means, $c = 0$ doesn't allow extracting; then, the function f uses binary search on $[0, c_{max}]$ and computes the interval $[c_1, c_2]$ such that:
- $c = c_1$ doesn't allow extracting,
- $c = c_2$ do allow extracting, and
- $|c_1 - c_2| < 0.2$;

(iii) The function f returns $c_{opt} = c_2$;

As mentioned before, the function f returns the optimal value c_{opt}. Recall that, optimal means that it is the smallest possible value which enables extracting $\pi^* = w$ from the image I_w. It is important to be the smallest one as that minimizes the additive information to the image and, thus, assures minimum drop to the image quality.

4 Experimental Evaluation

In this section we present the experimental results of the proposed watermarking codec algorithms which we have implemented using the general-purpose mathematical software package Matlab (version 7.7.0) [9]. We tested our codec algorithms on various 24-bit digital color images of various sizes (from 200×130 up to 4600×3700) and quality characteristics. Many of the images in our image repository where taken from a web image gallery [17] and enriched by some other images different in characteristics.

In this work we used JPEG images due to their great importance on the web, since they are small in size, while storing full color information (24 bit/pixel), and can be easily and efficiently transmitted. Moreover, robustness to lossy compression is an important issue when dealing with image authentication. It should be observed that the design goal of lossy compression systems is opposed to that of watermark embedding systems. The Human Visual System (HVS) attempts to identify and discard perceptually insignificant information of the image, whereas the goal of the watermarking system is to embed the watermark information without altering the visual perception of the image [21].

In order to evaluate the quality of the watermarked image obtained from our watermarking method we used two objective image quality assessment metrics, namely the Peak Signal to Noise Ratio (PSNR) and the Structural Similarity Index Metric (SSIM). Our aim was to prove that the watermarked image is closely related to the original (image fidelity [5]), because watermarking should not introduce visible distortions in the original image as that would reduce images' commercial value.

The PSNR metric is the ratio between the reference signal and the distortion signal, i.e., watermark, in an image given in decibels (dB). It is well known that, PSNR is most commonly used as a measure of quality of reconstruction of lossy compression codecs (e.g., for image compression). The higher the PSNR value the closer the distorted image is to the original or the better the watermark conceals. It is a popular metric due to its simplicity, although it is well known that this distortion metric is not absolutely correlated with human vision. The SSIM image quality metric, developed by [18], is considered to be correlated with the quality perception of the HVS [19]. The highest value of SSIM is 1, and it is achieved when the original I and watermarked image I_w are identical.

4.1 Performance

Initially, we had to choose the appropriate values for the parameters of the quality function f. In our implementation we set both of the parameters P_r and P_b equal to 2 (see, Sect. 3.3). Recall that, the value 2 is a relatively small value which allows us to modify a satisfactory number of pixels in order to embed the watermark and successfully extract it, without affecting images' quality. Note that, for great in size images, a smaller width reduces the strength of the watermark. There isn't a distance between the two ellipsoidal annuli as that enables the algorithm to apply a small additive information to the values of the "Red" annulus. The two ellipsoidal annuli are inscribed to the rectangle magnitude matrix, as we want to mark images' cells on the high frequency bands.

We mark the high frequencies by increasing their values using mainly the additive parameter $c = c_{opt}$ because alterations in the high frequencies are less detectable by human eye [20]. What is more, in high frequencies most images contain less information.

The quality function f returns the factor c, which has the minimum value c_{opt} that allows the extracting algorithm to successfully extract the watermark. In fact, this value c_{opt} (see, Formula 1) is the main additive information embedded into the image. Depending on the images and the amount of compression, we need to increase the watermark strength by increasing the factor c. The value of c increases as the quality factor of JPEG compression decreases. It is obvious that the embedding algorithm is image dependent. It is worth noting that, the c_{opt} values are small for images of relatively small size while these values increase as we move to images of greater size.

To demonstrate the differences on watermarked image quality, with respect to the values of the additive factor c, we watermarked the original image lena.jpg and we embedded a watermark with $c = c_{max}$ and $c = c_{opt}$, where $c_{max} \gg c_{opt}$ (see, Fig. 3); in the watermarked image in the middle we used $c = c_{max}$ for illustrative purposes.

4.2 Attack Issues

In this section we present the experimental results of our watermarking method under several attacks. In fact, we test the robustness of our method after applying the following attacks:

(A) JPEG Compression
(B) Gaussian Noise
(C) Geometric Transformations

Recall that, for the evaluation process we use the PSNR and SSIM metrics.

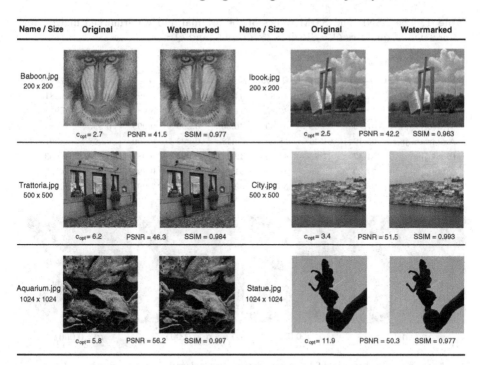

Name / Size	Original	Watermarked	Name / Size	Original	Watermarked
Baboon.jpg 200 x 200			Ibook.jpg 200 x 200		
	c_{opt} = 2.7 PSNR = 41.5 SSIM = 0.977			c_{opt} = 2.5 PSNR = 42.2 SSIM = 0.963	
Trattoria.jpg 500 x 500			City.jpg 500 x 500		
	c_{opt} = 6.2 PSNR = 46.3 SSIM = 0.984			c_{opt} = 3.4 PSNR = 51.5 SSIM = 0.993	
Aquarium.jpg 1024 x 1024			Statue.jpg 1024 x 1024		
	c_{opt} = 5.8 PSNR = 56.2 SSIM = 0.997			c_{opt} = 11.9 PSNR = 50.3 SSIM = 0.977	

Fig. 4. Some original images and their corresponding watermarked ones; for each image, its size and its c_{opt}, and PSNR and SSIM values are also shown, for $Q = 55$.

(A) JPEG Compression. The quality factor (or, for short, Q-factor) is a number that determines the degree of loss in the compression process when saving an image. In general, JPEG recommends a quality factor of 75–95 for visually indistinguishable quality difference, and a quality factor of 50–75 for merely acceptable quality. We compressed the images with Matlab using `imwrite` with different JPEG quality factors; we present results for $Q = 85$, $Q = 75$, $Q = 65$, and $Q = 55$.

Our watermarked images have excellent PSNR and SSIM values. In Fig. 4 we present six images of different sizes, along with their corresponding PSNR and SSIM values. Typical values for the PSNR in lossy image compression are between 40 and 70 dB, where higher is better. In our experiments, the PSNR values of 90 % of the watermarked images were greater than 40 dB. The SSIM values are almost equal to 1, which means that the watermarked image is quite similar to the original one, which explains the method's high fidelity.

In Table 1 we demonstrate the PSNR and SSIM values of some images that are used in this work. We observe that these values are decreasing on smaller quality factors. Also, as the additive value $c = c_{opt}$ increases for each quality factor, the quality decreases. Moreover, the additive value c that embeds robust marks for qualities $Q = 85$, $Q = 75$ and $Q = 65$, does not result in a significant image distortion as the tables suggest.

Table 1. The PSNR and SSIM values of the original and watermarked images, for compression of qualities $Q = 85$, $Q = 75$, $Q = 65$, and $Q = 55$.

Filename	PSNR				SSIM			
	$Q = 85$	$Q = 75$	$Q = 65$	$Q = 55$	$Q = 85$	$Q = 75$	$Q = 65$	$Q = 55$
Lena.jpg	54.04	50.10	46.82	44.86	0.997	0.993	0.986	0.981
Baboon.jpg	49.19	46.17	42.48	41.53	0.995	0.989	0.980	0.977
Trattoria.jpg	67.79	60.59	53.50	46.36	0.999	0.999	0.996	0.984
Aquarium.jpg	65.19	61.20	58.26	56.18	0.999	0.999	0.998	0.997
Ibook.jpg	51.47	47.78	44.76	42.21	0.994	0.987	0.976	0.963
City.jpg	57.20	52.86	48.63	51.54	0.998	0.995	0.987	0.993
Statue.jpg	63.58	58.40	54.90	50.30	0.998	0.995	0.990	0.977

original $\sigma^2 = 0.01$ $\sigma^2 = 0.001$ $\sigma^2 = 0.0001$

Fig. 5. The original image of Lena and its watermarked images with $\sigma^2 = 0.01$, $\sigma^2 = 0.001$ and $\sigma^2 = 0.0001$.

Table 2. The PSNR values of the original and watermarked images, for Gaussian noise with variance values $\sigma^2 = 0.01$, $\sigma^2 = 0.001$, and $\sigma^2 = 0.0001$.

Filename	$\sigma^2 = 0.01$	$\sigma^2 = 0.001$	$\sigma^2 = 0.0001$
Lena.jpg	24.94	34.75	44.62
Baboon.jpg	24.89	34.79	44.65
Trattoria.jpg	25.04	34.83	44.73
Aquarium.jpg	25.97	35.27	44.81
Ibook.jpg	25.01	34.79	44.62
City.jpg	24.89	34.76	44.70
Statue.jpg	25.37	35.12	44.92

(B) Gaussian Noise. We test the robustness of our watermarking model by adding Gaussian noise in the images with $mean = 0$ and deferent variances σ^2, that is, we use $\sigma^2 = 0.01$, $\sigma^2 = 0.001$ and $\sigma^2 = 0.0001$. Figure 5 illustrates the original image of Lena and the watermarked images with Gaussian noise of these three variance values. We have to mention that the watermark can be extracted successfully from the attacked image.

Table 2 presents the PSNR values of the original image and the watermarked image with Gaussian noise. As Table 2 and Fig. 5 indicate, although Gaussian noise with $\sigma^2 = 0.01$ introduces significant perceptual distortion in images, watermark remains imperceptible.

(C) Geometric Transformations. The robustness of the proposed model against geometric attacks was evaluated by applying common geometric attacks, which included rotation, cropping, and scaling.

C.1. Rotation Attacks

It is possible to detect whether the watermarked image has been subject to rotations, thanks to the following two properties of the 2DM representation of self-inverting permutations.

Due to the fact that the 2DM representation that has been used to mark the image is the result of a self-inverting permutation the sequence of the marked cells on the image is not random but there are the two properties that can be used to determine the angle of a watermarked image in respect with the original one and that has to do with the position of the marked cell in the main diagonal of the grid. The two properties are the following:

- The main diagonal of the $n^* \times n^*$ symmetric matrix A^* has always one and only one marked cell.
- The marked cell on the diagonal is always in the entry (i, i) of A^* where: $i = \lceil \frac{n^*}{2} \rceil + 1, \lceil \frac{n^*}{2} \rceil + 2, \ldots, n^*$.

In case the watermarked image has been subject to 90 degree rotation as demonstrated in Fig. 6(b) you may notice that the main diagonal has not any cells marked which means that we are dealing with a non valid watermark as there should have been exactly one marked cell.

The second case is when the watermarked image has been subject to 180 degree rotation as demonstrated in Fig. 6(c). In this case, beginning with the first property someone may notice that the main diagonal has one and only one marked cell meaning that the first property is satisfied confirming that the image has not been subject to 90 degree rotation.

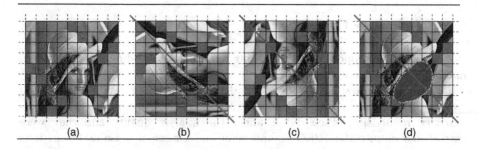

Fig. 6. (a) Watermarked image of Lena, (b) 90 degrees angled image, (c) 180 degrees angled image, and (d) cropped image.

The diagonal marked cell is situated in the grid's position (i, i); in our image $i = 3$ and thus $i < \lceil \frac{n^*}{2} \rceil$ since $n^* = 9$. It is against the second property meaning that the watermarked image has been subject to 180 degree rotation.

C.2. Cropping

Once again thanks to the fact that the 2DM representation a SiP has a symmetric property, i.e., the $n^* \times n^*$ matrix A^* is symmetric, our algorithm successfully extracts the watermark even marked parts of the watermarked image have been lost. This loss can be the result of cropping procedures to certain areas of the image. Recall that, this property is a consequence of the fact that at a self-inverting permutation, each element has its own inverse.

In Fig. 6(d) the removed marked part of the image can be recovered as marks using a SiP are symmetric on A^* with respect to the main diagonal. As a result, because of the fact that $A^*(4, 8)$ is marked, $A^*(8, 4)$ is marked as well. Taking that into account we conclude that the lost marked cell is $A^*(8, 4)$ and then we correctly extract the embedded watermark.

C.3. Scaling

In the case where a watermarked image has underwent significant scaling then extracting a watermark may be unsuccessful. In our model if an image has been scaled by a known ratio then each cell of the imaginary grid has underwent exactly the same scaling meaning that the magnitude cell has now a different size as well. Due to this fact, the width of the annuli will be incorrect making it impossible to calculate the appropriate difference between them. A solution to this would be to use different sized annuli in order to calculate the valid difference between them so that to spot marked areas.

The idea is simple, considering that we know the scaling ratio that the image has underwent we apply the same ratio calculating the new width for the two annuli. So if for example we used $P_b = 2$ and $P_r = 2$ for the width of the "Blue" and the "Red" annulus respectively when we performed the embedding procedure and the image has underwent 50 % scaling then in order to extract the embedded watermark from the image we have to use $P_b^* = 1$ and $P_r^* = 1$.

In order to calculate the difference between the same frequency bands, in the second case where the magnitude cell has 50 % of the initial size, we use annuli that have 50 % less width in comparison with the ones originally embedded.

5   Concluding Remarks

In this paper we propose a watermarking model for embedding invisible watermarks into digital images.

We experimentally tested our codec algorithms on color JPEG images with various and different characteristics. We obtained positive results as the watermarks were invisible, they didn't affect the images' quality and they were extractable despite the JPEG compression and Gaussian noise addition. It is worth noting that the proposed algorithms are robust against rotation or cropping attacks.

The study of our quality function f remains an interesting problem for further investigation; indeed, f could incorporate learning algorithms [22] so that to be able to return the c_{opt} accurately and in a very short computational time.

References

1. Garfinkel, S.: Web Security, Privacy and Commerce, 2nd edn. O'Reilly, Sebastopol (2001)
2. Chun-Shien, L., Shih-Kun, H., Chwen-Jye, S., Hong-Yuan, M.L.: Cocktail watermarking for digital image protection. IEEE Trans. Multimedia **4**, 209–224 (2000)
3. Davis, J.C.: Intellectual property in cyberspace - what technological/legislative tools are necessary for building a sturdy global information infrastructure? In: IEEE Proceedings of the International Symposium on Technology and Society, pp. 66–74 (1997)
4. O'Ruanaidh, J.J.K., Dowling, W.J., Boland, F.M.: Watermarking digital images for copyright protection. In: IEEE Proceedings of the Vision, Image and Signal Processing, vol. 143, pp. 250–256 (1996)
5. Cox, I.J., Miller, M.L., Bloom, J.A., Fridrich, J., Kalker, T.: Digital Watermarking and Steganography, 2nd edn. Morgan Kaufmann, San Francisco (2008)
6. Grover, D.: The Protection of Computer Software - Its Technology and Applications. Cambridge University Press, New York (1997)
7. Collberg, C., Nagra, J.: Surreptitious Software. Addison-Wesley, Upper Saddle River (2010)
8. Cox, I., Kilian, J., Leighton, T., Shamoon, T.: A secure, robust watermark for multimedia. In: Anderson, R. (ed.) IH 1996. LNCS, vol. 1174, pp. 317–333. Springer, Heidelberg (1996)
9. Gonzalez, R.C., Woods, R.E., Eddins, S.L.: Digital Image Processing using Matlab. Prentice-Hall, Upper Saddle River (2003)
10. Sedgewick, R., Flajolet, P.: An Introduction to the Analysis of Algorithms. Addison-Wesley, Reading (1996)
11. Golumbic, M.C.: Design Patterns: Algorithmic Graph Theory and Perfect Graphs. Academic Press Inc., New York (1980)
12. Chroni, M., Nikolopoulos, S.D.: Encoding watermark integers as self-inverting permutations. In: International Conference on Computer Systems and Technologies (CompSysTech'10), ACM ICPS 471, pp. 125–130 (2010)
13. Chroni, M., Nikolopoulos, S.D.: An efficient graph codec system for software watermarking. In: IEEE Proceedings of the 36th International Conference on Computers, Software, and Applications (STPSA'12), pp. 595–600 (2012)
14. Gonzalez, R.C., Woods, R.E.: Digital Image Processing, 3rd edn. Prentice-Hall, Upper Saddle River (2007)
15. Solachidis, V., Pitas, I.: Circularly symmetric watermark embedding in 2-D DFT domain. IEEE Trans. Image Process. **10**, 1741–1753 (2001)
16. Licks, V., Hordan, R.: On digital image watermarking robust to geometric transformations. In: IEEE Proceedings of the International Conference on Image Processing, vol. 3, pp. 690–693 (2000)
17. Petitcolas, P.: Image database for watermarking. http://www.petitcolas.net/fabien/watermarking/
18. Wang, Z., Bovic, A.C., Sheikh, H.R., Simoncelli, E.P.: Image quality assessment: from error visibility to structural similarity. IEEE Trans. Image Process. **13**, 600–612 (2004)

19. Hore, A., Ziou, D.: Image quality metrics: PSNR vs. SSIM. In: Proceedings of the 20th International Conference on Pattern Recognition, pp. 2366–2369 (2010)
20. Kaur, M., Jindal, S., Behal, S.: A study of digital image watermarking. J. Res. Eng. Appl. Sci. **2**, 126–136 (2012)
21. Zain, J.M.: Strict authentication watermarking with JPEG compression (SAW-JPEG) for medical images. Eur. J. Sci. Res. **2**, 250–256 (2011)
22. Russell, S., Norvig, P.: Artificial Intelligence: A Modern Approach, 3rd edn. Prentice-Hall, Upper Saddle River (2010)

Web Interfaces and Applications

Towards a Web of Semantic Tags

Geert Vanderhulst[(✉)] and Lieven Trappeniers

Alcatel-Lucent Bell Labs, Copernicuslaan 50, 2018 Antwerpen, Belgium
{geert.vanderhulst,lieven.trappeniers}@alcatel-lucent.com

Abstract. Folksonomies are widely used to classify content on the Web. However, plain text annotations hardly fit the vision of the Semantics Web, where an unambiguous understanding of the data by both user and machine is key. Ontologies underpinning the Web help to resolve the ambiguity problem, but a.o. the absence of a detailed world ontology still puts end-user tagging in the front seat for basic content classification. In this paper, we propose semantic tags to bridge the gap between plain text keywords and ontologies. Sematags define aliases (synonyms) and isas (hypernyms) to better cope with the issues traditional tags suffer from. We illustrate how sematags can be defined from scratch or extracted from existing lexicons and knowledge bases. To evaluate our approach, we composed sematags from Wikipedia concepts and used those to semi-automatically tag photos on Flickr.

Keywords: Tagging · Ambiguity · Soft semantics

1 Introduction

The basic premise of the Semantic Web is to represent knowledge in a meaningful way so that computers can function more effectively by being able to distinguish different meanings of data. This is achieved by describing data using languages with a logical entailment such as OWL and RDF. We refer to this approach using the term *hard semantics* since linked data is typically mapped on ontological resources by domain experts or agents. Besides, we witness an emerge of folksonomies to create order in a rapidly expanding Web of data [16,18]. The increasing popularity of tags as a flat space of keywords is both visible on websites such as Youtube, Flickr, Del.icio.us and across social networks (e.g. hashtags on Twitter). However, there are still a number of limitations of the current state of technology as identified in [5]: (i) tag ambiguity, (ii) missing links between multiple synonyms, spelling variants, or morphological variants, and (iii) variation in the level of granularity and specificity of the tags used caused by differences in the domain expertise of agents. These issues are due to the fact that tags typically have *no semantics* associated. In this paper we present TagNet, a framework that eases the task of annotating and searching for resources on the Web using *soft semantics*. Rather than defining hard links to ontological concepts, we add additional detail to a tag to remove ambiguity and

© Springer-Verlag Berlin Heidelberg 2014
K.-H. Krempels and A. Stocker (Eds.): WEBIST 2013, LNBIP 189, pp. 87–102, 2014.
DOI: 10.1007/978-3-662-44300-2_6

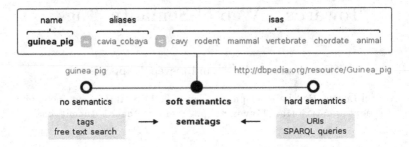

Fig. 1. A sematag consists of a name, *aliases* and *isas* which we label as soft semantics. Its purpose is to link tag-based systems (no semantics) with semantic knowledge bases (hard semantics).

facilitate automatic derivation of links to existing knowledge bases. In TagNet, tags (i.e. plain text keywords) are annotated in two dimensions: each tag (i.e. *sematag*) defines *aliases* and *isas* as illustrated in Fig. 1. Aliases are keywords that can be used as a synonym for a given tag (e.g. synonyms, acronyms, etc.) and isas are keywords that generalize the meaning of the tag (e.g. sport is an isa for tennis). The combination of aliases and isas helps us to understand and express the meaning of a tag using additional tags, similar to the approach taken in [5]. We distinguish between aliases and isas because it matches well with the detail of information contained in dictionaries (e.g. WordNet [4]) and ontologies (e.g. the DBpedia [2] ontology) which are suitable sources to extract tags from as outlined in Sect. 2. For instance, the WordNet lexicon expresses linguistic relations between words such as synonyms (aliases) and hypernyms (isas). Also in ontologies, there is a notion of similar concepts (aliases) – expressed in OWL using constructs such as `owl:sameAs` (instance level) and `owl:equivalentClass` (class level) – and 'isa' relations contained in an ontology which directly map on the isas of a tag in TagNet. TagNet advances the state of the art by exploiting soft semantics both in the annotation process of arbitrary resources on the Web and during search operations. To solve ambiguity for end-users, we explain the different senses of a keyword using the isas and aliases of tags matching the keyword (Sect. 3) which is also useful to refine search queries (Sect. 4). A unique advantage of sematags over hard URIs is their scalability to tag-based systems combined with the ability to map them on linked data, as illustrated in Sect. 5 by means of a case study.

2 Tagging Vocabularies

To stimulate reuse and sharing of existing sematags and relieve users of specifying aliases and isas manually, TagNet relies on vocabularies from which tags are extracted and suggested to users. Basically, a tag (i.e. entered keyword) is only valid if it can be found in a vocabulary compatible with TagNet. However, since this constraint would prohibit free tagging, we relax it by requiring that the

Fig. 2. A vocabulary takes a keyword as input and outputs one or more sematags.

name of the tag can be freely chosen, as long as it is annotated with at least one isa that appears in a controlled vocabulary. Hence, a user can annotate a picture of a pet using the sematag `mickey` (the name of the pet), provided that it is enriched with e.g. a known `dog` isa tag.

We consider WordNet and DBpedia as main, controlled vocabularies for Tag-Net thanks to their wide coverage of contemporary terms. A lexicon such as WordNet contains a rich set of words that are part of the English language, but it still lacks several concepts such as names of places, people, companies, television shows, etc. In addition to language-specific words, we also want to include commonly accepted terms that are introduced by a community of users. The DBpedia vocabulary extracts tags out of content that was published on Wikipedia. Examples of tag names that are supported by this vocabulary are `google`, `san francisco`, `madonna`, etc. Whilst Wikipedia covers a large set of generally accepted terms, it still excludes concepts that only matter to specific users such as names of family members or pets and highly specialized terms related to a particular domain (e.g. medicines). To share such specialized tags, custom user- or domain-specific vocabularies can be integrated in TagNet as discussed in Sect. 6. Figure 2 illustrates the main task of a vocabulary: taking a keyword as input, a vocabulary outputs one or more tags that attribute a meaning to the keyword using isas and aliases. Note that sematags do not contain direct references to concepts defined in the vocabulary's underlying knowledge base. For example, a tag extracted from the WordNet lexicon does not store a reference to a WordNet synset, nor does a DBpedia tag contain a link to a Wikipedia page. We opted for such a loose coupling because it allows us to describe and interpret all tags equally and independent of the semantics underlying a vocabulary. However, decoupling tags and vocabularies also introduces a new level of ambiguity between similar tags extracted from different vocabularies. For instance, the term `dog` is found both in WordNet and the DBpedia vocabulary with slightly different semantics. To overcome this ambiguity, we add a label to each tag that identifies the vocabulary from where the tag originates. In the next sections we outline how tags are extracted from WordNet and DBpedia.

2.1   WordNet Vocabulary

In WordNet, words are organized in synsets: sets of words with a similar meaning (i.e. synonyms). For each synset, hypernyms can be looked up (e.g. animal is a hypernym of dog). Hence, for each word in a synset, a sematag can be composed as follows:

1. the name of the tag is the name of the word;
2. the aliases of the sematag correspond to the names of all other words in the synset;
3. the isas of the sematag relate to the names of all direct hypernyms of the synset including hypernyms of hypernyms.

A keyword that is looked up in WordNet can appear in multiple synsets if it has several meanings and thus gives rise to multiple sematags, one for each sense. To improve the results, we filter out generic hypernyms such as `living thing`, `object`, `entity` and `whole` as they do not contribute to the differentiation of senses. The tag depicted in Fig. 1 is an example of a sematag produced by the WordNet vocabulary.

The WordNet vocabulary is further subdivided in the following subvocabularies: nouns, verbs, adjectives and adverbs. This allows users and agents to quickly distinguish between senses, knowing the lexical role of a keyword.

2.2   DBpedia Vocabulary

The DBpedia ontology organizes Wikipedia concepts in a structured hierarchy currently covering about 320 classes and 1650 different properties. There is an opportunity to generate sematags out of DBpedia classes (e.g. http://dbpedia.org/ontology/Person, instances (e.g. http://dbpedia.org/resource/Semantic_Web) and properties (e.g. http://dbpedia.org/ontology/birthDate). In this section, we will only elaborate on classes and instances, yet properties are briefly discussed in Sect. 8. To understand how sematags are extracted from DBpedia, we will first introduce the notion of redirects and disambiguates in the DBpedia ontology:

Redirects. The `dbo:wikiPageRedirects` property maps a resource on another resource. An example is the resource `Cow` which does not have its own page on Wikipedia, yet is redirected to the resource `Cattle`. Hence we can interpret `cow` as an alias for `cattle` and vice versa. Several redirects are also defined to support different descriptions of the same resource. For instance, the resource `Winston_Churchill` is also referred to as `Sir_Winston` and `Prime_Minister_Churchill`.

Disambiguates. The `dbo:wikiPageDisambiguates` property maps a virtual resource on a collection of relevant resources that could be intended by a particular term. An example is the `Bird_(disambiguation)` resource which links to o.a. `Bird` (animal), `Birds,_Illinois` (community in the USA) and `The_Birds_(film)` (a Hitchcock movie). These resources can be considered as distinct senses of the term `bird`.

For a given keyword, the DBpedia vocabulary will lookup resources that match the keyword, also following redirects. If a match results in a disambiguating resource, each linked resource is also added to the temporary result set. Next, for each resource aliases are collected including the name of the resource if distinct from the keyword. This is achieved by asking for all resources for which a redirect exists to the current resource. The isas of a DBpedia sematag are populated by analyzing the classes to which a resource belongs (indicated by the `rdf:type` relation). Whilst DBpedia concepts are also mapped on other ontologies such as the YAGO knowledge base [17], we currently require isas to be part of the DBpedia ontology. The reason for this is the level of detail provided by YAGO classes (e.g. `FilmsBasedOnShortFiction`, `1960sHorrorFilms`) as compared to DBpedia classes (e.g. `Film`). Too much detail compromises the general applicability of a sematag. Some examples of tags extracted from DBpedia resources are listed in Fig. 2. In addition, keywords are directly matched with classes in the DBpedia ontology. If a matching class is found, a sematag is created as follows:

1. the keyword that serves as name for the tag is substituted by an asterisk, indicating that the tag name does not matter;
2. no aliases are added (no relevant `owl:equivalentClass` relations are defined in the DBpedia ontology);
3. the class name is included as isa, as well as any parent classes.

The last sematag depicted in Fig. 2 is extracted from the `Bird` class in the DBpedia ontology.

3   Explaining Tags Using Tags

When a resource is annotated using TagNet, a tag keyword is looked up in available vocabularies. If the keyword is found and multiple senses are detected, the user is requested to select the proper meaning in the context of the resource. However, disambiguating between different meanings of a keyword is not always a trivial task. This is largely due to the fact that several words have multiple senses, many of which we do not use in daily life or even are aware of. For instance, according to WordNet the noun `dog` has seven senses of which most are less commonly used, e.g. 'informal term for a man' and 'metal supports for logs in a fireplace'. Similar, when looking up a keyword in DBpedia, several concepts with the same name yet a different meaning are typically returned. These often include unexpected results because the search term also corresponds to the name of an (infamous) music album, place or alike. A straight-forward approach to let users distinguish between multiple meanings is to present them with a list of explanations as lined up above, and let them pick the intended one. However, this approach postulates some issues preventing quick disambiguation. First, it clearly takes time for a user to read all sense descriptions of a word as to identify the intended sense. Descriptions are often verbose and/or expressed using scientific terms, making it hard to grasp what is meant exactly (e.g. describing a dog as 'a member of the genus Canis' is still confusing). Secondly, several senses only marginally differ in semantics from each other. This level of detail is redundant for most tagging purposes and causes uncertainty when trying to select the proper sense. To increase the efficiency of perceiving a tag's senses, we present

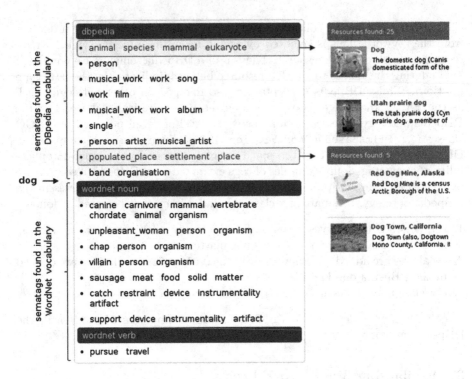

Fig. 3. Ambiguous senses of a keyword are explained to users by means of the isas of matching sematags. A dialog visualizes the results of a tag lookup in available vocabularies and allows users to pick the intended sense.

a filtered set of the isas of a tag – instead of sense descriptions – arranged by the (sub)vocabulary they originate from as illustrated in Fig. 3. These isas are fast to read and hence help to quickly differentiate between senses. Sematags are further organized by their aliases – e.g. dog, utah_prairie_dog, etc. – and can be picked on class level (only isas are included) as well as instance level (aliases are included that map on a unique resource, similar to a URI).

The reason we opted for isas as the primary means to distinguish between tags with a similar name is because we learned that (i) tags extracted from WordNet and DBpedia generally contain more indicative isas than alias and (ii) broader terms seem more helpful than similar terms to understand the semantics of a tag. However, additional user experiments are needed to validate this claim which is based on our own experience. Moreover, to improve the understandability of tags explaining tags, it might be useful to incorporate statistics about the popularity of words to decide which tags are best suited to explain the semantics of tags. Another option is to give up some semantic detail in favor of a simplified tagging experience; a proper balance is needed. A coarser filter could for instance group the WordNet tags with isas unpleasant_woman, chap and villain into a single tag with isas person and organism. Similar, we could prune the DBpedia tags

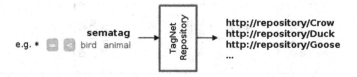

Fig. 4. A repository takes sematags as input and outputs resources matching a search query composed from the input.

and only display key terms such as `animal`, `person`, `song`, `album`, `place` and `band`.

4   TagNet as Search Tool

In this section we elaborate on the role of sematags to facilitate search operations in a repository populated by resources. We represent a resource by a URI, a name (label), a description and an optional image (thumbnail). Resources are annotated with sematags which are extracted from vocabularies as explained in Sect. 2. The extra information contained in sematags is exploited when retrieving resources. Search terms are not only compared to a tag's name, but are also matched with its aliases and isas such that searching for `animal` will also yield resources that are tagged as `bird` or `dog`. TagNet implements a meta-search algorithm that accepts a mix of sematags and keywords – encoded as sematags with no isas and aliases – to find resources in connected repositories. A sematag $t1$ matches a sematag $t2$ if and only if:

1. $t1$ and $t2$ originate from the same vocabulary, and;
2. $t1$ has the same name as $t2$ or an alias exists in $t2$ with the same name as $t1$ or an isa exists in $t1$ with the same name as $t2$[1], and;
3. all isas contained in $t1$ also exist in $t2$.

A search query tunnelled through TagNet can be refined dynamically. Initially, search keywords are passed to TagNet which are matched with the name and tags of resources in a target repository. If the results are considered too many and/or too diverse, the search results are narrowed down by indicating the actual meaning of one or more keywords. To this end, sematags representing the various senses of a keyword are looked up in available vocabularies and presented to the user in a dialog as depicted in Fig. 3. Finally, selected sematags are sent along with remaining keywords (that were not disambiguated) to a target repository and resources are returned. Hence sematags help users to resolve ambiguity *at search time* and refine a search query (Fig. 4).

In the next two sections we discuss how sematags can be used to search for resources in WordNet and DBpedia repositories. Note that the knowledge base underlying WordNet and DBpedia is used both for tag extraction (using vocabularies) and retrieval of resources (using repositories). Sematags originating from

---

[1] Note that wildcards are allowed in tag names. A * matches any tag name.

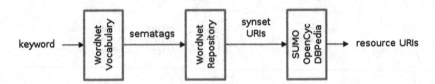

Fig. 5. Facts about resources can be inferred from WordNet sematags by first translating the tags into synset URIs and then using these URIs to locate resources in a knowledge base mapped on WordNet.

the WordNet vocabulary relate to synsets which can be considered as annotated WordNet resources. Similar, it makes sense to query a DBpedia repository using DBpedia sematags because resources in this repository are already (virtually) annotated with DBpedia sematags.

4.1 WordNet Repository

In the WordNet repository, each synset is identified by a URI that is composed of an identifier such as `dog-0` with `dog` being the name of the synset and 0 corresponding to its sense number. Searching for synsets using sematags is achieved by looking up all synsets matching the keyword of the sematag and filtering out the results by comparing aliases and isas. Figure 5 shows that the ability to search through WordNet via sematags is useful for finding resources in a knowledge base that is mapped on WordNet such as SUMO [12], OpenCyc [10], DBpedia, etc. Sematags originating from WordNet can be translated into synset URIs which can then be used to query for resources that are linked to particular synsets.

4.2 DBpedia Repository

In the DBpedia repository, Wikipedia content is seen as a collection of resources that are virtually annotated with sematags. Given a sematag, a search algorithm can look for resources annotated with a matching sematag. Although these sematags do not really exist, we can assume they do according to the following rules based on the tag extraction method outlined in Sect. 2.2:

- each resource is annotated with a sematag having the same name as the resource itself;
- the aliases of the sematag are derived from 'redirects' and 'disambiguates' pointing to the resource;
- the isas of the sematag relate to the class hierarchy of the resource in the DBpedia ontology.

The following SPARQL query collects resources that match this scheme:

```
SELECT DISTINCT ?r ?l ?c ?t
WHERE {
  ?r rdfs:label ?l; dbo:abstract ?c.
```

```
?r a <$tag.isa1>; a <$tag.isa2>.
FILTER (bif:contains(?1,'"$tag.name" or "$tag.alias1"')).
FILTER ((langMatches(lang(?1), "en")) && (langMatches(lang(?c), "en"))).
OPTIONAL { ?r dbo:thumbnail ?t }
}
```

This query does not include resources connected through `dbo:wikiPageRedirects` or `dbo:wikiPageDisambiguates` properties. We include these resources using separate queries to keep the queries simple and performant.

5   Evaluation

To evaluate the effectiveness of soft semantics to link tagged resources with a semantic knowledge base, we tested how tags used in Web services such as Del.icio.us, Flickr and Youtube can be dynamically mapped on DBpedia or WordNet resources and vice versa. With such links in place, we can infer facts about a photo or video using its tags and involve tagged resources in semantic queries. In a first step, we explored how additional tag detail can be introduced in Flickr. Next, we investigated which steps should be traversed to unambiguously link a collection of popular tags to related DBpedia or WordNet resources.

5.1   Introducing Sematags in Flickr

In Flickr, photos are classified by means of user-generated (ambiguous) keywords. Rather than substituting these tags for URIs of semantic resources – wich are incompatible with a tag-based system like Flickr – we aim to upgrade these tags to sematags and hence remove ambiguity and facilitate mappings to resources through TagNet. However, this means that sematags need to be stored in Flickr, when annotating a photo. We thus need a way to seamlessly inject isas and aliases in a legacy tagging system without breaking its core functionalities (e.g. search functionality). To this end, we consider two approaches:

1. sematags are encoded in a string notation such as `name|alias1|isa1;isa2` (e.g. `atlantis||db:space_shuttle`) and added as a single tag to a link, or;
2. sematags are flattened into an array of tags composed of the name of the tag and its isas (e.g. `name, isa1, isa2`) and added as distinct tags to a resource.

The former approach is compatible with Flickr (and a.o. also Del.icio.us) and results in a number of benefits: (i) free text searches in Flickr now also range over the synonyms and hypermyns of a tag, (ii) search queries can be passed through TagNet, semantically refined and forwarded to Flickr using Flickr's open API, (iii) unlike hard links, sematags can easily be understood by humans and machines and (iv) sematags can be mapped on linked data and vice versa. However, we acknowledge that a custom encoding of sematags is not recognized by existing systems, resulting in poor textual representations of sematags. Sematags could be rendered in a more visually appealing way by hiding aliases and isas by default and depicting those when hovering over a tag or clicking on it. Furthermore, if sematags are not natively supported, internal free text searches will also match vocabulary labels prepended to tags such as db: which is not desirable.

The latter approach gives up on aliases and loses information about relationships between tags. In a flattened array of multiple sematags, it is unclear which tags are actually isas and to which tag they belong. Hence it is impossible to unambiguously map multiple flattened sematags on semantic resources. Yet, matching a sematag with a set of flattened sematags (i.e. the other way round) will only yield false positives in rare cases if tags are compared as follows. A sematag t matches an array of tags T if and only if:

1. T contains t or T contains an alias that exists in t, and;
2. T contains every isa that exists in t.

A situation where false positives are possible occurs if a sematag $t2$ introduces keywords in T that compromise the semantics of a flattened sematag $t1$. For instance, if a link is tagged using a keyword dog in the sense of an animal and another tag introduces the keyword person, then searching for a dog in the sense of a person would incorrectly return the resource. Sematags with wildcards in their name (see Fig. 2) should also be avoided here. However, the main drawback of this approach is the lack of aliases which are needed by a machine to distinguish between resources annotated with the same set of isas.

5.2   From Tagged Photo to Linked Photo: A Case Study

We used a *public beta release of TagNet*[2] and the all time most popular tags on Flickr[3] as a starting point for our study. These comprise 142 tags, related to the broad domain of photography, and are listed in Fig. 6. We looked up each tag in TagNet using DBpedia as primary repository and assigned a score based on the relevance of the search results which were limited to 20 results per query for usability reasons. The results of this step are summarized in Table 1 and marked on Fig. 6. It shows that 110 tags received an A score, meaning that they were correctly mapped on a corresponding DBpedia resource in the first hit. For example, the tag fall is resolved into http://dbpedia.org/resource/Autumn and nyc maps on http://dbpedia.org/resource/New_York_City. To denote the connection with DBpedia, we added the db prefix to tags with an A score such that TagNet knows which repository to use to map the tag on a URI.

For tags with a B score, additional detail should be added to overcome ambiguity. For instance, canon is in the first place known by DBpedia as a city in Georgia, a priest, a list of topics related to Dutch history, etc., while in the context of photography it refers to a company specialized in the manufacturing of imaging and optical products. From the related DBpedia resource (http://dbpedia.org/resource/Canon_(company), two isas can be extracted (company and organisation) which

---

[2] http://sematags.belllabs.be/
[3] http://www.flickr.com/photos/tags/

animals, architecture, art, asia, australia, autumn, baby, **band**$_C$, barcelona, beach, berlin, **bike**$_C$, bird, birds, birthday, black, **blackandwhite**$_D$, blue, **bw**$_C$, california, canada, **canon**$_B$, car, cat, chicago, china, christmas, **church**$_B$, city, clouds, color, concert, dance, day, **de**$_C$, dog, england, europe, fall, family, fashion, festival, film, florida, flower, flowers, food, football, france, **friends**$_B$, fun, garden, geotagged, germany, girl, graffiti, green, halloween, hawaii, holiday, house, india, **instagramapp**$_D$, iphone, **iphoneography**$_D$, island, italia, italy, japan, **kids**$_C$, **la**$_C$, lake, landscape, light, **live**$_B$, london, love, **macro**$_B$, **me**$_D$, mexico, **model**$_B$, museum, music, nature, **new**$_C$, newyork, **newyorkcity**$_D$, night, nikon, nyc, ocean, **old**$_C$, paris, park, party, people, photo, photography, photos, portrait, **raw**$_B$, red, river, **rock**$_B$, **san**$_C$, **sanfrancisco**$_D$, scotland, sea, seattle, **show**$_C$, sky, snow, spain, **spring**$_C$, **square**$_B$, **squareformat**$_D$, street, summer, sun, sunset, taiwan, texas, thailand, tokyo, travel, tree, trees, **trip**$_C$, uk, **unitedstates**$_D$, **urban**$_B$, usa, vacation, **vintage**$_C$, **washington**$_C$, water, wedding, white, winter, woman, yellow, zoo

Fig. 6. By default, 110 out of 142 popular Flickr tags (77.5 %) are mapped correctly on a valid DBpedia resource through TagNet (A score). Tags that need additional attention to resolve ambiguity are marked in bold and labeled with a B, C or D score (see Table 1).

Table 1. Scores attributed to the search results of 142 random tags in TagNet using its DBpedia vocabulary.

Score	Description of score	Tags
A	The first hit matches a corresponding DBpedia resource.	110
B	The results contain a match, but not in the first hit.	10
C	None of the results correspond to a match.	14
D	No results were found.	8

give rise to a sematag `db:canon||company,organisation` – encoded in a Flickr-compatible format as discussed in Sect. 5.1 – that uniquely identifies the resource in TagNet. Similar, `friends` is recognized by default as a sitcom while the resource http://dbpedia.org/resource/Friendship is actually the best match for this tag's meaning. The `Friendship` resource has no specific isas, but by including its name as an alias to a `friend` tag (i.e. `friend|db:friendship`), TagNet can distinguish between the different senses. As such, each DBpedia resource can be described unambiguously by a human-understandable sematag that can be dereferenced to a URI via TagNet and vice versa. Note that we prefer to augment a tag with isas (if available) over aliases derived from a resource's label since these specific aliases often tend to be spelling variants of the tag name or informally refer to its isas. For instance, an alias of `canon` in the sense of the Japanese multinational would be `canon_(company)`.

Tags with a C or D score need extra attention. No resources with a matching name exist in DBpedia or they are not in line with the meaning of the tag. This leaves us with two options: i) lookup the tag in a secondary repository or ii) replace the tag by a similar tag or add A-rated aliases or isas to the tag. By relying on WordNet as secondary repository, seven more tags (**band**, **bike**, **kids**, new, old, show, washington) were attributed an A or B score and thus could be upgraded to sematags with a wn: prefix (e.g. wn:bike).

To clarify the semantics of the remaining 15 tags, we have to find at least one meaningful isa or alias for each tag. For instance, the tag me and iphoneography can be annotated with db:person and db:blog isas respectively. Tags like newyorkcity and sanfrancisco need an alias that is spelled differently (e.g. db:nyc, db:san_francisco) or substituted by this alias, while the tag instagramapp can be understood using an instagram alias.

Tags like blackandwhite (and by extension also typical Twitter hashtags such as #savetheplanet) are more difficult to map on linked data as they denote a very specific property, a state of mind or expression which is hard to describe using formal semantics. In summary, we showed that 127 out of 142 random tags (89.4 %) could be mapped with minimal effort on known concepts using DBpedia as primary and WordNet as secondary vocabulary. *By systematically enriching a tag with additional tags, a (sema)tag becomes an alternate notation for a URI that scales better to tag-based systems like Flickr, as it is human readable and supports free text queries (including synonym and hypernym matching).*

6   Architecture and Implementation

TagNet is developed as a Java Web application, using Servlet technology in the back-end and AJAX technology in the front-end. It offers a REST API and has an open-ended design such that custom vocabularies and repositories can easily be plugged in by implementing a Vocabulary and Repository interface respectively. An overview of the architecture is presented in Fig. 7. The WordNet vocabulary and repository make use of the WordNet 3.0 database files[4] while the DBpedia vocabulary and repository rely on the online DBpedia Virtuoso SPARQL endpoint[5]. The dependency on the DBpedia SPARQL query engine is a bottleneck in the current beta implementation. On the one hand, it allows TagNet to run on light-weight servers with limited memory available, but on the other hand we rely on live data which might not always be available in time. Each request for sematags or resources is translated into SPARQL queries which are directed to the online DBpedia SPARQL endpoint. Although a lot of effort was spent in optimizing these queries, we experienced huge differences in their processing time which is probably due to a variable load of the Virtuoso SPARQL engine over time. While the execution of a query can be considered relatively fast at one moment, the same query might time out moments later. To bypass these performance issues, we replicated the DBpedia database on a local server such that network latencies and processing delays caused by high loads were avoided. Furthermore, we could cache sematags that were looked up in the DBpedia vocabulary and pre-generate a repository of annotated resource URIs. This would dramatically speed up the matching of tags since additional queries are only needed to collect the data associated with matching resource URIs.

---

[4] http://wordnet.princeton.edu/wordnet/download/
[5] http://dbpedia.org/sparql/

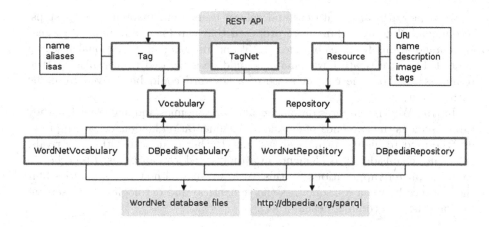

Fig. 7. TagNet architecture overview.

7   Related Work

Previous work that has been done in the area of tagging is quite diverse. For instance, models have been proposed to represent relationships between agents, resources and tags and augment user-contributed data [7,11]; frameworks were proposed to add meaning to tags [5,8,13]; sharing and reuse of social tagging data has been studied [6,9] as well as recommendation algorithms [1,14,15].

In the remainder of this section, we elaborate on the works with the closest match to TagNet and discuss how they differ or match. MOAT [13] extends an ontology designed for tagging [11] and aims to enrich free tags (i.e. any user-defined keywords) with additional meaning. Similar to TagNet, MOAT looks up the global meaning of keywords in a controlled vocabulary and allows users to select the appropriate meaning, or define a new meaning by referring to a Web resource (e.g. a DBpedia resource). Unlike tags in MOAT which are stored externally, sematags can be injected in real-world tagging systems and mapped on knowledge bases through TagNet.

Another approach to add meaning to tags is presented in Tags4Tags [5] where the underlying meaning of tag can be revealed by means of another tag. In this work, the typical meta-model in which a Web resource maintains one or more `hasTag` relations with tag literals is expanded with typed relationships between a pair of tags. The ideas postulated in Tags4Tags were reused in HyperTwitter [8]. Using so-called 'tripletweets', tag equivalence (e.g. `#webist13 = #webist2013`, tag specializations (e.g. `#tennis subtag #sports`) and predefined relations between tags (e.g. `#munich >translation #muenchen`) can be expressed. This is completely in line with the vision of TagNet: a Twitter vocabulary can process tripletweets and generate sematags out of them. Moreover, sematags could be incorporated in HyperTwitter to express that the hashtag `#webist13` is a subtag of a sematag `webist`.

To cope with large datasets and relieve users from manual tagging steps, recommendation algorithms were proposed that can (semi-automatically) generate annotations from Web pages [1,15] and images [14]. Additional research is needed to investigate how sematags could be generated from arbitrary Web resources, i.e. how the correct sense of a keyword could be derived from the current context.

In [19], Weller compares ontologies and folksonomies and suggests that they can be seen as the two ends of a scale of documentation languages ranging from unstructured to highly formalised systems. Rather than seeing them as rivals, they can be considered as elements in a toolbox which can be used together to support concrete applications. In this work, we showed how soft semantics blur the distance between folksonomies (no semantics) and ontologies (hard semantics) and help to complete each other.

8   Conclusions and Outlook

The key contributions of TagNet are twofold. First, TagNet introduces sematags which annotate regular keywords with isas and aliases, hence solving typical tag-related issues such as dealing with ambiguity, spelling variants and variations in the specificity of tags. Unlike other approaches, sematags do not include hard links to Web resources but rather contain a minimal set of information – extracted from pluggable vocabularies – that is used to lookup related resources in a repository. This loose coupling guarantees that folksonomies remain folksonomies (using richer tags) yet unambiguous links to concepts in formal knowledge bases can still be retrieved. By supporting WordNet and DBpedia as default vocabularies, we cover a wide range of contemporary meaningful tags. Second, TagNet serves as an extensible meta-search engine. We illustrated how TagNet is used to search through DBpedia using sematags and explained how other repositories can be supported. We also indicated how sematags can be scaled to support legacy tagging systems and give rise to enriched folksonomies.

In future work, we want to further explore and validate the effectiveness of using tags to explain the different senses of a keyword to users. Another interesting path to explore is the use of extended 'facets' (categories and subcategories to which resources belong) to narrow down search results. Sematags support basic faceted search by default as isas classify resources in categories. To better align with existing faceted search engines, we could indicate how many resources match a sematag while refining a search operation using the dialog depicted in Fig. 3. In [3], Ben-Yitzhak et al. also explained the importance of gaining insight in the data behind facets which is far richer than just knowing the quantities of resources that belong to each facet. We see an opportunity to include information about the properties of a resource in (intermediate) search results and (refined) search queries. For instance, we can also annotate properties of resources using sematags. Searching for e.g. 'birthplace artist' in DBpedia with 'birthplace' and 'artist' both being resolved to sematags – the former matching a property, the latter matching resources – would result in a list of instances of the DBpedia

`Artist` class for which a `birthPlace` property is defined (which is also included in the search results).

References

1. Araujo, S., Houben, G.-J., Schwabe, D.: Linkator: enriching web pages by automatically adding dereferenceable semantic annotations. In: Benatallah, B., Casati, F., Kappel, G., Rossi, G. (eds.) ICWE 2010. LNCS, vol. 6189, pp. 355–369. Springer, Heidelberg (2010)
2. Auer, S., Bizer, C., Kobilarov, G., Lehmann, J., Cyganiak, R., Ives, Z.G.: DBpedia: a nucleus for a web of open data. In: Aberer, K., et al. (eds.) ASWC 2007 and ISWC 2007. LNCS, vol. 4825, pp. 722–735. Springer, Heidelberg (2007)
3. Ben-Yitzhak, O., Golbandi, N., Har'El, N., Lempel, R., Neumann, A., Ofek-Koifman, S., Sheinwald, D., Shekita, E., Sznajder, B., Yogev, S.: Beyond basic faceted search. In: International Conference on Web Search and Web Data Mining (WSDM'08), pp. 33–44. ACM (2008)
4. Fellbaum, C. (ed.): WordNet: An Electronic Lexical Database. The MIT Press, Cambridge (1998)
5. Garcia-Castro, L.J., Hepp, M., Garcia, A.: Tags4Tags: using tagging to consolidate tags. In: Bhowmick, S.S., Küng, J., Wagner, R. (eds.) DEXA 2009. LNCS, vol. 5690, pp. 619–628. Springer, Heidelberg (2009)
6. Golder, S., Huberman, B.A.: The structure of collaborative tagging systems. J. Inf. Sci. **32**(2), 198–208 (2006)
7. Gruber, T.: Collective knowledge systems: where the social web meets the semantic web. Web Semant. Sci. Serv. Agents World Wide Web **6**(1), 4–13 (2007)
8. Hepp, M.: HyperTwitter: collaborative knowledge engineering via twitter messages. In: Cimiano, P., Pinto, H.S. (eds.) EKAW 2010. LNCS (LNAI), vol. 6317, pp. 451–461. Springer, Heidelberg (2010)
9. Kim, H.-L., Breslin, J.G., Yang, S.-K., Kim, H.-G.: Social semantic cloud of tag: semantic model for social tagging. In: Nguyen, N.T., Jo, G.-S., Howlett, R.J., Jain, L.C. (eds.) KES-AMSTA 2008. LNCS (LNAI), vol. 4953, pp. 83–92. Springer, Heidelberg (2008)
10. Matuszek, C., Cabral, J., Witbrock, M., DeOliveira, J.: An introduction to the syntax and content of cyc. In: AAAI Spring Symposium on Formalizing and Compiling Background Knowledge and its Applications to Knowledge Representation and Question Answering, pp. 44–49 (2006)
11. Newman, R.: Tag Ontology Design (2005). http://www.holygoat.co.uk/projects/tags
12. Niles, I., Pease, A.: Towards a standard upper ontology. In: International Conference on Formal Ontology in Information Systems (FOIS'01), pp. 2–9. ACM (2001)
13. Passant, A., Laublet, P.: Meaning of a tag: a collaborative approach to bridge the gap between tagging and linked data. In: WWW'08 Workshops: Linked Data on the Web (LDOW'08) (2008)
14. Sigurbjörnsson, B., van Zwol, R.: Flickr tag recommendation based on collective knowledge. In: 17th International Conference on World Wide Web, pp. 327–336. ACM (2008)
15. Song, Y., Zhuang, Z., Li, H., Zhao, Q., Li, J., Lee, W.-C., Giles, C.L.: Real-time automatic tag recommendation. In: 31st International Conference on Research and Development in Information Retrieval (SIGIR'08), pp. 515–522. ACM (2008)

16. Specia, L., Motta, E.: Integrating folksonomies with the semantic web. In: Franconi, E., Kifer, M., May, W. (eds.) ESWC 2007. LNCS, vol. 4519, pp. 624–639. Springer, Heidelberg (2007)

17. Suchanek, F.M., Kasneci, G., Weikum, G.: YAGO: a core of semantic knowledge. In: 16th International World Wide Web Conference (WWW'07), pp. 697–706. ACM Press (2007)

18. Vander Wal, T.: Folksonomy Coinage and Definition (2007). http://vanderwal.net/folksonomy.html

19. Weller, K.: Folksonomies and ontologies: two new players in indexing and knowledge representation. In: Applying Web 2.0. Innovation, Impact and Implementation, pp. 108–115 (2007)

Web Service Discovery and Execution Using a Dialog-Based Approach

Márcio Fuckner[1](✉), Jean-Paul Barthès[1], and Edson Emilio Scalabrin[2](✉)

[1] UMR CNRS 7253 Heudiasyc, Université de Technologie de Compiègne,
Centre de Recherche de Royallieu, 60200 Compiègne, France
{marcio.fuckner,barthes}@utc.fr
[2] Pontifícia Universidade Católica do Paraná, Programa de Pós-Graduação
em Informática - PPGIa, Rua Imaculada Conceição,
1155 - Prado Velho, Curitiba, PR, Brazil
scalabrin@ppgia.pucpr.br

Abstract. Several Semantic Web techniques applied in Service-oriented
architectures enable explicit representation and reasoning on service operations. Those techniques applied to the automatic discovery, selection
and execution of services are promising but still too complex to allow
a large-scale adoption. Consequently, the most widespread approach for
upgrading existing services to a semantic level is the usage of traditional
software engineering practices, resulting in complex and non-intuitive
interfaces in some cases. We propose an approach to leverage the service discovery, selection and execution processes for Web services without semantic annotations, using only the WSDL descriptor as a source.
In order to do so, we first identify candidates based on linguistic cues
extracted from the Web service descriptor. The generated proof-of-
concept allows users to select and execute service operations through
a personal assistant using restricted requests in natural language.

Keywords: Web services · Natural language · Personal assistants

1 Introduction

Web services and their standards, such as the SOAP message format and the
WSDL interface definition language have gained widespread adoption and
reduced the complexity of integration between heterogeneous systems. Lightweight Web services, such as REST also have encouraged the adoption of basic
and ad hoc integration scenarios. As a result, many development tools adopted
such standards and now can reduce the complexity of developing applications.

The semantic Web vision proposed by Berners-Lee [1] has brought new opportunities to leverage the Web services, moving them from a syntactic to a semantic level. Standards such as OWL-S [2] and WSMO [3] have created a common
entry point to different proposals for discovery, composition and execution of services. However implementing them using a bottom-up approach is still complex,

© Springer-Verlag Berlin Heidelberg 2014
K.-H. Krempels and A. Stocker (Eds.): WEBIST 2013, LNBIP 189, pp. 103–118, 2014.
DOI: 10.1007/978-3-662-44300-2_7

where thousands of services are already available within and outside enterprises [4]. Allowing the leverage of even simple Web services from the syntactic level to the semantic level at a large scale still remains a major challenge. Service wrapping requires traditional software engineering steps, in some cases leading to the creation of complex and non-intuitive interfaces with end-users.

A paper by Chai et al. [5] presents a case study aiming at validating the usage of natural language by end users, in comparison with traditional point-and-click systems. The study reveals a reduction of 33 percent in time to execute the same task, as well as a reduction of 63 percent regarding the quantity of mouse clicks. Companies are also working on better end-users interfaces in order to improve their efficiency. An example of this behavior was presented in a recent post of MIT Technical Review Magazine [6]: an international bank reveals that around 65 percent of the time is used by their branch staffers with customer information desk. As a response, the bank is installing a new personal assistant using natural language through a chat window added as a mashup in their customer's Internet banking software. Thus, the customer can send sentences like "How about my investments today?" to the assistant.

Having those issues in mind, we propose an approach for wrapping independent Web services to end-users using a natural language dialog approach. We call independent services, those services executed directly, without semantic dependencies on other services. We built a proof-of-concept system using NLP techniques, running in a multi-agent environment with dialog-based human-interaction facilities. The system allows end-users to make requests in natural language sentences representing what they are looking for. The system identifies and understands key concepts from the user's input and leads the user through an appropriate dialog, which is finished when a service is executed. The proof-of-concept shows the viability of usage, given that the web service descriptors are the only source of input data.

The rest of the paper is organized as follows: In Sect. 2 we present some background information regarding the techniques used in our work. In Sect. 3 we describe in detail our approach. The outcomes of a usage example are shown in Sect. 4. A discussion of related work is presented in Sect. 5. Some conclusions presenting what we have learned from the study and proposed future work are presented in Sect. 6.

2   Background

In this section we briefly describe two key areas related to this work: (i) Personal assistants, which use multidisciplinary approaches to improve the interface between a human and a software component, such as natural language processing. (ii) Web service description languages, which present key information to build the basic vocabulary and information model.

Personal Assistants. In Multi-Agent Systems, the Personal Assistant Agent (PA) is an agent built to be an assistant of one user, its master. The term "digital butler," coined by Negroponte [7] is also commonly used to describe a PA.

It aims at simplifying the interface between a human and an agent in a multi-agent system. This approach is promoted by projects like the PAL Program [8] (Personalized Assistant that Learns) proposed by DARPA, with contributions from SRI and several other laboratories with the CALO project [9]. The CALO framework provides assistant components, such as the CALO Express (CE), a lightweight personal desktop assistant that uses learning techniques to identify relevant information on the desktop, such as documents, presentations, emails and agenda. Meeting Express (ME) is another component example, designed to help a user in a meeting.

One special interest to the personal assistant approach in this work is the frequent usage of natural language (NL) written or spoken as a common interface. Natural language processing (NLP) is a field of computer science and linguistics concerned with the interactions between computers and humans. In this work we use the available tools to deal with NL and also improve the personal assistant vocabulary. Techniques such as stemming, part of speech tagging and word sense disambiguation are explored in our proof-of-concept application.

Web Service Description Languages. Several specifications were proposed during the Web service history. For the sake of clarity, we listed some important standards using Vitvar et al. taxonomy [4], which proposes a stack with two levels, namely a *semantic* and a *non-semantic level.*

- At a *non-semantic level*, WSDL is the de-facto standard for Web services specification. It specifies the interface, operations, the data types using XML Schema, and non-functional descriptions, such as communication protocol and physical endpoint information. Behavioral aspects can also be specified, for example, using WS-BPEL.
- At a *semantic level*, OWL-S and WSMO provide a framework for describing semantics for services, adopting a domain ontology, a formalism to describe the service capabilities, the effects and goals of Web services.

This clear separation between semantic and syntactical information on Web services is only conceptual, revealing in practice a thin line between them in industry. As a response to the difficulty to implement them in a large-scale, the work from W3C called Semantic Annotations for WSDL and XML Schema [10] was initiated. It provides a model where the WSDL could be annotated with semantic information. It could be interpreted as a bridge between the non-semantic layer and the semantic one, using the WSDL as a non-marginal source of information. WSMO-Lite [4] creates an extension of SAWSDL, addressing the need of a concrete service ontology as its next evolutionary step.

3   Overall Approach

In this section we present a detailed description of our approach to Web service discovery and execution using a multi-agent platform. We could summarize it in two high-level processes:

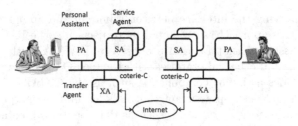

Fig. 1. A typical configuration of an OMAS multi-agent system.

1. service parsing, in order to create a knowledge representation of the service and its dialog;
2. discovery and execution using a personal assistant with natural language understanding skills.

First, we present the OMAS multi-agent platform, used to implement the proposed solution. The subsequent sections describe each high-level process separately.

3.1 Multi-Agent Platform

To implement our proof-of-concept, we selected OMAS[1] as a multi-agent platform [11]. This platform was designed for building cognitive agents and provides several types of agents: service agents (SA), transfer agents (XA) and personal assistant agents (PA). They are organized around a single net local loop and share messages using broadcast mode (UDP). A physical loop is called a *local coterie* and transfer agents are responsible to connect different physical loops or different platforms. A set of loops in a particular application is called a *coterie*. All the communications are P2P meaning that there is no central directory nor a single point of failure (SPOF). These are mandatory features when talking about service oriented and loosely coupled architectures. To illustrate the architecture, a typical configuration of an OMAS multi-agent system is shown in Fig. 1 containing service agents, transfer agents and personal assistants.

Personal Assistant Agents. An agent targeted to this work is the personal assistant (PA). This agent has a very specialized task: it makes an interface with a person or its master and delegates more specific tasks to other types of agents present in the environment. As a design principle, a PA has very superficial technical skills and for technical problems relies on other agents called service agents. This design approach leads to modularization and easier maintenance, since the technical expertise is distributed in separate agents. As a good design practice, service agents answer their PA and no other agents. However, a service agent can access any other agent.

---

[1] The platform and the documentation are available at http://www.utc.fr/~barthes/OMAS/.

A personal assistant agent in OMAS has a set of functions to deal with the user through a natural language dialog (NL). It has a standard top-level dialog that determines what the user wants to do: a request, an assertion or a command for example. The agent reacts executing the underlying task or invokes an ELIZA-like dialog to analyze the input and either produces an adequate answer or tells the master that it did not have enough information to process the input. The ELIZA-like dialog is a special dialog inspired by the work of [12].

The framework allows the creation of nested sub-dialogs. Such sub-dialogs are modeled by a conversation graph, having a set of nodes representing states of the conversation. Each node contains a set of rules that apply to a fact base containing information obtained from the master's input or resulting from the analysis steps of the previous states. The fact base is similar to the fact base of a rule-based system. At a given node, applying the rules triggers either a transition to a new state or an action (e.g. a message sent to some agent) [13]. These features will be explored in more details in the next sections, when an automatic dialog is created, based on the Web service structure.

3.2   Service Parsing

This process aims at extracting relevant keywords and structural information of Web services using a descriptor as an input. Each step contributes to construct a representation for service discovery and execution. The diagram shown in Fig. 2 provides an overview of the process and also of the relevant information used and generated during each step.

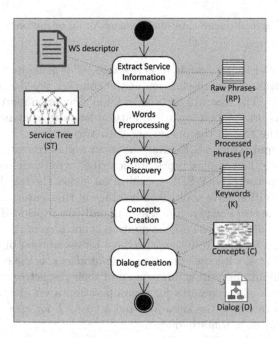

Fig. 2. Service parsing diagram.

Extract Service Information. This is the starting step, which uses a Web service descriptor as an input parameter, as shown in Fig. 2. The goals of this step are: (i) extract keywords from a Web service descriptor; and (ii) build a tree representing the service. As presented in the Background Section, there are many different standards for the specification of Web services. As a result, one must build specific parsers to provide input for goals (i) and (ii). For our first prototype we created a parser for the WSDL specifications, focusing on the operations and their parameters. For the operations, we extract the values from the nested documentation tags. For the parameters, we extract the input and output representation, described as XML Schema types.

The *documentation* tag value related to the operation is used to build a set of raw phrases $RP = \{rp_1, rp_2, ...rp_n\}$. A raw phrase rp in this context is interpreted as the original phrase with spaces and stop words. Figure 3 shows a fragment of a WSDL document with a documentation tag inside the operation. In this case, the resulting set RP would be: { "Get a share price quote on any listed NY stock", "Requires one valid stock identifier" }.

```
<wsdl:operation name="getSharePrice" ... >
  <wsdl:documentation>
      Get a share price quote on any listed NY stock.
      Requires one valid stock identifier.
  </wsdl:documentation>
  ...
</wsdl:operation>
```

Fig. 3. A documentation fragment for an operation.

During the breadth-first search, a service tree ST is generated for each operation found containing a representation of the complex types in the input and output parameters. The tree will be used to build a common representation and an automatic goal-oriented dialog, using natural language sentences.

The root of the tree is the operation, with two branches representing the input and the output structure. Finding the input and output structure is not a complex task, once the complex types are described with their respective types in the WSDL structure The WSDL specification allows the tag documentation in all element definitions. We took the advantage of this feature to improve the experience with the user and give him a user-friendly description of such pieces of information in the dialog. If the documentation is not present, the name defined in the type will be used. A resulting graphical representation of the generated tree is shown in Fig. 4, with the operation *GetSharePrice* as the root of the tree, followed by the input and output branches and their respective attributes.

To sum up, this step generates for each operation a set of raw phrases RP that will be used to create the keywords and a tree ST for creating a common representation and an automatic dialog.

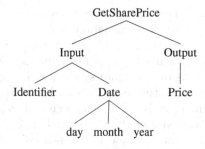

Fig. 4. Generated tree.

Preprocessing Words. After extracting the service information, a set of raw phrases $RP = \{rp_1, rp_2, ...rp_n\}$ is used in this step as an input. This process aims at preparing the set of words using some NLP techniques, described in the Background Section.

First, a word segmentation of each raw phrase (rp) is done, using white space, tabs and new line characters as delimiters. Second, a filter removes all the stop words. Third, in order to improve the accuracy of the word synonym lookup process, a Part of Speech (POS) is executed for each word, identifying nouns, verbs, adverbs and adjectives.

Finally, a stemming algorithm is invoked, transforming the original words into root words. As a result a new set of phrases called $P = \{p_1, p_2, p_n\}$ is generated, where each p is a set of instances $\{(w_1, t_1), (w_2, t_2), ..., (w_j, t_j)\}$, w is the word, t is their respective type (noun, verb, adverb or adjective) and j is the quantity of words in the given phrase.

Synonyms Discovery. The goal of this step is to collect as many synonyms as possible for each word extracted from the service descriptor. Discovering a word synonym is a complex action, due to the multiple meanings of the same word in different contexts (aka polysemy). Therefore, two minimum components are necessary to work on this problem of word sense disambiguation: (i) a dictionary or a thesaurus; and (ii) a method of disambiguation.

For (i), we chose WordNet [14,15]: an electronic lexical database for the English language, developed at Princeton University. WordNet groups noun, verbs, adjectives and adverbs by means of conceptual semantic and lexical relations. Each grouping is called *synset*, and a wide range of tools is available to deal with such structures.

For (ii) we chose one of the first works related to the theme, proposed by Lesk [16]. Lesk uses an unsupervised method that disambiguates two words by finding the pair of senses with the greatest overlap in their dictionary definitions. This algorithm presents a low computing overhead because it explores only the sense of the words present in the phrase, avoiding a deep navigation in the graph.

The algorithm receives the set of phrases P generated in the previous section as an input. Then, for each word processed, it looks for the set of senses in

WordNet. To clarify the concept of sense, each sense has a dictionary definition that will be used by the disambiguation process. Giving an example, we
try to disambiguate the word "risk" in the set of words $p = \{\{project, noun\},$
$\{risk, noun\}\}$. The word risk has 6 senses for noun and each one points to at
least the original word plus one or more synonyms. Using the algorithm, the
chosen sense of risk was "a venture undertaken without regard to possible loss
or injury," instead of "the probability of being exposed to an infectious agent."
This is an effect of the presence of the word "undertaken" in both definitions
(risk and project). As a result two new words, related to the same sense were
added: "peril" and "danger," expanding the vocabulary.

Lesk's approach is sensitive to the exact wording of definitions. In certain
cases, words in the definition do not link in fact the words. The absence of a
certain word or a presence of a frequent word can radically change the results.
Several proposed methods achieve good results for disambiguation, but require
a preprocessed dependency knowledge database as presented in [17] or make
deep explorations in the glosses graph as presented in [18,19]. They should be
considered in future experiments.

In short, at the end of this step, a set of keywords are generated for the
service called $K = \{k_1, k_2, k_n\}$, where each k_n is a word (original or synonym)
and n is the number of keywords for the underlying service.

Concepts Creation. A representation language is necessary to model the services, the dialogs and the input and output parameters to deal with the service.
We use a representation language called MOSS[2] [11], summarized in the next
paragraphs.

MOSS is a complex frame-based representation language, allowing the description of concepts, individuals, properties, classless objects, default values, virtual
concepts or properties. It includes an object-oriented language, a query system,
multilingual facilities and many other features described in the online documentation. MOSS is centered on the concept of property and adopts a descriptive
(typicality) rather than prescriptive approach, meaning that defaults are priv-
ileged and individuals may have properties that are not recorded in the corresponding concept. Reasoning is done via a query mechanism. We only present
here the features used for the creation of a general concept representing the
service and its structure.

Concepts, Attributes and Relations. The service tree generated in Sect. 3.2, called
ST, will be used as a source to create a representation of the service using the
MOSS language. Given the tree, if a visited node is a leaf, then it will be transformed into a final attribute. On the other hand, if the node is intermediary,
then it will be transformed into a new concept, and also a relationship with
this new concept will be created in the current concept. This approach could
result in possible redundancies when a complex type is used more than once.
However it simplifies the transformation and also prevents the occurrence of

---

[2] available at http://www.utc.fr/~barthes/MOSS/

```
(defconcept "GetSharePriceConcept"
    (:rel "Input" (:to "InputConcept"))
    (:rel "Output" (:to "OutputConcept")))

(defconcept "InputConcept"
    (:att "Identifier")
    (:rel "Date" (:to "DateConcept")))

(defconcept "OutputConcept"
    (:att "Price"))

(defconcept "DateConcept"
    (:att "day") (:att "month") (:att "year"))
```

Fig. 5. Generated concepts (:att specifies an attribute, :rel a relation).

circular references. To give an example of the creation of nested concepts, let's use the tree of Sect. 3.2. In this example we have four nodes as candidates to concepts: The toplevel node *GetSharePrice*, the standard *Input* and *Output* nodes and the *Date* node. Figure 5 shows the generated concepts using the MOSS syntax. The *Date* node was transformed into a concept called *DateConcept*, once the node is intermediary. It also influenced the creation of the *InputConcept*, which had a relationship with the concept *DateConcept* instead of a simple attribute.

Concepts (*C*) when created are incorporated into the OMAS environment, allowing the creation of individuals during any dialog session.

Dialog Creation. The goal of this step is to build an automatic sub-dialog based on the concept set (*C*), created during the previous step. To allow a conversation between the user and the PA, this goal-driven dialog is modeled as a finite state machine as shown in Fig. 6. The goal of this type of dialog is the fulfillment of all of the attributes and relations of an individual representing the input.

Selection State. The sub-dialog starts in the *Selection* state. This state aims at finding empty input attributes. Our technique proceeds along the following assumptions: (i) One individual or instance related to the service context is created for each dialog. (ii) For each relationship, at least one individual corresponding to the type of the relationship is created and associated to the underlying individual.

If all of the attributes of the input are filled, the next state will be *Execution*, responsible for the execution of the service, as well as displaying the execution outcomes represented by the output individual. The *Selection* state does not have interaction with the user and only uses the input individual for making the inference.

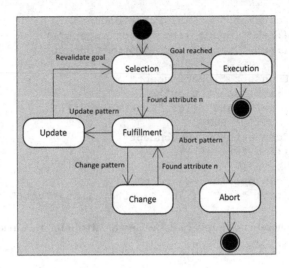

Fig. 6. Service execution state machine.

Fulfillment State. If an empty attribute n is found, the control is transferred to this state, which aims at asking the master to fulfill the information. A question/answer dialog is started, asking the user to fill the attribute n.

Update State. The control is transferred to this state if the algorithm detects an update pattern. Knowledge engineering processes using unstructured natural language texts are still an expert task and are sensitive to the context. We choose a discovery process that extracts the attribute value from the sentence based on simple grammatical constructions. We used a small subset of the proposal made by Hahn and Schnattinger [20] called *Linguistic Quality Labels*. They reflect structural properties of phrasal patterns in which unknown lexical items occur. We assume here that the type of grammatical construction exercises a particular interpretative force on the unknown item. Based on this idea, we used the traditional triple noun-verb-noun phrase to detect sentences like "My age is 23" or "The window has a size of 3×5 m." Apposition is also a source of information. The apposition almost unequivocally will determine the attribute in our case. An example of apposition phrase could be "The user Mary," where *user* is the attribute name and *Mary* is the correspondent value.

Abort State. When the PA detects abort patterns in the master's phrase, it interrupts the process confirming their action. If the user confirms, then the service execution is aborted. If not, the control returns to the *Selection* state. An abort pattern could be interpreted as a set of words such as $\{cancel, quit, \ldots\}$. The sets were made empirically during this preliminary phase and must be evaluated in the future in order to improve their accuracy.

Change State. This state enables the user to change the sequence of the fulfillment and for example, ask to change the value of any other attribute. Let's use the phrase "Sorry, I made a mistake when giving my age" during the

Fulfillment state. The sentence does not fit in the requirements of the *Abort* state nor the *Update* state. It also presents linguistic cues indicating the desire to change something such as {*mistake, sorry, ...*}. If the algorithm matches one attribute in the phrase, then the control returns to the *Fulfillment* state. If there is no correspondence, the control returns to the *Selection* state.

Execution State. The control is transferred to this state when the master has filled all the attributes. Here, the PA sends a message to the service agent (SA) responsible for the SOAP envelope creation, transportation and response decoding. The PA waits for the response and then presents the output to the end user, terminating the sub-dialog.

3.3   Discovery and Execution

The discovery and execution process is tailored to identify the user needs based on linguistic cues and conduct a dialog conversation. This process was inspired by the work on multi-agents task selection and execution using personal assistants dialogs described in [13].

During this stage, we assume that the PA is currently associated with an end-user. That is to say, the user now has a channel opened with the personal assistant to make requests and also see the PA responses. It is important to point-out that the conversation between a PA and the end-user starts in a generic top-level dialog, described in the diagram shown in Fig. 7. Any other dialog in the PA is considered a nested or sub-dialog, even our special sub-dialog used here. The starting point of the top-level dialog, namely *Entry State* allows users to input their requests. The next state is called *Service Discovery*.

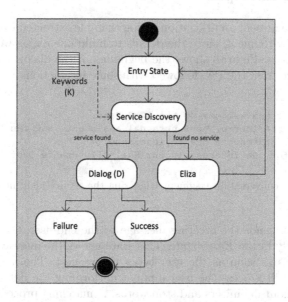

Fig. 7. Discovery and execution activity diagram.

Service Discovery. Using the service keywords (K), the service discovery is done as follows:

1. The user asks something to the PA (e.g., "Give me the project risks and their financial reserves")
2. The phrase is segmented into a set of words, removing spaces, words separators and empty words. For example, the resulting list of words would be $\{give, project, risk, financial, reserves\}$;
3. A stemming algorithm is executed for each word, transforming them into root words.
4. For each known service, the PA matches the user set of words with the set of keywords (K), using a MYCIN-like formula to compute a score. This is a simple but efficient approach, since each match of a subexpression reinforces the overall match score;
5. Services are then ordered by decreasing scores;
6. The service with the highest score is selected.

If a task cannot be determined, the PA enters in the state *Eliza*, in order to analyze the input and either produces an adequate answer or tells the user that it did not have enough information to process the input.

Dialog Execution. Once the top-level dialog has identified the target service to execute, a nested sub-dialog associated with the service is instantiated and started. The creation of this goal-oriented dialog was detailed in Sect. 3.2. After the execution of the sub-dialog the control is then returned to the main dialog.

4   A Dialog Example

In this section we present an utilization dialog example extracted from one ready-to-use OMAS environment, since the details to build one dialog were presented in previous sections. Figure 8 shows the beginning of the dialog, started with a welcome message from the PA, followed with some interactions.

```
P: Good morning and welcome to the ACME Bank.
        I am Ariberto, your personal assistant. How can I help you?
U: I'd like to contract a health insurance.
P: Thank you for the interest in our Health Insurance Quote service.
```

Fig. 8. A conversation fragment triggering the service identification.

When the PA sends the greeting message to the end-user, the conversation graph is currently in the *Entry state*. This state allows the interaction with the user and changes as soon as the user types the request. The next state, *Service Discovery*, will process the user input, transforming the data into a set of root words, without delimiters and stop words. A matching process is then executed for each known service in the environment, using a MYCIN-like formula

$(a+b-ab)$. Given the set of words provided by the user, the selected service was the *Health Insurance Quote Service*. For demonstration purposes the environment had a few services, related to health, travel and vehicle insurance quotes.

As a result, a sub-dialog related to the health service was created. As a preparation process, an individual representing the service concept was created, as well as individuals to fill its relationships. To be more specific in this case, an individual was created for both input and output concepts, once the types related to this service are simple attributes. All service sub-dialogs start in the *Selection* state. It means that the sub-dialog behavior is to look for empty attributes in the input individual. In this example, the PA found the *name* and transferred the control to the *Fulfillment* state, which always waits for the user input.

As shown in Fig. 9, the user sent the sentence "My name is John Doe" to the PA. The pattern found by the PA was compatible with an update, which in turn, extracted only the fragment "John Doe". This context information was then available in the *Update* state. As a result, the PA changed the value to "John Doe." returning the control back to the *Selection* state.

```
U: My name is John Doe.
P: Thank you for the information. Confirming your name as John Doe.
P: Could you please tell me your age?
U: No, sorry, the name is not correct.
P: Your current name is John Doe. Could you please tell me your name again?
U: The name is John Malbec Doe
P: Thank you for the information. Confirming your name as John Malbec Doe.
          Could you please tell me your age?
U: I'm 23.
P: Your age is 23.
```

Fig. 9. A conversation fragment that identifies a user intervention.

The user can change the order of fulfillment at any time. The same dialog of Fig. 9 shows the PA asking for the user's age. In the dialog example, the user refused the fulfillment answering: "No, sorry, the name is not correct." The pattern found in the phrase matched the *Change* state. This state found the attribute *name*. Hence, the control was transferred back to the *Fulfillment* state, which allowed the user to change his name and transfer the control to the *Update* state. The control was then returned back to the *Selection* state. Finally, the Web service was executed after the fulfillment process, as show in Fig. 10.

5   Related Work

Many research efforts have been made to propose approaches for discovery, composition and execution of Web services. In general, the proposals use semantic-based approaches on semantic descriptors and domain-specific ontologies. To give some examples, the paper by Rivera et al. [21] presents a framework for building applications targeted to end users who have no previous technology

```
P: Now, I have all of the information to process your request.
          I would like your attention to check the following information
          before confirming your request.
          ...
P: Could you please confirm the request?
U: yes
P: Service requested successfully.
                    Process number : 9992323231.
                    Insurance price : \$ 150.00.
```

Fig. 10. A conversation fragment that shows the service execution.

experience. One of the features is the service discovery, which is based on pre and post-conditions expressed in RDF graph patterns. It also presents a solution to service execution using a wrapper figure. This approach uses a dummy service execution in order to match the messages with domain specific data and wraps it into an application widget, which could be used as a common component for application modeling. The paper of Lim and Lee [22] presents a sophisticated mechanism to discover and execute web services using semantic Web service information described in OWL-S. Different workflow templates are extracted, and then the algorithm selects the most suitable workflow by calculating similarities between sub-workflows. Adala et al. in [19] use a similar Web service discovery mechanism, using NLP techniques such as word disambiguation. However, the approach used to match the user natural language request and their knowledge representation is slightly different. It uses SUMO (Suggested Upper Merged Ontology) as a source to calculate the distance between the user request and the representation.

As can be seen, most of these solutions use semantic descriptors as an input. We have a great amount of services lacking semantic descriptors, normally found by third-party providers or even traditional Web services published in UDDI directories. It opens an opportunity for other techniques based on non-semantic information.

6   Conclusions

The work proposed in this paper provides an approach for discovery and execution of Web services. The approach presented here is both simple and efficient, particularly in environments with independent Web services without a proper domain-ontology and semantic annotations describing the service capability. It presents a discovery mechanism based on expanded keywords presented in a Web service descriptor and a fulfillment process using natural language. The sentences are provided by and end-user without previous knowledge about the physical location and structure of the service. The approach leverages the usage of several Web services constructed in a bottom-up fashion where only operational descriptors are available.

The generated proof-of-concept is a preliminary outcome and we are working on improvements of the approach in order to: (i) allow more sophisticated dialogs, specially when dealing with complex representation of input data and (ii) allow more complex scenarios using composite Web services.

The OMAS platform containing all the machinery for implementing multi-agents and dialogs, and the corresponding documentation can be downloaded from http://www.utc.fr/~barthes/OMAS/

References

1. Berners-Lee, T., Hendler, J., Lassila, O.: The Semantic Web. Scientific American (2001)
2. Web-Ontology Working Group, W.: OWL-S: Semantic Markup for Web Services. W3C Member Submission (2004). http://www.w3.org/Submission/OWL-S/
3. WSMO Working Group, W.: Web Service Modeling Ontology (WSMO). W3C Member Submission (2005). http://www.w3.org/Submission/WSMO/
4. Vitvar, T., Kopecký, J., Viskova, J., Fensel, D.: WSMO-lite annotations for web services. In: Bechhofer, S., Hauswirth, M., Hoffmann, J., Koubarakis, M. (eds.) ESWC 2008. LNCS, vol. 5021, pp. 674–689. Springer, Heidelberg (2008)
5. Chai, J., Lin, J., Zadrozny, W., Ye, Y., Stys-budzikowska, M., Horvath, V.: The role of a natural language conversational interface in online sales: a case study. Int. J. Speech Technol. 4, 285–295 (2001)
6. Simonite, T.: Siri's new cousin works as a bank teller. MIT Technology Review - The Future of Work (2012). http://www.technologyreview.com/
7. Negroponte, N.: Being Digital. Knopf Doubleday Publishing Group, New York (1996)
8. DARPA PAL Program, D.: Personalized Assistant that Learns. SRI International (2012). https://pal.sri.com/Plone/framework
9. Tur, G., Stolcke, A., Voss, L., Peters, S., Hakkani-Tur, D., Dowding, J., Favre, B., Fernandez, R., Frampton, M., Frandsen, M., Frederickson, C., Graciarena, M., Kintzing, D., Leveque, K., Mason, S., Niekrasz, J., Purver, M., Riedhammer, K., Shriberg, E., Tien, J., Vergyri, D., Yang, F.: The CALO meeting assistant system. IEEE Trans. Audio, Speech, Lang. Process. 18, 1601–1611 (2010)
10. SAWSDL Working Group, W.: Semantic Annotations for WSDL and XML Schema. W3C Recommendation (2007). http://www.w3.org/TR/sawsdl/
11. Barthès, J.P.A.: OMAS - a flexible multi-agent environment for CSCWD. Future Gener. Comput. Syst. 27, 78–87 (2011)
12. Weizenbaum, J.: ELIZA - a computer program for the study of natural language communication between man and machine. Commun. ACM 9, 36–45 (1966)
13. Barthès, J.-P.A.: Flexible communication based on linguistic and ontological cues. In: Babin, G., Stanoevska-Slabeva, K., Kropf, P. (eds.) MCETECH 2011. LNBIP, vol. 78, pp. 131–145. Springer, Heidelberg (2011)
14. Miller, G.A.: WordNet: a lexical database for English. Commun. ACM 38, 39–41 (1995)
15. Stark, M.M., Riesenfeld, R.F.: WordNet: an electronic lexical database. In: Proceedings of 11th Eurographics Workshop on Rendering. MIT Press (1998)
16. Lesk, M.: Automatic sense disambiguation using machine readable dictionaries: how to tell a pine cone from an ice cream cone. In: Proceedings of the 5th Annual International Conference on Systems Documentation, SIGDOC '86, pp. 24–26. ACM (1986)

17. Chen, P., Ding, W., Bowes, C., Brown, D.: A fully unsupervised word sense disambiguation method using dependency knowledge. In: Proceedings of Human Language Technologies: The 2009 Annual Conference of the North American Chapter of the Association for Computational Linguistics, NAACL '09, pp. 28–36. Association for Computational Linguistics (2009)

18. Navigli, R., Velardi, P.: Structural semantic interconnections: a knowledge-based approach to word sense disambiguation. IEEE Trans. Pattern Anal. Mach. Intell. **27**, 1075–1086 (2005)

19. Adala, A., Tabbane, N., Tabbane, S.: A framework for automatic Web service discovery based on semantics and NLP techniques. Advances in Multimedia - Special issue on Web Services in Multimedia 2011 (2011)

20. Hahn, U., Schnattinger, K.: Towards text knowledge engineering. In: Proceedings of the Fifteenth National/Tenth Conference on Artificial Intelligence/Innovative Applications of Artificial Intelligence, pp. 524–531. American Association for Artificial Intelligence (1998)

21. Rivera, I., Moller, K., Handschuh, S., Zundorf, A.: Web service wrapping, discovery and consumption - more power to the end-user. In: 7th International Conference on Web Information Systems and Technologies (2011)

22. Lim, J., Lee, K.H.: Constructing composite web services from natural language requests. Web Semant. Sci. Serv. Agents World Wide Web **8**, 1–13 (2010)

Comparison of Mobile Web Frameworks

Henning Heitkötter[✉], Tim A. Majchrzak, Benjamin Ruland,
and Till Weber

Department of Information Systems, University of Münster,
Münster, Germany
{heitkoetter,tima}@ercis.de,
{benjamin.ruland,tillweber1986}@gmail.com

Abstract. When developing mobile applications for more than one platform, developers often use cross-platform development approaches based on Web technologies such as mobile Web apps instead of native development. While the single, platform-independent source code reduces development effort, Web apps still need to be optimized for mobile particularities such as limited screen size and touch-based interaction. Developers may choose from a variety of mobile Web frameworks that support them in this regard, each with different strengths and weaknesses. In this paper, we intend to guide the decision of developers for a Web framework based on a set of criteria expected from high-quality frameworks.

Keywords: App · Mobile Web app · Framework · Cross-platform · Comparison · Evaluation · User interface

1 Introduction

For software developers, the popularity of mobile devices is a blessing and a curse at the same time. There is a demand for new *apps* that utilize novel possibilities. At the same time, the heterogeneity of mobile platforms such as Android or iOS [22] makes it cumbersome to implement apps for multiple platforms.

This leads to a need for *cross-platform* development. Due to the prevalent knowledge of Web technologies, Web apps are an interesting choice for supporting multiple platforms. In general, they only require a browser and often offer sufficient functionality. Native apps developed using a platform's software development kit (SDK) need only be employed if truly native performance and look & feel are desirable. Unfortunately, the requirements for Web apps on mobile devices differ from Web apps in general. To effectively implement them or to make existing Web apps suitable for mobile devices, sophisticated framework support is advisable. An abundance of available frameworks hampers an easy selection, though. Moreover, there is hardly any guidance for informed decision-making.

To fill this gap, it is important to evaluate frameworks based on sound criteria. In this paper, we describe our criteria-based evaluation process, which can

© Springer-Verlag Berlin Heidelberg 2014
K.-H. Krempels and A. Stocker (Eds.): WEBIST 2013, LNBIP 189, pp. 119–137, 2014.
DOI: 10.1007/978-3-662-44300-2_8

be sketched as follows: Based on typical requirements of apps, we derive eleven qualitative criteria. These criteria, accompanied by corresponding assessment guidelines, are then used to evaluate four frameworks. Background information and, more importantly, own experience are the foundation for judging to what degree a framework fulfills a certain criterion.

Our paper makes a number of contributions. First, we describe a novel set of evaluation criteria useful beyond their application in this paper. Second, we evaluate the frameworks in detail and give operationalizable decision advice. Third, we contribute to the theory with a discussion of implications of our research. By outlining which approaches look promising and where current frameworks lack features, we highlight areas for further research and development.

This article is structured as follows. Related work is studied in Sect. 2. Section 3 introduces the concept of mobile Web apps and presents the frameworks analyzed later, including their general characteristics. Our evaluation criteria are developed in Sect. 4 and then used in Sect. 5 to evaluate the frameworks. Section 6 discusses and summarizes the findings, before we conclude in Sect. 7.

2   Related Work

Our research is literature-driven. Therefore, relevant citations are provided in the corresponding paragraphs throughout this paper. In this section, we distinguish our work from existing approaches. The main observation is that there are no all-encompassing reviews based on scientific criteria. Rather, many papers evaluate single frameworks in isolation, most likely due to the novelty of this field. Nevertheless, these papers provide valuable contributions.

Several papers evaluate core technologies for Web apps such as HTML5 [16]. With additions like offline support, HTML5 is particularly suited for mobile Web apps. This is also reflected in recently published textbooks (e.g., [27]) and in the positive assessment of HTML5 [24]. It is mature enough for widespread usage and typically used together with CSS and JavaScript.

Reports on app development often evaluate a single mobile Web framework, but do not compare it to competing ones. For example, a comparison of Web and native apps mentions jQuery Mobile [2] and a paper on a smart-metering app describes its use in a real-world scenario [44]. A study of HTML5 presents several frameworks [5]. Smutny goes a step further and briefly compares selected frameworks [37]. However, he does not propose a set of criteria for doing so.

Our previous paper on evaluating cross-platform development approaches in general [15] presents complementary work. It thereby helps to make a higher-level decision: Web app *or not*. The research design is similar to this article, while the object under study differs. Ohrt and Turau [28] present a broad comparison of cross-platform development tools, but do not consider mobile Web apps.

3   Mobile Web Apps

This section examines mobile Web apps as a cross-platform approach to app development and introduces four frameworks that will be analyzed in Sect. 5.

3.1   General

A Web application, short *Web app*, is a Web site that provides an application within browsers, as opposed to static content [4, Sect. 1.3.2]. It is built with Web technologies such as HTML5, CSS, and JavaScript. A *mobile* Web app is intended to be used on mobile devices. It may be a mobile-optimized version of an existing Web app. In contrast to standard mobile apps, mobile Web apps are not installed on the device (e.g., via an *app store*) but accessed through the browser. Special requirements due to the mobile environment call for a different approach and specific optimizations compared to ordinary Web apps.

Mobile-specific requirements mainly stem from limited screen size available on mobile devices and from a different style of user interaction through touch gestures. The smaller screen of smartphones and, to a lesser extent, of tablets requires a different user interface (UI) layout and mobile versions of typical HTML elements. Touch interaction replaces the traditional pointer-based interaction combined with keyboard input. This requires several adaptations. UI elements have to be of sufficient size if users shall select them. Mobile Web apps should not expect the user to enter a large amount of text. They should, however, support gestures as an additional means of interaction. The mobile context includes additional particularities that have to be accounted for such as limited hardware resources and unstable or slow network connections. Hence, mobile Web apps should *optimize* network requests.

Combined with nearly 100 best practices recommended by the World Wide Web Consortium (W3C) for developing mobile Web pages [4, 31], the aforementioned requirements highlight the need for Web frameworks that support the development of mobile Web apps. In order to select promising frameworks for evaluation, we studied Web sites and literature dealing with mobile Web frameworks. *jQuery Mobile* and *Sencha Touch* were mentioned most often and will be analyzed in the following. Third-placed *jQTouch* bears close resemblance to jQuery Mobile and is not investigated further, because its evaluation would not provide additional insight. Several frameworks followed with significantly less mentions, of which we selected *The-M-Project* as a promising alternative. *Google Web Toolkit* combined with *mgwt* completes the set of candidates. As apps using GWT are programmed in Java, this combination represents a differing approach to mobile Web development.

As they run within a browser, mobile Web apps have limited access to device-specific features and hardware. Depending on requirements, they are *not always* the optimal choice for cross-platform app development, as demonstrated by Heitkötter et al. [15]. Several popular cross-platform development frameworks are based on Web technologies. They follow a so-called hybrid approach and package mobile Web apps with a runtime that gives access to device features. Such development projects may often utilize mobile Web frameworks as well. Hence, we analyzed in how far frameworks can be combined with PhoneGap [30], also named Apache Cordova, a popular hybrid framework.

3.2 jQuery Mobile

jQuery Mobile [18] makes the interface of Web pages *responsive* and, thus, accessible on mobile devices. With jQuery Mobile, developers merely need to use HTML5, quite similar to Web development in general. HTML elements with specific attributes and values are transformed into mobile-optimized UI elements or get a certain role, such as *header* or *button*. jQuery Mobile enhances the HTML markup based on values of these attributes by adding additional markup and CSS classes prior to rendering. Besides UI components, jQuery Mobile provides animations and JavaScript support for touch events. It does not include an API for advanced features such as data binding or internationalization. It does, however, incorporate the popular JavaScript library jQuery [17].

jQuery Mobile aims to deliver a uniform user interface to all popular operating systems, namely Android, iOS, BlackBerry OS, Windows Phone and Symbian. Mobile Web apps using jQuery Mobile can also be packaged with PhoneGap. The framework uses *progressive enhancement* [7], which adjusts the presentation according to supported features of displaying devices.

Created in November 2010 by the jQuery Project [20], jQuery Mobile is since maintained as open source under MIT license. Beneath the jQuery Project, it is supported by companies like Adobe, Mozilla Corporation, Palm, BlackBerry, and Nokia. It is part of a large ecosystem, which, besides others, includes a *ThemeRoller* for developing custom styles. Our review assesses version 1.3.2.

3.3 The-M-Project

The-M-Project [40] provides a JavaScript framework for creating mobile Web apps with a Model-View-Controller (MVC) architecture. Apps, including their UI, are written entirely in JavaScript, without HTML or CSS. The framework constructs HTML at runtime, resorting to jQuery Mobile for creating the UI. In addition to means for programmatic UI definition, the API provides features such as data binding, event handling, AJAX requests, and internationalization.

The-M-Project is licensed under MIT License and primarily developed by Panacoda. The first version was released in 2011. Our evaluation examines version 1.4. The-M-Project is available for all platforms where jQuery Mobile is supported and can also be packaged with PhoneGap [39]. The-M-Project includes Espresso, a build tool simplifying the development lifecycle. It sets up the initial project structure and creates required components. Furthermore, Espresso supports optimizing, packaging, and deploying the mobile Web app.

3.4 Sencha Touch

Sencha Touch [36] enables the structured development of mobile Web apps by only using JavaScript, similar to The-M-Project. The main elements of the framework are *components*: an extensive inheritance hierarchy of components contains all functionality. Hence, developing with Sencha Touch mostly consists of instantiating and configuring these components. Since most components allow nesting other components or docking them to their sides, even complex structures can be realized. This procedure applies to creating the user interface, where layouts determine how nested components are aligned, and to dynamic parts. An MVC architecture supports modularity and the utilization of dynamic data.

Sencha Touch was announced in June 2010 and is developed by Sencha Inc. We examine Version 2.2. It is compatible with Android, iOS, BlackBerry, and Windows Phone 8, but provides no explicit support for Symbian. Packaging with PhoneGap is possible [6]. Sencha Cmd is a build tool for projects using Sencha Touch. It can be used to set up, build, and deploy a project.

3.5   Google Web Toolkit with Mgwt

Google Web Toolkit (GWT) [11] allows to develop complex Web apps in Java, which GWT then compiles to JavaScript that can be run in most up-to-date browsers. GWT's Java API abstracts from browser differences and low-level AJAX or DOM operations, aiming to increase productivity. In addition to the extensive features of Java, it offers support for AJAX requests, management of browser history, and internationalization. Several libraries extend GWT with additional widgets and functionality. GWT lacks UI elements optimized for mobile devices. *mgwt* extends GWT with corresponding features, putting a strong focus on native look & feel and performance. To this end, mgwt provides developers with an additional, mobile-specific API for building up the user interface programmatically in Java, including animations.

GWT was released in 2006 by Google and is now steered by several contributors. Developed since 2011, mgwt mainly relies on a single developer. Both are licensed under Apache License 2.0. Versions examined are GWT 2.5.1 and mgwt 1.1.2. GWT supports most modern desktop browsers [13]. mgwt focuses on mobile browsers based on WebKit, which are available for iOS, Android, and Blackberry. Native themes are provided for iOS and Android. GWT apps can be packaged as PhoneGap applications with GWT-PhoneGap [14]. For GWT, there are numerous tools helping developers in all phases of the development lifecycle, including plug-ins for the popular Eclipse IDE, debugging facilities, and a graphical UI builder. Setting up a project that uses mgwt is slightly more complicated. No UI builders for mgwt are available.

4   Criteria

Selecting a Web framework from a set of alternatives constitutes an optimization problem to maximize the utility of a decision-maker or company. To deal with the complexity of measuring utility directly, most decision-making methods split up the utility-wise consequences of a selection into the consequences of disjoint criteria on utility [43], which can later be combined using an additive function [8] or complex functions such as the *Analytic Hierarchy Process* [32]. In any case, identifying separate criteria simplifies evaluation because each criterion can be examined on its own. Moreover, it improves decision-making because the decision process is dissected into manageable components. Decision-makers can weight criteria according to their needs. Combining all requirements of mobile Web frameworks into a single measure would prove rather difficult and opaque. Hence, the first step of our evaluation consisted of developing a set of criteria.

In order to arrive at meaningful criteria, a goal hierarchy guided our criteria elicitation. The overall goal was to allow decision-makers to select the optimal mobile Web framework depending on differing requirements. Two mostly separate sub-goals further define the quality of such a framework: first, functionality and usability of mobile apps created with the framework and second, the developer experience when developing mobile Web apps using the framework.

Table 1. Criteria of the developer's perspective (1/2).

D1 **License and Costs.** Costs for obtaining a framework and employing it in commercial apps influence whether a framework is suitable for a certain app or a particular company. Hence, this criterion examines licensing costs that accrue for developing and publishing a commercial app based on the respective framework. Additionally, costs of support inquiries are considered (actual development costs are assessed by criterion *D5*). The optimal case would be an open source framework under a permissive license such as MIT License [26] or Apache License [1]. Copyleft licenses [34] such as GNU General Public License [9] might complicate commercial, closed source projects. This criterion is especially relevant for smaller companies

---

D2 **Long-term Feasibility.** The decision for a framework represents a significant investment because specific know-how needs to be acquired and apps will be tied to the framework. Hence, developers will prefer a framework that will most likely be available in the long term. A framework needs continuous updates, especially in view of rapidly changing browsers and Web technologies. Indicators of long-term feasibility are popularity, update behavior, and the development team. Popularity can be assessed through a high diffusion rate among app developers and recognition in the developer community. A positive update behavior is marked by short update cycles and regular bug-fixes. A framework with a strong development team, ideally backed by several commercial supporters, is more likely to prosper in the future

---

D3 **Documentation and Support.** Documentation and further support channels assist developers in learning and mastering a framework. Assistance is not only required when getting started, but also to conquer the API. Therefore, a documentation of good quality provides tutorials and a comprehensive, well-structured reference. For popular frameworks, textbooks might provide a starting point. Other means of support such as community forums or paid assistance help in case of special problems

---

D4 **Learning Success.** Time and effort needed to comprehend a framework directly affect its suitability. While a good documentation (*D3*) may enhance learning success, learning inherently depends on the inner characteristics of a framework, i.e., its accessibility and comprehensibility. Hence, learning success is examined separately. It mainly depends on the subjective progress of a developer during initial activities with a framework. Intuitive concepts, possibly bearing resemblance to already known paradigms, can be mastered quickly. To a minor extent, this criterion also considers the effort needed for learning new concepts after initial orientation

---

Table 2. Criteria of the developer's perspective (2/2).

D5 **Development Effort.** The cost for developing apps mostly depends on the development effort needed, assuming a basic familiarity with the framework. While certain development phases such as requirements elicitation or design are largely independent of the framework used, it directly influences the implementation. Hence, the development effort is characterized by the time needed for implementing apps with the framework. Indicators for a framework that ease development are expressive power, an easy-to-understand syntax, reusability of code, and good tool support. The latter includes an Integrated Development Environment (IDE), which facilitates implementation and possibly GUI design, as well as debugging facilities

---

D6 **Extensibility.** In view of both evolving requirements and a changing environment, it may be necessary to extend a framework with additional functionality, either during initial implementation or in later iterations. This will be easier and more stable if a framework offers corresponding features such as a plug-in mechanism, or, as a last resort, is open to modification as open source. Besides considering the existence of extensibility measures, this criterion assesses their usefulness and accessibility

---

D7 **Maintainability.** Web apps can and will be updated regularly. Therefore, their implementation must be maintainable over a longer period. This criterion is positively correlated with comprehensibility of the source code and its modularity. Both indicators depend on the framework used to implement the app. A framework that allows for concise but understandable code will improve comprehensibility. Modularity requires the possibility to separate different parts of an app into distinct units

---

The first focuses on the users' perspective and their experience using an app, which literature considers an important factor of acceptance [10]. The user perspective is of course highly relevant for the developer as well, but only mediated through the requirement to build a user-friendly app. In contrast, the latter goal takes into account the developers' perspective and other decision-relevant factors that foremost affect developers and the development costs of an app project. Based on these two goals we grouped the criteria into *user* and *developer* perspective.

Our process of deriving a set of criteria suitable for evaluating mobile Web frameworks included several sources of information. We set out with a review of existing articles and Web sites that give decision advice for choosing frameworks related to Web *or* mobile development in general [15,21,29]. Since those areas have some overlap with our topic, the comparisons provided some insights into typical requirements of frameworks, which influenced our criteria. Special consideration was given to particularities and challenges due to the mobile environment and to Web-specific requirements, both already outlined in Sect. 3.1. Our experience developing apps further contributed to the set of criteria, as well as expectations discussed with partners from industry.

This process resulted in two kinds of criteria: *binary* and *qualitative*. Binary criteria are concerned with questions *whether* a framework possesses a required property, or not. They can be answered with *yes* or *no*. These include, for example, if a framework supports a certain mobile platform or its compatibility with

Table 3. Criteria of the user's perspective.

U1 **User Interface Elements.** Elements of the user interface need to be well-designed and optimized for mobile usage. On the one hand, this criterion assesses whether a framework offers mobile versions of common UI elements and layouts, as well as their quality. Structural elements need to address limited screen sizes and particularities of touch-based interaction. On the other hand, a framework should support behavioral UI elements such as animations and gestures

---

U2 **Native Look & Feel.** User acceptance of a Web app, also compared to a native app, often depends on a native look & feel. In contrast to a typical Web site, apps with a native UI have a platform-specific appearance and behavior. As this is an often mentioned requirement of apps [23], this criterion assesses whether a framework supports a native look & feel. Optimally, a framework would provide different, platform-specific themes, at least for Android and iOS. If that is the case, we examine how closely these resemble truly native UIs. Otherwise, the framework should provide means to efficiently style its UI elements and implement themes

---

U3 **Load Time.** The time required to load a Web app is important to users in view of slow and instable network connections on mobile devices. In contrast to native apps, Web apps moreover are not installed but retrieved upon access. Load times partly depend on the code size of the framework and on the typical verbosity of code using the framework. A framework might provide means to reduce initial load time such as support for asynchronous requests (AJAX) or storing application and user data locally on the device (via features of HTML5)

U4 **Runtime Performance.** The performance at runtime (after loading) informs the overall impression of an app. Since they run in a *sandbox*, Web apps might suffer from a comparatively low performance. Hence, the overall performance of a framework, as subjectively experienced by users, is important. The UI elements need to react quickly to user interactions and animations should be smooth

---

PhoneGap. Applicable criteria have mostly been answered in Sect. 3. Binary criteria restrict the set of suitable frameworks prior to an evaluation. Qualitative criteria deal with the *quality* of a framework with respect to its fulfillment of requirements. Typically, quality is graded on an ordinal scale. Qualitative criteria are less obvious and can typically not be inferred reliably from descriptions of a framework. Instead, evaluating a framework with respect to these criteria requires intensive engagement with a framework. At the same time, they are highly decision-relevant. Hence, this article focuses on qualitative criteria.

Tables 1, 2 and 3 display our resulting set of qualitative criteria, divided into developer and user perspective. Each criterion has a name and is identified through a letter for the perspective and a running digit. A short description motivates each criterion and lists indicators, i.e., factors influencing its evaluation.

5   Evaluation

In this section, we present the results of our evaluation. We assessed the four mobile Web frameworks according to the criteria outlined in Sect. 4. Results are described

Table 4. Assessment summary.

Symbol	Criterion	jQuery Mobile	The-M-Project	Sencha Touch	GWT + mgwt
D1	License and Costs	1	1	2	1
D2	Long-term Feasibility	1	3	2	4
D3	Documentation and Support	2	2	1	3
D4	Learning Success	1	3	3	3
D5	Development Effort	4	3	2	2
D6	Extensibility	3	5	1	2
D7	Maintainability	4	2	1	2
U1	User Interface Elements	2	1	1	2
U2	Native Look & Feel	5	6	4	1
U3	Load Time	2	3	3	1
U4	Runtime Performance	3	3	2	1

separately for each framework in the following subsections. Beforehand, the next subsection outlines our evaluation process. Table 4 gives an overview of all individual assessments in terms of grades, organized along frameworks and criteria.

5.1 Evaluation Process

Our evaluation of each framework consisted of two steps: collecting information about the framework in question and using it to develop prototypical apps. Publicly available information such as documentation and community resources was helpful in gaining a first impression of the quality. Certain criteria, for example license, costs, and long-term feasibility, can even solely or best be assessed in this way. For other criteria, the information represented a starting point for the ensuing in-depth scrutiny through development experience. For example, typical problems discussed by the community or feedback from our industry partners hinted at potential benefits and drawbacks. We developed mobile Web apps for managing contacts and schedules. These apps were intentionally prototypic. Their set of requirements had been compiled to gain profound insight while implementing them. Requirements included multiple screens with a native look & feel, advanced widgets and layout, local storage, and asynchronous loading.

Based on these experiences, two reviewers jointly assigned grades on a scale from 1, *very good*, to 6, *very poor* for each criterion. They complement the textual evaluation for a quick overview. As highlighted in Sect. 4, each criterion is associated with a set of requirements and guidelines, which formed the basis of the assessment of each framework. This process ensured that evaluation was as objective as possible given the qualitative nature of the task at hand.

128   H. Heitkötter et al.

5.2   jQuery Mobile

jQuery Mobile uses the MIT License, which supports both open source and closed source projects. As no other costs accrue for support or development tools, *License and Costs* are suitable for any project (grade 1). In terms of *Long-Term Feasibility*, jQuery Mobile meets the demand of high popularity as it is frequently mentioned in reviews, literature, and general developer forums. jQuery Mobile cites several notable references such as Ikea or Disney World. As evident from the success of jQuery and thanks to several supporting firms, the development team promises a stable and steady further development. Furthermore, short update cycles in recent times predict a positive update behavior in future, so that, overall, jQuery Mobile should remain viable long-term (1).

The documentation covers all available features in a concise but understandable way. While it does not showcase sample applications or step-by-step tutorials, several textbooks, articles, and tutorials by third-party authors are referenced. Support is available from the highly frequented jQuery Mobile Forum [19] with about 200 topics per month and from external support forums, in which jQuery Mobile seems to be a relevant topic [38]. Thus, the criterion *Documentation and Support* is assessed as good (2).

Looking at the *Learning Success*, one can easily implement a simple application with jQuery Mobile, as only standard HTML and few custom, intuitive attributes are needed. For developing a richer dynamic app, skills in JavaScript and jQuery are required in addition. As Web developers are likely to have such previous knowledge, a quick learning success can be achieved with minor effort. Further education mostly requires little effort due to the familiarity of concepts. All in all, learning and mastering jQuery Mobile is easy (1).

Developing static applications solely in HTML required little time and effort. A simple syntax and easy debugging also speed up development. Dynamic applications, however, require pages to be altered prior to rendering, typically by the use of DOM manipulation. While this is no obstacle to small applications, the *Development Effort* might increase for bigger projects. There are no special IDEs that support development with jQuery Mobile. jQuery Mobile does not provide APIs for advanced functionality such as data binding or internationalization and focuses on creating mobile user interfaces. In consequence, it helps little when developing complex Web apps (4).

jQuery Mobile can be extended via plug-ins that either add custom methods to jQuery Mobile's JavaScript API or provide additional widgets. jQuery Mobile reuses the plug-in mechanism of jQuery but does not state its corresponding API comprehensively. Only a medium number of extension is referenced on the project's homepage. Hence, the framework's *Extensibility* is satisfactory (3). The source code of a Web app built with jQuery Mobile mainly consists of HTML code, which tends to be comprehensive. As other parts of the source code are mainly written in JavaScript and no structural concepts are provided, the readability of these parts depends on the programming style of the developer. In terms of modularity, jQuery Mobile lacks support to separate different parts of an app into individual sections, so that, overall, *Maintainability* is limited (4).

jQuery Mobile provides various *User Interface Elements* such as form elements, lists, tool bars, and grid layouts. Their quality is sufficient as they are adapted to small screen sizes and touch-based interaction, but does not reach the quality of native UI elements. Page transitions can be enhanced by a set of animations and touch gestures can be detected by specific JavaScript-events. All in all, the support for mobile UIs is good (2). jQuery Mobile aims for a unified user interface. Therefore, the look & feel intentionally differs from the native appearance of each platform and no platform-specific templates are provided. A custom adaption of native designs is possible, since the design is mainly influenced by CSS, but tends to be rather complex, even when assisted by the ThemeRoller. Hence, the criterion *Native Look & Feel* is not well-fulfilled (5).

The *Load Time* of a jQuery Mobile application as experienced by users is rather short. On the one hand, this effect is due to the small size of the framework, which is less than 100 KiB in its *minified* form. On the other hand, jQuery Mobile reduces the processing time of browsers, so that the Web app is displayed faster. Several techniques like AJAX and prefetching help to reduce interruptions during usage, while keeping the initial load time short. Storing the whole application data on a mobile device is possible but not assisted. In summary, jQuery Mobile applications load comparatively quickly (2). On high end devices such as Apple's iPhone 4S or Samsung's Galaxy S2, experienced runtime performance can hardly be distinguished from native apps, since animations run fluid and response to user interaction is almost immediate. Mid-end devices show, however, performance issues, as scrolling occurs bumpy and animations are barely visible. On average, *Runtime Performance* is satisfactory (3).

5.3 The-M-Project

License and Costs of The-M-Project are favorable for all kinds of projects (1). *Long-term Feasibility* heavily depends on the major backer of the project, Panacoda. New versions appeared regularly in 2012/13 [41]. The-M-Project's popularity is difficult to assess as the homepage presents no references. Its forum [42] shows steady, moderate interest (approximately 15 topics per month in the first half of 2013), its repository is favorited by more than 500 developers. All in all, The-M-Project's long-term view is solid (3).

The-M-Project's documentation provides tutorials as well as a reference of concepts and of the API. Overall, the documentation is well-structured and extensive; at times, in-depth information is missing, e.g., on the class *Model*. Several sample apps accompany the documentation. Additional support is available through the mentioned community forum, which usually provides timely answers. In summary, *Documentation and Support* are good (2). When familiarizing themselves with the framework, Web developers need to get used to programming only in JavaScript without HTML or CSS, and, hence, also learn The-M-Project's API. The build tool Espresso helps with getting started, as does the documentation. Mastering the concepts needs detailed information, which the documentation does not provide for all parts. The overall *Learning*

Success achieved with The-M-Project is slowed due to the extensive API knowledge required and the particular approach to Web development (3).

The-M-Project advocates many structural requirements on Web app projects, partly due to the MVC architecture. For smaller projects, this overhead might complicate development more than necessary, while The-M-Project's advanced concepts help when implementing complex apps. In general, a large amount of boilerplate code is required, which partially can be generated by Espresso. Defining the UI programmatically in JavaScript is quite verbose and cumbersome. On the other hand, advanced features of The-M-Project, such as content binding, free developers from implementing complex logic manually. JavaScript in general and The-M-Project in particular lack sophisticated development environments that offer code completion and other helpful features. Since JavaScript gives developers great flexibility, a larger code base requires strict development guidelines to maintain structure. On average, *Development Effort* with The-M-Project is slightly increased (3), mainly due to the programmatic UI creation.

The-M-Project offers no means for extending the framework. The only way to adapt the framework is modifying the openly available source code. Hence, *Extensibility* is poor (5). Thanks to the well-defined architecture prescribed by The-M-Project, apps can be maintained quite well. They typically have a modular design and separated concerns. The rather verbose source code might decrease comprehensibility, but overall, *Maintainability* is good (2).

As The-M-Project reuses jQuery Mobile for the UI, most of the assessment of jQuery Mobile with respect to widgets, animations, and gestures applies here as well. The-M-Project provides additional widgets not available in jQuery Mobile such as a date picker or a map view. Hence, the set of *User Interface Elements* is even better than jQuery Mobile's (1). The-M-Project uses the default theme of jQuery Mobile and allows optional adaptation with CSS. Hence, a *Native Look & Feel* is not supported, either, and changing the style is less comfortable (6).

The complete The-M-Project framework is rather large with a size of close to 400 KiB (minified JavaScript, CSS, and images) because it bundles several libraries with its own source code. Apps built with The-M-Project tend to be comparatively large, in part owed to the boilerplate code required for model, view, and controller. At the same time, The-M-Project provides good support for minifying and making apps available offline via HTML5's *application cache*, as Espresso generates required manifests automatically. This simplifies reducing the *Load Time* to acceptable levels (3). The *Runtime Performance* of apps is satisfactory and similar to jQuery Mobile (3); no obvious lag is discernible.

5.4 Sencha Touch

Sencha Touch is licensed under either GPL or a free-of-charge commercial license that allows closed source distribution. Enhanced support and a specialized development tool can additionally be purchased at extra charge, so that the criterion *License and Cost* is well-fulfilled (2), although Sencha Touch is less open than the other frameworks. Long-term feasibility of Sencha Touch relies almost exclusively on Sencha Inc. Since the framework is a major product of Sencha, suspension is unlikely at the moment. Sencha Touch has an equally high popularity as jQuery Mobile. Frequent and major updates in the past year point to a short update cycle. Summing up, *Long-term Feasibility* seems stable, but is heavily dependent on a single, albeit established company (2).

The documentation extensively covers the API, with helpful, modifiable examples and good structure. In addition, one can access several tutorials and sample apps. A support forum shows high activity (more than 500 topics created per month in the first half of 2013). Besides, Sencha Touch offers a special support forum and charged telephone assistance, so that the criterion *Documentation and Support* is covered well (1). When learning Sencha Touch, one has to deal with JavaScript and the framework's API. Developers need to familiarize themselves with the component structure and the way in which components are instantiated and linked to each other. As this differs from common Web development approaches, initial learning progress is quite slow. After being familiar with the API, further learning is, however, easier, due to good documentation and well-structured components. Overall, *Learning Success* is satisfactory (3).

Sencha Touch requires a lot of effort for developing small applications due to structural overhead by concepts like MVC. In contrast, larger applications benefit from these concepts. Both MVC and the possibility to nest components simplify structuring an app. Additionally, an IDE is available with costs [35]. It provides a UI editor, a code editor, and supplementing tools. Summarizing, the average *Development Effort* is low, mainly due to the structured approach (2).

In terms of *Extensibility*, custom components inherit from other components. Besides, Sencha Touch provides an interface for adding plug-ins to components that alter their functionality. Thus, the framework's extensibility is very good (1). The expressive API, as evident for example in self-explanatory parameters, leads to comprehensible source code. As separation of concerns and the allocation into various files facilitate modularity, *Maintainability* is, overall, very good (1).

The set of UI elements such as widgets and charts is wide and of high quality. It can be compared to that of The-M-Project. As nesting of elements is a basic concept of the framework, complex structures are realizable. Since Sencha Touch also provides support for gestures and animations, it fulfills the criterion *User Interface Elements* very well (1). The look & feel of a Sencha Touch app resembles that of iOS apps. Sass [33], an extension to CSS, can be used for customization. Though Sass allows powerful and easy design adjustment, a *Native Look & Feel* would require high effort (4).

Sencha Touch provides a tool to merge and minimize source code, and to embed icons into CSS. Thus, unused components are omitted and the number of HTTP requests is reduced. Additionally, the framework uses an update process similar to that of a native app by storing data in HTML5's application cache combined with versioning and incremental updates. However, an app can be as large as 800 KiB, leading to a significant loading time. Summing up, the experienced *Load Time* on first launch can be rather high, but caching may reduce it on further launches (3). Runtime performance of a Sencha Touch application is close to native performance, as no lag or stuttering is observable (2).

5.5   Google Web Toolkit with Mgwt

GWT and mgwt are open source and free of charge, also for commercial projects. Extensive support is also freely available, at least for GWT, so that the criterion *License and Costs* is fulfilled well (1). Since development has so far mainly been sponsored by Google, GWT depends on the company's steady contribution to the framework. There have been some concerns about Google's long-term strategy with respect to GWT [3] and the number of updates has decreased. GWT is now operated by a dedicated open source project, which might ensure its viability for the near future. mgwt, however, relies on a single developer and has no advanced project structure. In the first half of 2013, no new version appeared. Overall, *Long-term Feasibility*, especially of mgwt, has to be seen as uncertain (4).

While GWT's documentation is comprehensive and easily comprehensible, mgwt lacks a thorough documentation. Information is scattered among various resources, namely mgwt's wiki, blog, API documentation, and a showcase. mgwt lacks a tutorial that allows developers to learn how to develop with it. The GWT community [12] is large and offers support in a forum and on external sites. The community forum of mgwt [25] is also rather active, with approximately 50 topics per month in the first half of 2013, and mgwt's developer answers questions on a daily basis. The active support partially offsets the mediocre documentation, so that *Documentation and Support* are satisfactory (3).

The initial steps with mgwt are rather hard, because a newly created project already contains more than ten classes and still needs additional ones to work properly. In this situation, the lack of a complete tutorial becomes especially noticeable. However, after mastering the initial hurdles, further familiarization is easy thanks to mgwt's clear structure and its easy-to-understand API. Web developers need to learn Java, while GWT provides an advantage for Java developers. In summary, *Learning Success* is hindered at first but fast later (3).

Developing Web apps, even complex ones, with GWT is comparatively easy. Programming in Java enables developers to use first-class development environments such as Eclipse, which offer code completion and compile-time type checking. Hence, tool support is considerably better than it is for JavaScript programming, partly due to Java's static typing. Java's object-oriented nature offers sophisticated means for structuring the source code of an application. GWT imposes no restrictions on the architecture of applications, making it suitable for smaller and larger projects alike. At the same time, the framework provides a large set of often-needed features such as AJAX handling and internationalization. The API of mgwt is also directly accessible. Hence, implementing the UI programmatically is not as cumbersome as it is in other approaches. The development life cycle of GWT is slightly more complex, because an additional compilation of Java to JavaScript takes place. However, Google offers free plugins for Eclipse that handle these steps. Furthermore, extensive debugging facilities are available. In contrast, setting up new mgwt projects is complicated and requires several shell commands. All in all, the *Development Effort* is acceptable for all kinds of projects (2), especially for developers with experience in Java.

As the existence of mgwt itself demonstrates, GWT is extensible by everyone, mainly through object-oriented means. Google and third-parties provide plug-ins for a wide range of functionality such as maps and geo-location. *Extensibility* is good, although there is no formalized plug-in mechanism (2). Java source code of GWT- and mgwt-based apps lends itself well to a modular organization with separation of concerns. Although some boilerplate code is necessary, overall *Maintainability* is good (2).

The user interface is primarily influenced by mgwt's mobile-optimized widgets and behavioral elements. The set of widgets provided by mgwt is limited and smaller than that of jQuery Mobile: It includes only standard buttons, one default list widget, and fewer form elements, most with a default appearance only. There are no advanced widgets such as map views. The behavior of widgets is noticeably optimized for mobile usage, for example with pull-to-refresh functionality for lists. Additionally, typical animations for page transition are available. All in all, mgwt provides good functionality with respect to mobile *User Interface Elements* (2), since the limited set of widgets is well-optimized.

mgwt has a particular focus on native appearance of Web apps. Therefore, it supplies CSS themes for different mobile platforms and devices, including iPhone, iPad, Android, and Blackberry. The widgets adapt to the respective platform and mimic the appearance of native UI elements as precise as possible. As developers may further change the appearance using CSS, mgwt achieves a *Native Look & Feel* (1).

The compiler of GWT tries to reduce the number of files to download and their size by removing unused code and optimizing the generated JavaScript. Hence, a mobile Web app with GWT and mgwt can be as small as 200 KiB. Additional support for HTML5's application cache ensures a fast *Load Time* (1). In addition to a native appearance, mgwt also tries to match the feeling of native apps by focusing on a strong performance of the underlying JavaScript code. As a result, the *Runtime Performance* of mgwt apps is very good and in most cases close to native apps (1).

6 Discussion

This section summarizes the strengths and weaknesses of each framework. We then analyze which framework tends to be best suited for typical scenarios. Eventually, we examine which promising approaches and which pitfalls currently exist, also outlining further need for research.

jQuery Mobile is a popular framework for building mobile user interfaces. It is easily accessible thanks to its documentation and by being based on HTML markup. By focusing on mobile UI elements, it neglects advanced requirements such as data binding or patterns for complex applications. Hence, smaller application with only little business logic can be created with ease, but larger applications do not benefit from jQuery Mobile. Integrating frameworks that provide such functionality is no simple task.

The-M-Project's JavaScript API supports such advanced requirements. Mobile Web apps are completely implemented in JavaScript. jQuery Mobile is only used in the background to create the UI and is not apparent to developers. The-M-Project is better suited for advanced requirements and large apps, at the cost of being less accessible at first. Extending it, also with respect to a native look & feel, is difficult. Load and runtime performance are average at best.

Web apps with Sencha Touch are also developed solely in JavaScript. Developers can learn and master the framework and its high-quality API quickly. As the API is extensive and powerful, Sencha Touch is suitable for large and complex apps. These also benefit from good maintainability. For smaller apps with simple requirements, Sencha Touch's overhead may reduce efficiency of development.

Google Web Toolkit takes a different approach to Web development, as apps are written in Java and compiled to JavaScript. mgwt extends GWT with mobile-optimized widgets. Developing with GWT is easy, also due to good development environments. From a user's perspective, mgwt yields high-quality mobile Web apps with good performance and a native look & feel on Android and iOS. In contrast to GWT, mgwt's documentation and accessibility is below average. The long-term outlook is rather unstable.

These summaries already suggested some frameworks for certain requirements. The selection of a framework should be based on weighting the criteria according to their importance in the respective app project. Afterwards, the frameworks can be ranked with respect to their suitability for the project at hand. Table 4 provides a good starting point for the selection process. In general, small projects with only limited user interaction and logic tend to be well-supported by jQuery Mobile. As UI design is based on HTML markup, jQuery Mobile is easily accessible to teams skilled in Web development. An app with a restricted feature set suffers less from the lack of advanced functionality in jQuery Mobile. Full-fledged mobile Web apps with complex user interaction and advanced requirements are a different scenario. They need support for data binding, history management, modularity, and possibly internationalization. Sencha Touch is well-equipped for developing this kind of app.

If developers are used to Java, GWT might be a viable alternative, although it so far does not support mobile Web apps directly. mgwt adds this support, but is not as stable. If a look & feel is desired that to some extent resembles native apps, GWT and mgwt might also be suitable. However, in that case, a different approach to cross-platform mobile development than Web apps might be preferable. Which framework to choose also depends on the long-term importance of mobile Web apps. For a one-time development project, the adjustment time needed for a more complex framework such as Sencha Touch might not pay off, so that jQuery Mobile is a natural choice. In case of ongoing mobile development, using the more extensive frameworks might pay off.

Our evaluation highlighted promising approaches but also several areas of potential improvement. Weaknesses outlined in the individual evaluation sections are left up to the developers of each framework. Furthermore, we have identified several areas where additional research and exploration seem worthwhile. The examined frameworks either concentrate on building a mobile UI with HTML, not providing advanced functionality (jQuery Mobile), or implement UI and logic solely in JavaScript (The-M-Project, Sencha Touch). A combination of these approaches in the mobile context seems worthwhile, because it would allow developers to use well-evaluated technologies such as HTML and CSS to implement the UI, while resorting to JavaScript APIs for more complex logic. Such a combination would require means to connect mobile HTML components with corresponding JavaScript APIs, e.g., for data binding.

A better combination of technologies for native development and for Web apps is desirable. How future technology could combine the strengths of today's competing technologies is an open question. Research needs to deal not only with technology but also with its application. To our knowledge, development best practices for mobile Web apps hardly exist. Further research needs to examine whether existing processes designed for Web development can be transferred and it should compile specific guidelines.

7 Conclusions

We presented an evaluation of frameworks for creating mobile Web apps. Based on typical requirements of apps, we derived a set of criteria that can be used to evaluate (and design) these frameworks. The criteria were applied to evaluate jQuery Mobile, The-M-Project, Sencha Touch and Google Web Toolkit combined with mgwt. Sencha Touch is deemed suitable for complex apps, while jQuery Mobile is sufficient in case of smaller projects focused on UI aspects.

While we designed our approach to be as objective as possible, some threats to validity remain: Each framework was evaluated by two of the authors as reviewers. To nevertheless ensure a diversified knowledge base, each reviewer brought a different area of expertise to the evaluation. They were experienced with software development in general as well as Web and mobile development in particular. However, developers with another background might weigh the strengths and weaknesses of framework differently. We incorporated feedback from industry partners and community sources to address this issue. Furthermore, we examined one specific version of each framework. Thus, as quality changes over time, the individual assessment might not stay accurate. For the near future, however, it should hold. The general statements as part of the assessment will likely be true for an even longer period.

To overcome the issues mentioned above and to expand our research, future work includes enlisting more experts with diverse backgrounds for reviewing the frameworks, updating the evaluation to new versions, and addressing issues mentioned throughout the assessment and discussion. Moreover, we would like to give even more detailed decision advice.

References

1. Apache License 2.0 (2004). http://www.apache.org/licenses/LICENSE-2.0
2. Charland, A., Leroux, B.: Mobile application development: web vs. native. Comm. ACM **54**(5), 49–53 (2011)

3. Comments on Google Web Toolkit Steering (2012). https://groups.google.com/d/topic/gwt-steering/qO9MW9lSL5Y
4. Connors, A., Sullivan, B.: Mobile web application best practices. Technical report, W3C (2010). http://www.w3.org/TR/mwabp/
5. Curran, K., Bond, A., Fisher, G.: HTML5 and the mobile web. IJIDE 3(2), 40–56 (2012)
6. Dougan, R.: Packaging Sencha Touch 2 with PhoneGap (2012). http://robertdougan.com/posts/packaging-sencha-touch-2-with-phonegap-cordova
7. Firtman, M.: jQuery Mobile: Up and Running. O'Reilly, Sebastopol (2012)
8. Fishburn, P.C.: Additive utilities with incomplete product sets: application to priorities and assignments. Oper. Res. 15(3), 537–542 (1967)
9. GNU General Public License (2007). http://www.gnu.org/licenses/gpl-3.0
10. Gong, J., Tarasewich, P.: Guidelines for handheld mobile device interface design. In: Proceedings of the DSI 2004 Annual Meeting (2004)
11. Google Web Toolkit (2012). http://www.gwtproject.org/
12. GWT Community (2012). http://www.gwtproject.org/community.html
13. Gwt, FAQ. Get Started (2012). http://www.gwtproject.org/doc/latest/FAQ_GettingStarted.html
14. GWT-Phonegap (2013). http://code.google.com/p/gwt-phonegap/
15. Heitkötter, H., Hanschke, S., Majchrzak, T.A.: Comparing cross-platform development approaches for mobile applications. In: Proceedings of the 8th WEBIST (2012)
16. HTML5 (2012). http://www.w3.org/TR/html5/
17. jQuery (2012). http://jquery.com/
18. jQuery Mobile (2013). http://jquerymobile.com/
19. jQuery Mobile Forum (2013). http://forum.jquery.com/jquery-mobile
20. jQuery Project (2012). http://jquery.org/about/
21. Lennon, J.: Compare JavaScript frameworks (2010). http://www.ibm.com/developerworks/java/library/wa-jsframeworks/
22. Lin, F., Ye, W.: Operating system battle in the ecosystem of smartphone industry. In: Proceedings of the 2009 International Symposium on IEEC (2009)
23. Majchrzak, T.A., Heitkötter, H.: Development of mobile applications in regional companies: status quo and best practices. In: Proceedings of the 9th WEBIST (2013)
24. Melamed, T., Clayton, B.: A comparative evaluation of HTML5 as a pervasive media platform. In: Phan, T., Montanari, R., Zerfos, P. (eds.) MobiCASE 2009. LNICST, vol. 35, pp. 307–325. Springer, Heidelberg (2010)
25. mgwt User Group (2013). http://groups.google.com/group/mgwt
26. The MIT License (1988). http://opensource.org/licenses/mit-license.php
27. Oehlman, D., Blanc, S.: Pro Android Web Apps. Apress, Berkeley (2011)
28. Ohrt, J., Turau, V.: Cross-platform development tools for smartphone applications. IEEE Comput. 45(9), 72–79 (2012)
29. Olaru, A.: Selection Criteria for Javascript Frameworks (2007). http://www.infoq.com/news/2007/12/choosing-javascript-frameworks
30. PhoneGap (2013), http://phonegap.com/
31. Rabin, J., McCathieNevile, C.: Mobile web best practices 1.0. Technical report, W3C (2008). http://www.w3.org/TR/mobile-bp/
32. Saaty, T.: Axiomatic foundation of the analytic hierarchy process. Manag. Sci. 32(7), 841–855 (1986)
33. Sass (2013). http://sass-lang.com/

34. Sen, R., Subramaniam, C., Nelson, M.L.: Open source software licenses: strong-copyleft, non-copyleft, or somewhere in between? Decis. Support Syst. **52**(1), 199–206 (2011)
35. Sencha Architect (2013). http://www.sencha.com/products/architect/
36. Sencha Touch (2012). http://www.sencha.com/products/touch/
37. Smutny, P.: Mobile development tools and cross-platform solutions. In: Proceedings of the 13th ICCC (2012)
38. Stack Overflow. Tag jQuery Mobile (2013). http://stackoverflow.com/questions/tagged/jquery-mobile
39. The-M-Docs. Native Packaging (2012). http://panacodalabs.github.com/The-M-Docs/#espresso/native_packaging
40. The-M-Project (2013). http://the-m-project.org/
41. The-M-Project. github repository (2013). https://github.com/mwaylabs/The-M-Project
42. The-M-Project. Google Groups (2013). https://groups.google.com/group/themproject
43. Triantaphyllou, E., Mann, S.H.: An examination of the effectiveness of multi-dimensional decision-making methods: a decision-making paradox. Decis. Support Syst. **5**(3), 303–312 (1989)
44. Zibula, A., Majchrzak, T.A.: Developing a cross-platform mobile smart meter application using HTML5, jQuery Mobile and PhoneGap. In: Proceedings of the 8th WEBIST (2012)

Improving Search Engines' Document Ranking Employing Semantics and an Inference Network

Christos Makris[1], Yannis Plegas[1(✉)], Giannis Tzimas[2], and Emmanouil Viennas[1]

[1] Department of Computer Engineering and Informatics, University of Patras, Patras, Greece
{makri,plegas,biennas}@ceid.upatras.gr
[2] Department of Applied Informatics in Management and Economy, Faculty of Management and Economics, Technological Educational Institute of Messolonghi, Messolonghi, Greece
tzimas@teimes.gr

Abstract. The users search mainly diverse information from several topics and their needs are difficult to be satisfied from the techniques currently employed in commercial search engines and without intervention from the user. In this paper, a novel framework is presented for performing re-ranking in the results of a search engine based on feedback from the user. The proposed scheme combines smoothly techniques from the area of Inference Networks and data from semantic knowledge bases. The novelty lies in the construction of a probabilistic network for each query which takes as input the belief of the user to each result (initially, all are equivalent) and produces as output a new ranking for the search results. We have constructed an implemented prototype that supports different Web search engines and it can be extended to support any search engine. Finally extensive experiments were performed using the proposed methods depicting the improvement of the ranking of the search engines results.

Keywords: Search engines · Semantic-enhanced web applications · Re-ranking model · Wordnet senses · Inference network

1 Introduction

The global availability of information provided by the World Wide Web in the past few decades has made people's lifes easier in terms of time saving and accuracy in information seeking. Commercial search engines have provided the necessary tools to the average Internet user to search for information about any topic he/she might be interested in and their everyday use rises constantly.

However there are still circumstances where one finds himself/herself wondering around the information maze posed to him/her by the Web. For example a user might be interested in "rockets" and missiles, but get highly ranked results after performing a query in a search engine about the famous NBA basketball team, or interested in animals and specifically in "jaguars", but get results about cars. Polysemy can be

© Springer-Verlag Berlin Heidelberg 2014
K.-H. Krempels and A. Stocker (Eds.): WEBIST 2013, LNBIP 189, pp. 138–153, 2014.
DOI: 10.1007/978-3-662-44300-2_9

clarified by the general context of one's speaking, but search engines do not provide the necessary functionality to address this problem. Moreover, it often happens for the first set of results returned by a search engine to contain irrelevant information.

To overcome these drawbacks, in this paper we propose a new technique aiming to provide the necessary tools for the refinement of search results, taking into account feedback provided by the user. Besides the keywords provided from the initial query and the set of choices the user makes, we also utilize the semantic information hidden inside the returned pages. We feed this enriched combination of information in a probabilistic model and re-rank the results, without having to gather or import any additional data, thus making the whole concept simple and efficient.

Overall in this work, we describe the SerfSIN system (Search Engines results ReFinement using a Sense-driven Inference Network), that uses a re-ranking model based on inference networks and enhances it, in order to form an effective system for efficient reorganization of search results based on user choices. Moreover, we utilize the WordNet knowledge base in order to clarify the various senses that the terms might carry and thus enrich our model with semantic information. Except from the WordNet, we are proposing also the use of the Wikipedia knowledge base and particularly the Wikipedia Entities/Articles semantic information, as a second way to clarify the different senses of the terms. Our techniques are not restricted to WordNet and Wikipedia, but they can also be extended to support other knowledge bases, such as YAGO [29] and BabelNet [24].

The main idea of the paper is to transfer the belief of the user to the selected documents through the constructed network to the other documents that contain the senses of the selected documents. The re-ranking of the results is based on a vector that contains a weight for each document that represents the probability of the document to be relative for the user. We construct a probabilistic network from the terms and the senses of the documents, so when the users select a document, the weights of the documents that contain these senses are taking bigger values and so they are ranked higher. Detailed experiments depict the superiority of the proposed system in comparison to the initial ranking and to previously relevant proposed techniques.

The rest of the paper is organized as follows. Section 2 overviews related literature and Sect. 3 highlights the overall architecture. Next, in Sect. 4 we present the re-ranking process, whereas the proposed approach is analytically covered in Sect. 5. Section 6 analyzes an extension of this work and Sect. 7 depicts the results of our experiments. Finally, Sect. 8 concludes the paper and provides future research directions.

2   Literature Overview

The last decade has been characterized by tremendous efforts of the research community to overcome the problem of effective searching in the vast information dispersed in the World Wide Web [5]. A standard approach to Web searching is to model documents as bags of words, and a handful of theoretical models such as the well-known vector space model, have been developed employing this representation. An interesting alternative is to model documents as probabilistic networks (graphs), whose vertices represent terms, documents and user queries and whose edges represent relations between the involved entities defined on the basis of any meaningful statistical or linguistic relationships. Many works explore the usefulness of such graph-based text representations for IR like [6, 7] and Bayesian Networks are prominent in them.

Bayesian Networks [25] are increasingly being used in a variety of application areas like searching [2, 10, 31], Bioinformatics [3], and many others. An important subclass of Bayesian Networks is the Bayesian Inference Networks (BIN) [32] that have been employed in various applications [1, 20, 30]. Moreover, BINs form a major component in the search engine Indri's retrieval model [23].

In this work we introduce a semantically driven Bayesian Inference Network, incorporating semantic concepts in order to improve the ranking quality of search engines' results. Related approaches were presented in [1, 18]. The authors in [18] enrich the semantics of user-specific information and documents targeting at efficient implementation of personalized searching strategies. They adopt a Bayesian Belief Network (BBN) as a strategy for personalized search since they provide a clear formalism for embedding semantic concepts. Their approach is different to ours, since they use belief instead of inference networks and they employ the Open Directory Project Web directory instead of WordNet. In [1] the authors enhance the BINs using relevance feedback information and multiple reference structures and they apply their technique to similarity-based virtual screening, employing two distinct methods for carrying out BIN searching: reweighting the fragments in the reference structures and a group fusion algorithm. Our approach aims at a different application and employs semantic information, as a distinct layer in the applied inference network.

On the other hand and concerning search result's re-ranking, an interesting approach is to exploit information from past user queries and preferences. The relevant techniques range from simple systems implementing strategies that match users' queries to collections results [16, 22] to the employment of the machine learning machinery exploiting the outcomes of stored queries, in order to permit more accurate rankings, the so called "learning to rank" techniques [19]. There is also related but different to our focus work [8] combining diversified and interactive retrieval under the umbrella of dynamic ranked retrieval.

The main novelty of our work centers in the transparent embedding of semantic knowledge bases to improve search engine results re-ranking. Also in order to achieve our purpose we create a new probabilistic model which takes as input different semantic knowledge bases. The most relevant to our work is the system presented in [4] embedding instead of Bayesian inference network, techniques based on the exploitation of semantic relations and text coverage between results. Our work outperforms [4] improving its search performance, while it is based on a solid theoretical framework.

3 The Proposed System

In Fig. 1 a high level overview of the overall system architecture is depicted. As shown the system is decomposed into the following core subsystems:

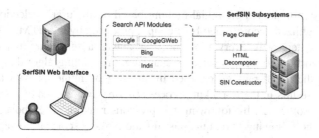

Fig. 1. SerfSIN high level system architecture.

1. The **SerfSIN Web Interface** that interacts with the end users in order to provide searching and search refinement services.
2. The **Search API Modules** which are responsible for the communication with various search engines' APIs, in order to retrieve the relevant results. At present three search engines are supported, namely:

    – Google Search API, with two options provided to the user for the first set of retrieved results; the use of the Google deprecated API and the option of parsing the pages of the Google results.
    – Bing Search API.
    – Indri Search Machine [28] over the ClueWeb09 Dataset [9].
3. The **Page Crawler** that fetches the content of the search engine results after the end user poses his first query.
4. The **HTML Decomposer** that parses the HTML code of a page and exports useful data, such as the title, keywords, metatags, highlighted text etc.
5. The **Sense Interference Network (SIN) Constructor** that creates the Network from the previous steps and reorganizes the search engines results.

The subsystems work in a sequential manner and the first three interact with the users and the various Web sources. In order for a user to utilize the services provided by SerfSIN, he/she simply makes a query after setting the basic search parameters (explained in Sect. 7) in the SerfSIN Web Interface. Every time the user clicks on a result, the core module is utilized producing the new improved ranking. In particular, the core subsystems work real-time and in parallel, rearranging the initial order and the algorithms utilized are presented in detail in the following sections.

4   The Re-ranking Process

The whole process is initialized by the initial query performed by the user through the SerfSIN Web Interface. The query keywords are imported to the search engine selected (Google, Bing or Indri) through the relevant API and the results are collected by the Page Crawler. After this step, the initial results' ranking is the same as the one given by the search engine selected.

The next step improves the initial ranking based on the user's selections; the SIN Constructor is utilized accompanied by the input produced by the HTML Decomposer. This step runs iteratively every time the user makes a selection. In particular the proposed network is utilized, either as a standalone re-ranking algorithm, or in combination with the initial ranking returned by the search engine, or with the previous ranking of the results in the re-ranking process (if we have a series of re-rankings). In all cases we resolve ties, by following the previous ranking. The above options are expressed by the following two equations, for the ranking score of document d_i:

$$New\, Ranking\, Score_i = R_i \tag{1}$$

$$New\, Ranking\, Score_i = (n - previous\_rank(i) + 1) * (1 + \beta * R_i) \tag{2}$$

where R_i denotes the re-ranking weight provided by the network for d_i (its computation is described in the next section), previous_rank(i) stands for the previous rank position of d_i, n is the number of results retrieved and β is a user defined weight factor. Intuitively, when the factor β is raised the re-ranking process results in major rank changes. The equation $(n - previous\_rank(i) + 1)$ introduces a factor based on the previous ranking of a result in the list. Equation (1) is used in the case of the network use as a standalone re-ranking system, while Eq. (2) is used for the composite case where the new ranking system is composed with the previous ranking of search results. In the new ranking produced, the results are ranked according to the above calculated score. When the user selects further results, the same procedure is followed with the difference that the ranking produced by the previous phase is used as input for the next reordering.

Even though we assume that most results selected by a user are relevant, our scheme incorporates smoothly the previous ranking, hence it is robust to user misselections. A misselection of a result leads to the inclusion of its relevant information to the ranking process, but still can be made to not affect significantly the produced ranking.

5   Re-ranking Weight Calculation

Our extension of inference network, the Sense Inference Network (SIN), as depicted in Fig. 2, consists of four component levels: the document level, the term level, the sense level, and a fourth level that represents the documents nodes and the value they take in order to re-rank the results; the fourth level can be considered to play the role of the query layer in the traditional inference network model and its presence signifies that we are not interested to model specific information needs, but re-rankings based on users' reaction. The SIN is built once for the retrieved documents of the query's results and its structure does not change during re-ranking. The document level contains a node (d_i's) for each document of the query's results. For each term of the documents nodes texts, we add terms nodes (t_j's) to the network and we interconnect the documents nodes with the terms nodes with arcs. The terms are induced by the retrieved pages by applying to them sequentially: (i) HTML stripping, (ii) removal of the stop words and finally, (iii) stemming using the Porter stemming algorithm [27]. For each term node we also

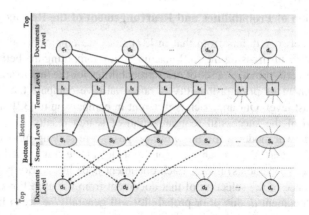

Fig. 2. The Sense Inference Network.

find its different senses using WordNet [14] and we add them to the network. WordNet is a lexical database for the English language. It groups English words into sets of synonyms called synsets, provides short, general definitions, and records the various semantic relations between these synonym sets. The term nodes are connected through arcs to their different senses nodes (S_i's). Finally, all the senses nodes which are contained in a document are connected to the respective document node at the last level. The formed network is a four level directed graph in which the information flows from the documents nodes of the first level to the term nodes and then through the senses nodes to the documents nodes of the last level.

The innovative idea in our network is the existence of the level of senses (concepts) based on the WordNet knowledge base. The term nodes are connected to their different senses through directed arcs. The existence of a directed path between a document node and a sense node denotes that this sense is appearing in the respective document and more formally to the event that a sense has been observed in the documents collection. Similarly, a single sense node might be shared by more than one term. The dependence of a sense node upon the respective term node is represented directly in the network through an arc. The final process for the construction of SIN is the creation of the arcs from the senses nodes to the document nodes at the last level. The last level's nodes are different from the nodes of the first layer; they represent the same entities (documents) but in different time instances (we depict this fact by drawing the arcs from the sense nodes to the nodes at the last layer as dashed, just to depict the fact that we are moving at a different time instances; this is a common practice that breaks cycles in Bayesian networks).

The sense level models the hidden semantics and the belief of the network that the senses of a document are the senses that the user looks for. The senses nodes are connected to every node at the last level representing a document where this sense appears (this can be validated if there exists a path from the document node at the first level to the sense node). The document nodes at the last level have an accumulated belief probability that is used for re-ranking. The value of this belief is estimated based on the different senses of the document and denotes the conceptual similarity between the document and the information need of the user.

5.1   Estimation of Probabilities and Rearrangement of the Results

Our inference network differs from that in [32] since we employ it only as a weight propagation mechanism, using the [32] machinery for computing the beliefs at the last level of the network, provided a set of prior probabilities for the first level; when a user selects a document its prior probability is raised and we compute the change at the beliefs at the last level. Our approach is different in comparison to [32] and is adapted to the problem of the successful reorganization of search results. [32] proposed an information retrieval model while our work proposes a re-ranking model.

In order to estimate the probabilities for the nodes of the constructed SIN, we first begin at the root (documents) nodes. Each document node has a prior probability that denotes the chance of the selection of that document from the user. For our collection and for each document d_i this prior probability will generally be set to be:

$$p(d_i) = \frac{1}{n}, \ i \in [1...n] \tag{3}$$

where n is the number of the query results. This probability will change into 1, when a result is selected in order to denote that this document is relevant from the user's point of view. This belief is transferred through the network to the senses nodes and then to the final layer representing the document nodes and changes the values of the classification weights, re-ranking the results.

For all non-root nodes in the SIN we must estimate the probability that a node takes, given any set of values for its parent nodes. We begin with the term nodes. Each term node contains a specification of the conditional probability associated with the node, given its set of parent document nodes. If a term node t has a set of parents parst = $\{d_1, ..., d_k\}$, we must estimate the probability $P(t|d_1, ..., d_k)$. Here we follow the inference network machinery described in [32] employing the tf-idf weights for the term nodes and setting:

$$p(t|d_i) = 0,5 + 0,5 * ntf(t, d_i)nidf(t) \tag{4}$$

where ntf() and nidf() are the normalized term frequency and normalized inverse document frequency components for term t. In particular, if tf(t,d_i) denotes the number of times term t appears in d_i, f_t the number of its occurrences in the collection and max_tf(d_i) the maximum number of a term's occurrences in d_i then:

$$ntf(t, d_i) = \frac{tf(t, d_i)}{max\_tf(d_i)}, \ nidf(t) = \frac{\log(\frac{n}{f_t})}{\log n} \tag{5}$$

Based on these weights we can collect the belief for a term node from its father set by employing the formed weighted sum link matrix [32]. The next step is the estimation of the probabilities for the sense nodes. If a sense node S has a set of parents parsS = $\{t_1, ..., t_k\}$, we must estimate the probability $P(S|t_1, ..., t_k)$. The probability of a sense node denotes the importance of the sense for each term. Initially, the different meanings for each term are calculated using WordNet. The probability of a sense to be the unique sense of a term is equally likely among the different senses and is defined to be 1/(number of different senses) for each term, hence we set.

$$p(S|t_i) = \frac{1}{m_i} \tag{6}$$

where S is a sense of t_i and m_i is the number of the different senses of the term t_i. Based on these weights we collect the belief for the sense node from its father set, by employing a weighted sum link matrix.

Finally, we estimate the probability for a document node at the last level to be relative to the user's interests, based on the network's structure. The parents of the documents nodes at the last level of the network are the senses nodes. Therefore, the selection from the user of a result gives the network the ability to distinguish the senses, which interest the user and the document nodes at the last level get new weights signifying this knowledge. The senses nodes are affecting the document nodes according to their semantics as these are represented through arcs. We do not give weights but instead use a simple sum link matrix and the probability/belief for a document d at the last layer with q father senses is simply the sum of the beliefs of its father senses divided by q. The Senses nodes are connected to the documents nodes for which there exist paths between the documents and the senses (through the term nodes). Final step is the computation of the weights at last level that entail the belief of the relatedness of the documents to the selected document.

The values of the beliefs at the last level of document nodes $W_i = bel(d_i)$ compose a vector $(W_1, W_2, \ldots, W_n)$. Let $(W_1^0, W_2^0, \ldots, W_n^0)$, be the vector of beliefs at the last level before the selection of any results from the user (initial probabilities at the first level are all equal). For each result that the user selects, a new vector is estimated. In particular when the user selects a single result d, its probability at the first level is raised to 1, and a new belief for every document in the last level is computed. After this weight propagation, the re-ranking weight R_i for document d_i is defined as $R_i = W_i - W_i^0$. Similarly as the user selects further results, the probabilities of the respective nodes at the first level are raised to 1 and the beliefs are recalculated. By repeating this process and computing the re-ranking weights using formulae (1) and (2) (note that we always subtract from the initial weights) we reorganize the results accordingly.

The innovative idea is the use of the senses (nor the terms) in order re-rank the results. The importance of the terms modulates the importance of the senses. When the user selects a result, the terms of this document get higher values, thus the respective senses get higher values. Consequently, all the documents that have these senses get higher values in the final ranking process. The more senses (from the selected document) a document has, the higher ranking value it takes. Thus, the documents which contain the more senses (and the more times) from the selected document, are ranked higher.

6 Extensions

In this section, we extend the method described previously by embedding Wikipedia articles instead of the senses of the WordNet. Particularly we automatically annotate the terms of the documents with entities/articles of the Wikipedia, a process that is commonly known as *Wikification*. In terms of the scheme presented in Fig. 2 we have to change the third level using as senses the articles of the Wikipedia that assigned to each term using the *Wikification* process. This procedure as we can see in [15, 21] assigns one article to each term. Our transformed method as described below assigns to each term a small set of articles (2 or 3 mainly). Like previous approaches [15, 21] the cross-reference of the terms in the documents to Wikipedia articles is based on local compatibility between the terms around the term and textual information embedded in the article. In our method we replace the terms around the text with the most representative words for the document and we apply this process for each term of the documents. We select for each document/result a small set (about five to ten) of words sorting the terms according to their occurrences and selecting the top-k of them.

The text annotation methods are facing the named entity disambiguation problem, in which a term has as possible annotations multiple Wikipedia articles. We employ the best method (method C) from paper [21] which utilizes the TAGME approach [15], and an extra vote in the disambiguation procedure which is given to a Wikipedia article based on the WordNet and the PageRank value of the article. The final disambiguation score is computed by linearly combining the disambiguation score, with the relatedness (as computed in [15]) and thus producing a global score. Then, we select for a given spot, the Wikipedia article with the largest score as chosen disambiguation. Finally in order to disambiguate a term we follow the disambiguation by threshold approach (DT) from [15], which for a specific term selects the Wikipedia article with the maximum relatedness weight [15] plus the set of all other Wikipedia articles that are at a chosen threshold distance from the selected article. Finally, from this pool of articles we disambiguate to a small set of articles, the articles (commonly 2 or 3) with the highest commonness value (as computed in [15]). The possibility of an article to be the dominant article is equivalent between the articles and for this reason in the network for each arc from a term to an article we assign as weight this value. Based on these weights we collect the belief for a sense node (article) from its father set (terms which disambiguate to this article), by employing a weighted sum link matrix.

Next we proceed with the same way as in Sect. 5.1 in order to re-rank the results based to the Wikipedia Articles.

7   Evaluation of Serfsin's Performance

To carry out our evaluation, we explored 150 web queries; 50 queries from the TREC WebTrack 2009 [11], 50 queries from the TREC WebTrack 2010 [12] and 50 queries from the TREC WebTrack 2011 [13] datasets respectively. All tracks employ the 1 billion page ClueWeb09 collection [33]. These ranked lists of results contain, for every page, relevance judgments made by human assessors.

We assessed our network performance by comparing the rankings it delivered to the rankings search machines returned for the same set of queries and results. For our comparisons, we relied on: (i) the available relevance judgments and (ii) the Normalized Discounted Cumulative Gain (nDCG) measure [17], which quantifies the usefulness, or gain, of a document based on its position in the result list. The assumption in nDCG is that the lower the ranked position of a relevant result, the less valuable it is for the user; because it is not likely that it will be examined by the user. Formally, the nDCG accumulated at a particular ranking position p is given by:

$$DCG_p = rel_1 + \sum_{(i=2)}^{p} \frac{rel_i}{log_2 i}, \; nDCG_p = \frac{DCG_p}{IDCG_p} \tag{7}$$

where rel_i are the document relevance scores and $IDCG_p$ is the Ideal DCG, i.e. the DCG values when sorting the documents by their relevance.

We set the re-ranking experiment by selecting randomly a relevant document, after posing each query and then performing re-ranking; we used nDCG before and after re-ranking to estimate the ranking performance. The experiments carried out can be distinguished according to three basic parameters (all of the parameters can be accessed through the SerfSIN Web Interface [34]):

- The search engine selected to perform the initial query.
- The percentage of the resulting pages text used to identify the terms that feed the second level of the constructed network (SIN).
- The participation of the initial ranking returned by the search engine, or the previous ranking of the results after a user's selection, in the re-ranking process, that is the significance of the proposed network compared to the initial ranking.

Our experiments were carried out using the Indri search engine over the ClueWeb09 Category B Dataset. We also utilized two different general purpose search engines, namely Google and Bing. We used 50 results in the case of Indri and Bing, while in the case of Google we used 20 in order to test if the chosen result set size has any affect on the attained performance. The queries used, as well as the relevant judgments rely on the ClueWeb09 Dataset and this is the reason why we selected Indri as our main experimental search engine. In the case of the general purpose search engines, there are no relevant judgments for all the returned pages; hence we ignored these pages in our measurements. In relation to the second parameter, that is the text percentage of the resulting pages used to extract the network terms, we employ two distinct approaches: we either use the whole text stemming from the HTML pages, or we use the most important text contained in the pages (e.g. keywords, meta description, Google description, h1, h2 tags, strong words etc.).

In the following, we depict the most representative experimental results from the vast material that we collected. In the following, we depict the most representative experimental results from the vast material that we collected. Since our aim is to depict the improvement semantic information provides to search results we experimentally investigated only our main proposal (use of WordNet); in future work we plan to extensively experiment with Wikipedia entities and compare our findings with the experiments using WordNet. We summarize all the depicted configurations (Table 1) and then we particularize presenting the average nDCG values for every case (Table 2). We note that the proposed network has significantly better overall performance by 0.061962413, since the average nDCG values of the search engines and the proposed network are 0.264370611 and 0.326333024 respectively. We present twelve experiments with alternative configurations based on the parameters analyzed in the previous paragraphs (Table 1). For every experiment we calculated the total average of nDCG

Table 1. Parameters' configuration for the twelve experiments (Most Important Parts: MIP, Full Text: FT).

Exp.	Search engine	Text coverage	Use of initial ranking	Web track queries
1	Indri	MIP	Yes ($\beta = 1$)	2009
2	Indri	MIP	Yes ($\beta = 1$)	2010
3	Indri	MIP	Yes ($\beta = 1$)	2011
4	Indri	MIP	Yes ($\beta = 2$)	2011
5	Indri	FT	Yes ($\beta = 1$)	2010
6	Indri	FT	Yes ($\beta = 1$)	2011
7	Google	FT	No	2010
8	Google	MIP	No	2009
9	Google	MIP	Yes ($\beta = 1$)	2010
10	Bing	MIP	No	2011
11	Bing	MIP	Yes ($\beta = 1$)	2011
12	Bing	FT	No	2011

Table 2. nDCG Averages for every experiment.

Exp.	nDCG Aver. (Before)	nDCG Aver. (After)	Difference
1	0.259444438	0.309425945	0.049981506
2	0.236960647	0.285369305	0.048408658
3	−0.09917842	0.055169266	0.154347686
4	−0.100722072	0.011697012	0.112419084
5	0.062907506	0.120053429	0.057145923
6	−0.103749409	−0.03013304	0.073616369
7	0.538630812	0.591288965	0.052658153
8	0.525453777	0.593815908	0.068362132
9	0.549054511	0.575225518	0.026171007
10	0.43777936	0.486484735	0.048705375
11	0.434751776	0.468521246	0.033769469
12	0.43111441	0.449078004	0.017963594
Avg:	0.264370611	0.326333024	0.061962413

values, for every rank position of the results. We also calculated their difference, in order to depict the corresponding improvement that is evident in all cases.

In the next figures the experiment's graphs are depicted, where for every rank position of the results, the average nDCG values of the search engine are compared to the average nDCG values of the proposed network. We started our analysis with the Indri search engine, where the experiments took place in a "controlled" environment employing the ClueWeb09 Dataset and its relevant judgments and we continued by studying the proposed network's performance for the cases of general purpose search engines. In the performed experiments we measured the proposed network's behavior, as a standalone re-ranking system as well as for the composite case, where the previous ranking of the results is counted in the re-ranking process.

As the figures depict, the proposed network performs well in both cases: when used as a standalone re-ranking system (Experiments 7, 8, 10 and 12), or in the case where the previous ranking is taken into account. Especially in the Experiments 8, 10 where the network was used as the primary re-ranking engine in contrast to the general purpose search engines Google and Bing, the performance was excellent. It is worth noticing that when the network takes into account the previous ranking (Experiments 1–6, 9 and 11), it behaves better than the search engines and generally smoother (less rank changes when reordering) than the case where it acts as a standalone re-ranking system (Fig. 3, 4, 5, 6, 7, 8, 9, 10, 11, 12, 13, 14).

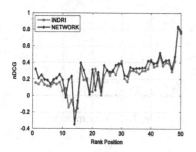

Fig. 3. Experiment 1.

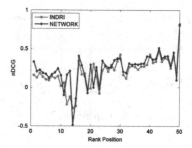

Fig. 4. Experiment 2.

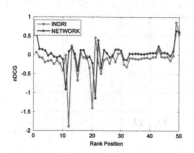

Fig. 5. Experiment 3.

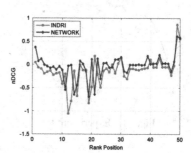

Fig. 6. Experiment 4.

Another interesting observation is that the overall network performance did not deescalate when the most important text parts were used for the terms extraction process, instead of utilizing the full text. Moreover, as shown in experiment couples (1, 2), (2, 3) and (7, 8) the query sets employed did not play an important role in the quality of the results, as the network behaves equivalently in all configurations.

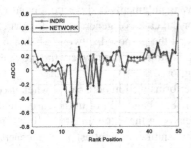

Fig. 7. Experiment 5.

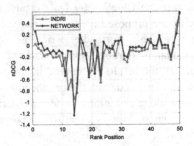

Fig. 8. Experiment 6.

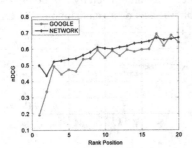

Fig. 9. Experiment 7.

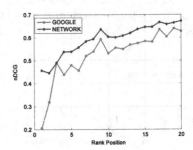

Fig. 10. Experiment 8.

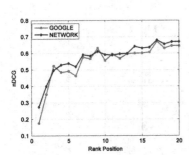

Fig. 11. Experiment 9.

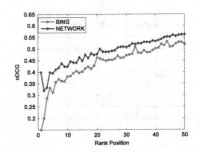

Fig. 12. Experiment 10.

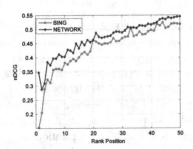

Fig. 13. Experiment 11.

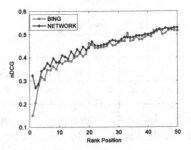

Fig. 14. Experiment 12.

Finally, in our Experiments (we indicatively depict Experiments 3 and 4) we notice that when the β factor, increases from 1 to 2 the results remain the same, so in most of the cases the experiments were performed with β equal to 1; moreover our technique leads to better performance irrespectively of the result set size.

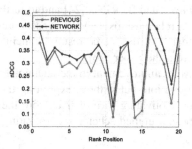

Fig. 15. A comparison between the two approaches.

We have employed in our experiments the system described in [4] and in Fig. 15 a diagram comparing their technique with ours is depicted, assessing the total average nDCG values of all the above experiments for the first 20 ranking positions. It is clear that the new approach performs better in all positions by 0.033364065, since the average nDCG values of the previous approach and the proposed network are 0.284028022 and 0.326333024 respectively.

Moreover, the approach presented in this paper differs in the way the relevant information is retrieved, as well as the re-ranking process. The techniques employed in [4] are based on the exploitation of semantic relations and text coverage between results, while we employ a variant of a Bayesian inference network. The main advantages/features of our technique can be summarized as follows:

- Employment of a solid theoretical framework that can be tuned and be enhanced and not just heuristic use of terms and senses and their overlap.
- Ability to transparently enhance the inference network with other ontologies.
- Due to the inference network employed and our weight parameter, our technique is more robust to user errors, and a misselection of a result cannot affect significantly the final ranking.

It should be finally noted that we employed the paired t test, and the computed one tailed p-values were found to be very small (in all cases less than 0.01), proving that the results have significant differences and thus signifying the superiority of our technique in a strict statistical sense, and for a significance level of a = 0.05.

8   Conclusions and Future Work

In this work we have presented a novel framework for re-ranking the search results of user queries employing a sense inference network in combination with semantic based techniques exploiting WordNet. The framework was applied in three search engines, and the attained results are quite encouraging depicting the ability of the proposed technique to capture the user preferences and produce a preferable ranking. A minor disadvantage seems to be the re-ranking process execution time; we plan to reduce the execution time by carefully tuning our code, without affecting the search quality. Moreover we aim to incorporate in our technique other knowledge bases besides WordNet, such as YAGO [29], and BabelNet [24] and to further enhance our inference network by embedding in it relationships between synsets present in WordNet. Finally we plan to improve the quality of the search results reducing the redundancy in their texts following methods from the paper [26].

Our approach comes as an improvement to the technique that was proposed in [4], and embeds semantic information, but without exploiting the machinery of the inference networks. It could be motivating to further explore the connection between the two approaches, and propose a unified scheme incorporating both of them.

Acknowledgements. This research has been co-financed by the European Union (European Social Fund-ESF) and Greek national funds through the Operational Program "Education and Lifelong Learning" of the National Strategic Reference Framework (NSRF)-Research Funding Program: Heracleitus II. Investing in knowledge society through the European Social Fund.

This research has been co-financed by the European Union (European Social Fund-ESF) and Greek national funds through the Operational Program "Education and Lifelong Learning" of the National Strategic Reference Framework (NSRF)-Research Funding Program: Thales. Investing in knowledge society through the European Social Fund.

References

1. Abdo, A., Salim, N., Ahmed, A.: Implementing relevance feedback in ligand-based virtual screening using Bayesian inference network. J. Biomol. Screen. **16**, 1081–1088 (2011)
2. Acid, S., de Campos, L.M., Fernandez, J.M., Huete, J.F.: An information retrieval model based on simple Bayesian networks. Int. J. Intell. Syst. **18**, 251–265 (2003)
3. Ahmed, A., Abdo, A., Salim, N.: Ligand-Based Virtual Screening Using Bayesian Inference Network and Reweighted Fragments. Sci. World J. **2012**, 1–7 (2012). Article ID 410914
4. Antoniou, D., Plegas, Y., Tsakalidis, A., Tzimas, G., Viennas, E.: Dynamic refinement of search engines results utilizing the user intervention. J. Syst. Softw. **85**(7), 1577–1587 (2012)
5. Baeza-Yates, R., Ribeiro-Neto, B.: Modern Information Retrieval: The Concepts and Technology Behind Search. Addison Wesley, Essex (2011)
6. Blanco, R., Lioma, C.: Graph-based term weighting for information retrieval. Inf. Retrieval **15**(1), 54–92 (2012)
7. Boccaletti, S., Latora, V., Moreno, Y., Chavez, M., Hwang, D.U.: Complex networks: structure and dynamics. Phys. Rep. **424**, 175–308 (2006)
8. Brandt, C., Joachims, T., Yue, Y., Bank, J.: Dynamic ranked retrieval. In: WSDM '11 (2011)
9. Callan, J.: The ClueWeb09 dataset. http://boston.lti.cs.cmu.edu/clueweb09 (2009). Accessed 1 Aug 2012)
10. Chapelle, O., Zhang, Y.: A dynamic Bayesian network click model for web search ranking. In: Proceedings of the 18th International Conference on WWW, pp. 1–10. ACM, New York, USA (2009)

11. Clarke, C.L.A., Craswell, N., Soboroff, I.: Overview of the TREC 2009 web track. In Proceedings of the 18th TREC Conference (2009)
12. Clarke, C.L.A., Craswell, N., Soboroff, I., Cormack, G.: Overview of the TREC 2010 web track. In: Proceedings of the 19th TREC Conference (2010)
13. Clarke, C.L.A., Craswell, N., Soboroff, I., Voorhees, E.M.: Overview of the TREC 2011 Web Track. In: Proceedings of the 20th TREC Conference (2011)
14. Fellbaum, C.: WordNet, an electronic lexical database. The MIT Press, Cambridge (1998)
15. Ferragina, P., Scaiella, U.: TAGME: on-the-fly annotation of short text fragments (by wikipedia entities). In: Proceedings of the 19th ACM International Conference on Information and Knowledge Management (CIKM '10), pp. 1625–1628. New York, USA, (2010)
16. Howe, A.E., Dreilinger, D.: SavvySearch: a meta-search engine that learns which search engines to query. AI Mag. 18(2), 19–25 (1997)
17. Jarvelin, K., Kekalainen, J.: IR evaluation methods for retrieving highly relevant documents. In: Proceedings of the 23rd International ACM SIGIR Conference, pp. 41–48 (2000)
18. Lee, J., Kim, H., Lee, S.: Exploiting taxonomic knowledge for personalized search: a bayesian belief network-based approach. J. Inf. Sci. Eng. 27, 1413–1433 (2011)
19. Liu, T.-Y.: Learning to Rank for Information Retrieval. Springer, Heidelberg (2011)
20. Ma, W.J., Beck, J.M., Latham, P.E., Pouget, A.: Bayesian inference with probabilistic population codes. Nat. Neurosci. 9, 1432–1438 (2006)
21. Makris, C., Plegas, Y., Theodoridis, E.: Improved text annotation with Wikipedia entities. SAC 2013, 288–295 (2013)
22. Meng, W., Yu, C., Liu, K.: Building efficient and effective metasearch engines. ACM Comput. Surv. 34(1), 48–89 (2002)
23. Metzler, D., Turtle, H., Croft, W.B.: Indri: A language-model based search engine for complex queries (extended version). IR 407, University of Massachusetts (2005)
24. Navigli, R., Ponzetto, S.P.: BabelNet: building a very large multilingual semantic network. In: Proceedings of the 48th Annual Meeting of the Association for Computational Linguistics (ACL 2010), pp. 216–225 (2010)
25. Niedermayer, D.: An introduction to Bayesian networks and their contemporary applications. In: Holmes, D.E., Jain, L.C. (eds.) SCI. Studies in Computational Intelligence SCI, vol. 156, pp. 117–130. Springer, Heidelberg (2008)
26. Plegas, Y., Stamou, S.: Reducing information redundancy in search results. SAC 2013, 886–893 (2013)
27. Porter, M.F.: An algorithm for suffix stripping. Program 14(3), 130–137 (1980)
28. Strohman, T., Metzler, D., Turtle, H., Croft, B.: Indri: a language model-based search engine for complex queries. In: Proceedings of the International Conference on Intelligence Analysis (May 2–6, 2005), McLean, VA (2005)
29. Suchanek, F.M., Kasneci, G., Weikum, G.: YAGO: a core of semantic knowledge. In: Proceedings of the 16th International Conference on WWW, pp. 697–706 (2007)
30. Tebaldi, C., West, M.: Bayesian inference of network traffic using link data. J. Am. Stat. Assoc. 93, 557–573 (1998)
31. Teevan, J.B.: Improving information retrieval with textual analysis: Bayesian models and beyond. Master's Thesis, Department of Electrical Engineering, MIT Press (2011)
32. Turtle, H.R.: Inference networks for document retrieval. Ph.D. Thesis (1991)
33. ClueWeb09 collection. http://lemurproject.org/clueweb09/
34. SerfSIN Web Interface. http://150.140.142.5/research/SerfSIN/

Category-Based YouTube Request Pattern Characterization

Shaiful Alam Chowdhury and Dwight Makaroff[(✉)]

Department of Computer Science, University of Saskatchewan,
Saskatoon, SK, S7N 5C9, Canada
sbc882@mail.usask.ca, makaroff@cs.usask.ca
http://www.cs.usask.ca

Abstract. Media content distribution systems make extensive use of computational resources, such as disk and network bandwidth. The use of these resources is proportional to the relative popularity of the objects and their level of replication over time. Therefore, understanding request popularity over time can inform system design decisions. As well, advertisers can target popular objects to maximize their impact.

Workload characterization is especially challenging with user-generated content, such as in YouTube, where popularity is hard to predict *a priori* and content is uploaded at a very fast rate. In this paper, we consider category as a distinguishing feature of a video and perform an extensive analysis of a snapshot of videos uploaded over two 24-h periods. Our results show significant differences between categories in the first 149 days of the videos' lifetimes. The lifespan of videos, relative popularity and time to reach peak popularity clearly differentiate between news/sports and music/film. Predicting popularity is a challenging task that requires sophisticated techniques (e.g. time-series clustering). From our analysis, we develop a workload generator that can be used to evaluate caching, distribution and advertising policies. This workload generator matches the empirical data on a number of statistical measurements.

Keywords: Workload characterization · Multimedia applications · Content distribution · Time-series clustering

1 Introduction

YouTube and other user generated content (UGC) sites have altered the way people watch Internet video. YouTube was the 4th most accessed Internet site in 2007 [6], and its use was increasing over time in a power-law manner. Recent studies support two central observations: (1) increasing number of videos/users [8,16] and (2) dissatisfying experiences of users in watching YouTube videos [13]. Other studies [10,14,15] suggest that YouTube is the most bandwidth intensive service of today's Internet, accounting for 20–35 % of Internet traffic.

© Springer-Verlag Berlin Heidelberg 2014
K.-H. Krempels and A. Stocker (Eds.): WEBIST 2013, LNBIP 189, pp. 154–169, 2014.
DOI: 10.1007/978-3-662-44300-2_10

Much research has been done investigating request characteristics from both client [11,19] and server perspectives [2,5,8,9] in order to enable improved service. However, none of this earlier work considered the categories of video objects. This aggregate data may not tell the whole story.

A proper understanding of YouTube's workload will aid in the design of new systems, as well as capacity planning, and network management for similar types of systems. The methodology we have developed is useful for UGC sites that have a single cache for the region of requests captured. YouTube itself operates on such a global scale that a single cache would not be sufficient. Rather, multiple regional caches satisfy regional demand patterns that have been shown to differ between different regions in the world [3]. If regional request data was available through the standard API, we could account for multiple caches in our analysis.

In this paper, the time-varying global viewing patterns of a sample of YouTube videos from their upload time are analyzed, considering video category.[1] We present the results of one data collection period (5 months of views of videos uploaded in 2 consecutive days). We show that different categories exhibit different viewing patterns in terms of overall popularity and detailed popularity over time. In fact, it is possible to predict the future popularity of some categories of videos at very early ages, because of correlations over time. We confirmed that the number of views of the popular videos follows a Zipf distribution for most categories, whereas views of the unpopular videos follow a light tail section. We also find that the uploading trends in YouTube have changed over time. People are now uploading more user generated content (UGC) compared to earlier observations. We also show that time-series clustering can be successfully used to understand the growth patterns for the categories where early popularity cannot be used to predict popularity in the rest of the measurement period.

These observations contribute to a better understanding of the popularity dynamics of YouTube videos, enabling realistic testing scenarios for developing and evaluating various design parameters for UGC sites. Request patterns for different categories may vary around the world; our dataset and analysis provide a case study that shows that global category differences persist, and therefore, will exist in each region. Our analysis enables the development of category-specific workload generators which can be combined to form the input for simulators and prototype systems. While developing and evaluating a comprehensive workload generator remains as future work, we have a strategy for generating synthetic requests on a category basis and present preliminary results which match reasonably well for two categories: News and Music.

The remainder of the paper is organized as follows. Related work is described in Sect. 2. Section 3 explains the data collection methods. Request patterns are discussed in Sect. 4, and we use views over time to develop a workload generator in Sect. 5. Section 6 provides conclusions and future work.

---

[1] As defined by the uploader.

2   Related Work

Previous request characterization and video popularity analysis has been used to investigate the feasibility of different content delivery streaming techniques, and to design and evaluate caching policies/systems for UGC sites. Our work leverages this research to investigate *category* popularity over time.

YouTube video request traffic was captured at the packet level at the University of Calgary over a 4 month period [11]. They investigated video popularity properties, usage patterns, and transfer behaviours as measured from the client edge of the distribution network. The traces examined contained data from both completed and incomplete requests. Their analysis suggests that appropriate caching decisions not only can improve end user experience, but also reduce network bandwidth usage. Another study [19] observed the traffic of YouTube videos between a university campus and the YouTube server. Approximately 25 % of the videos in the trace were requested more than once, leaving a long tail in the distribution. Three different content delivery techniques were analyzed: P2P based distribution, proxy caching and local caching. Proxy-caching outperformed the other techniques, and P2P based distribution sometimes exhibited worse performance than local caching. These two results can be biased by the measurement locations that restrict the context of the studies and the proposed solutions. For instance, it is claimed that video requests in YouTube follow a Zipf distribution [11], which is different from other works that consider global request patterns [1,5]. For our purposes, global access patterns are essential.

2.5 million YouTube videos were obtained using related video links [6] in a study at Simon Fraser University. Access patterns of the popular videos did follow a Zipf-like distribution. This indicated that the YouTube network is similar to small world networks, and P2P techniques could be successfully applied, contradicting earlier findings [19]. Their dataset is likely to be biased to popular videos because of the crawling approach, and popularity over time is not investigated.

A recent approach to investigate growth patterns in YouTube video requests was to use Google charts to collect views over time [9]. They analyzed the time-varying viewing patterns of popular videos, deleted videos and randomly selected videos. Popular videos usually experience a huge number of views on a single peak day or week. Unfortunately, using the Google charts API is not sufficient to have a proper, fine-grained understanding of the dynamics of video popularity as Google charts API always returns 100 data points, regardless of video age.

Recent work was done on nearly 30,000 videos, collected by using the recently uploaded standard feed provided by the YouTube API [2]. Their collection procedure claims to have an unbiased dataset; the *Most Recent* standard feed returns video information randomly that are uploaded recently. Most of these videos experienced their peak popularity within fewer than six weeks of their uploading time. Video collection based on keyword search is shown to be biased to popular videos, suggesting that the method of data collection is important.

3   Data Collection

No prior work measures the daily views of different categories of YouTube videos from the first day of their uploading time. We modified previous unbiased data collection methods [2], since we speculate that the first week since uploading deserves more investigation, even though this may expose day-of-week effects. Moreover, similar numbers of videos from all the categories are needed for appropriate comparison between different categories.

Multiple crawlers were deployed to obtain the data used in our analysis:

(1) Most Recent Crawlers. 15 crawlers were deployed on March 3rd, 2012 (a Saturday) to collect video IDs for 15 different categories,[2] by restricting each crawler's queries to a single category from those available for upload on that date. Though a video may be assigned to more than one category, we use the categories selected by the YouTube API. All crawlers collected video information for 24 h. The *Most Recent* standard feed provides video information randomly, reducing bias. A similar procedure was followed on March 4th, 2012. After two days, 71,208 videos' information was obtained. The dataset size is limited by the YouTube API, returning information for at most 100 different videos to each crawler every 1 or 2 h.

(2) Video View Collection Crawlers. Video view collection using two separate crawlers was started from March 4th, 2012 and March 5th, 2012. This continued for 149 consecutive days (approximately 5 months). The crawlers ensured a 24-h difference between view collections. Normalization was performed on the first day's views. Due to network connection failures, some video views on days 20 and 58 of the measurement period were not captured. Fortunately, those days are not that important for most of the videos; most significant events occur very early. Thus, 147 day's views are analyzed. After 149 days, the number of videos in the dataset fell from 71,208 to 47,711 (an average deletion rate of 33 %). Table 1 shows the summary of our dataset. Howto, Film, Entertainment and Tech videos experience the highest deletion rates.

(3) Uploading Rate Crawlers. Another crawler was developed that collected category names of videos provided by YouTube's *Most Recent* standard feed. The crawler ran for 5 months, starting from February 2nd, 2012 and collected approximately 365,000 unique videos' information. This allows us to estimate the short-term current category-specific uploading rates. While not an accurate representation of the entirety of YouTube, it does give some insight.

4   Video Request Analysis

4.1   Time-Varying Category Popularity

Figure 1 shows the cumulative distribution functions (CDF) of time-to-peak for the videos from different categories with at least 100 views; a video with a very

---

[2] https://developers.google.com/youtube/2.0/reference#YouTube_Category_List. Last accessed: 09-05-13.

Table 1. Categories and number of videos.

Category	Number of videos (Day 1)	Number of videos (Day 149)	Deleted videos Pct
Howto	4773	1772	62.87
Film	4654	2346	49.59
Ent.	4991	2528	49.34
Tech	4942	2682	45.73
Games	4711	2966	37.04
People	4310	2730	36.65
Autos	4714	3245	31.16
Comedy	4744	3467	26.91
News	4623	3432	25.76
Travel	4918	3698	24.80
Sports	4812	3733	22.42
Music	4774	3477	21.93
Nonprofit	4624	3691	20.17
Education	4710	3801	19.29
Animals	4908	4143	15.58
Total	**71208**	**47711**	**33.00**

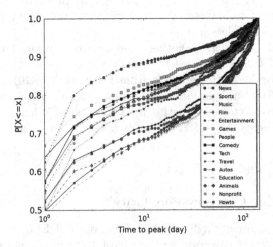

Fig. 1. CDF of time-to-peak.

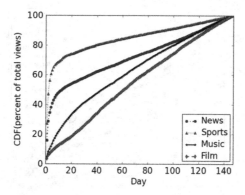

Fig. 2. Percent of total views over time.

small number of views has no actual growth pattern. One consequence of this restriction is that the number of videos in each category is significantly reduced, down to 42 % for News and Sports and 18 % for Animals and Travel. We define *time-to-peak* as the day in which a video experienced the most views [2].

Time to reach peak popularity is not the same for all categories. News and Sports categories follow a similar distribution with the shortest time to reach their peak. Approximately 85 % of News and Sports videos peak within the first 4–5 days of their lifetimes. As well, between 50 % and 60 % of the videos in almost every category experience their peak viewing on the first day.

Other categories such as Music, Film, Howto, Tech and Education follow similar patterns and many videos in these categories reach peak popularity much later. The remaining categories follow similar distributions, and peak distributions of these categories lie within the previous two groups.

The significance of time-to-peak can be enhanced by considering the CDF of total views over time for all videos in a subset of categories (Fig. 2). Music and Film videos experience relatively fewer views early in their lifetime. Film videos follow an almost constant viewing rate for the entire measurement period. News and Sports videos, however, experience a significant portion of the total views early.

It is important to understand if the peak day differs significantly from other days of a video's lifetime in order to determine if our previous statistic is helpful. Figure 3 shows the complementary cumulative distribution function (CCDF) of the most distant day x after the peak such that the views on day x is at least 50 % of the peak views, defined as follows:

$$x = max(i) : view(i) \geq 50\% \times view(peak) \land (i > peak) \qquad (1)$$

where $view(i)$ is the views on day i and $view(peak)$ is the number of views on the peak day. Only videos with more than 100 views are considered. Figure 3 shows the peak day as a unique point in the lifetime of videos for faster-growing

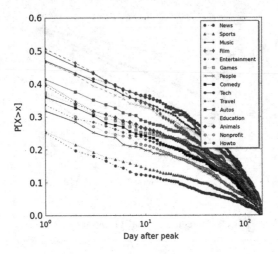

Fig. 3. CCDF of time-after-peak.

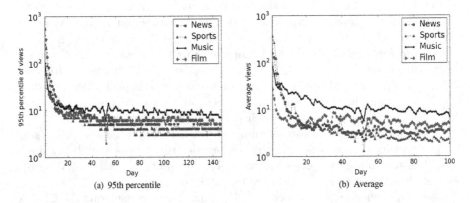

(a) 95th percentile   (b) Average

Fig. 4. Views per day.

categories (e.g., News and Sports). These categories experience a popularity burst, and quickly decline to a lower viewing rate.

Many Music, Film, Howto, Education and Tech videos that reach peak popularity comparatively lately do not have that drop in their popularity (Figs. 1 and 3), so time to reach peak popularity is proportional to the active lifespan of a video. For example, over 75 % of the News and Sports videos *never* experience half of their peak days' views after the peak day (Fig. 3), but fewer than 50 % for Film and Tech videos have this characteristic. The stability of Film and Tech videos suggests that a longer measurement period would increase the difference between these categories and News/Sports.

We are also interested to know if the categories that reach peak popularity faster than others also experience differing numbers of views. Figure 4(a) depicts the 95th percentile of views of selected categories over time. We show the 95th

percentile to remove the potential effect of outliers. This shows the minimum percentage of popular videos (5 %) during the first 100 days of data collection and the relative popularity of the categories for those popular videos.

These graphs illustrate how viewing patterns of different categories change throughout the early part of their lifetimes. Although the most similar dataset collected [2] indicates that the views of Music category exceeds all other categories within their 8-month measurement period,[3] our dataset shows that popular News, and Sports videos enjoy higher viewing rates than any other types of videos for the first couple of days since publication. Almost all categories have at least 5 % of their videos experience a high initial viewing rate, but after these few peak days, views for most of the categories become very low, except Music, Film and Tech, showing the variations in active life spans of different categories.

Although similar results can be observed from the average views per day (Fig. 4(b)), the high variance of views may distort the statistic. The most popular video in the dataset is a Sports video, (24 times the 2nd most popular Sports video), increasing the early average views of Sports videos substantially.

4.2   Fractions of Popular Videos

The percent of videos with different views of the YouTube categories are shown in Table 2. Only approximately 10 % of the Music videos enjoy *fewer* than 10 views; this value is over 30 % for Howto, People, Autos, Comedy, and Travel. Music, News, Sports, and Film contain most of the popular videos in our dataset

Table 2. Relative video popularity.

Category	≤10 views		11-100		101-1000		1001-10000		10001-100000		> 100000	
	Pct	Num	Pct	Num	Pct	Num	Pct	Num	Pct	Num	Pct	Num
Music	10.4	363	48.7	1694	32.9	1143	6.4	222	1.29	45	0.29	10
News	18.9	647	39.6	1358	31.6	1085	8.4	289	1.4	48	0.15	5
Sports	20.8	776	46.0	1717	26.1	975	6.0	223	1.04	39	0.08	3
Tech	22.6	605	47.3	1268	24.6	660	4.9	130	0.63	17	0.07	2
Film	23.1	541	49.5	1162	20.8	489	5.5	128	1.07	25	0.04	1
Entertainment	27.8	702	46.9	1185	20.6	521	3.9	98	0.75	19	0.12	3
Howto	43.8	776	34.6	613	17.0	302	4.0	71	0.45	8	0.11	2
Nonprofit	24.1	890	48.0	1773	23.5	867	3.9	142	0.46	17	0.05	2
Education	24.7	940	48.8	1856	21.7	825	4.3	165	0.37	14	0.03	1
Animals	25.6	1060	56.5	2340	15.5	643	2.1	85	0.34	14	0.02	1
Games	27.5	816	49.4	1464	19.1	566	3.4	102	0.51	15	0.1	3
People	29.5	806	49.9	1363	17.7	483	2.4	66	0.4	11	0.04	1
Autos	30.6	992	41.5	1345	23.2	752	4.1	132	0.68	22	0.06	2
Comedy	32.3	1121	51.1	1771	14.1	488	2.1	72	0.35	12	0.09	3
Travel	33.8	1248	48.9	1808	15.4	571	1.8	65	0.14	5	0.03	1

---

[3] We used another crawler to collect categories for the videos which remained.

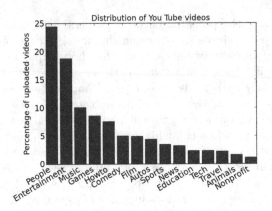

Fig. 5. Category uploading rate (365,000 videos).

(>1.11 % with over 10,000 views). The most unpopular videos are in the Travel category, followed by Comedy and Animals. Only 0.44 % of the People videos had more than 10,000 views, in spite of the highest uploading rate (shown later). Although uploaders currently upload more UGC videos, users are still not attracted to UGC videos compared to UCC (user copied content) videos.

4.3   Current Uploading Rate

In order to design a request generator for YouTube, the category uploading rate must be known. In 2007, Music was in the top position in number of uploaded videos followed by Entertainment, Comedy, Sports and Film [6]. Manual sampling revealed that these categories are now dominated by UCC rather than UGC content; most of the videos in YouTube were likely UCC then as well.

Figure 5 shows the current uploading trend of YouTube videos obtained by crawler 3. The uploading trend in YouTube has changed over time. The People category is at the top position with approximately 24 % of all the new videos, which was at the 6th position in 2007, only 8 % of all the videos. Samples from the People category contain comparatively more UGC objects than other categories.

4.4   Category Popularity Distributions

Figure 6 shows the Rank-frequency distribution for the 6 categories that showed the most interesting patterns. Other categories followed one of these patterns. Previous studies [1,6] showed that although requests for popular YouTube videos follow a Zipf-like distribution, a Weibull distribution fits better because of the light tail section, indicating a large number of very unpopular YouTube videos. After considering video categories, only News videos follow a Weibull distribution (and first 80 % with better accuracy), because of the comparatively flatter head section of News access pattern. This is consistent with *fetch-at-most-once* behaviour [12], as expected in watching News videos. For all the other categories,

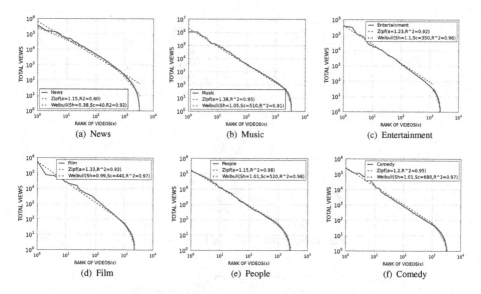

Fig. 6. Number of views against rank for categories.

request distributions of only the popular videos follow a Zipf-like distributions and the tail sections of these categories can be fitted to a Weibull distribution with a high goodness of fit (R^2). Our dataset indicates a very light tail. The number of videos exhibiting Zipf behaviour differs between the categories.

Another measure that we calculated was the CCDF of total views over the measurement period. There were a substantial number of videos in certain categories that had at most 1 view, potentially skewing the popularity measures. The HowTo and Autos category had 17 % and 12.6 % of videos with at most 1 view, respectively, while 9 % of HowTo videos had 0 views. There is a section of completely unpopular videos that get published, but never viewed. Figure 7 shows the CCDF of the total views for a selected number of categories. We truncate the x-axis to see the behaviour of views for unpopular videos more clearly. Entertainment is used as an example of a group of categories that had very similar CCDFs. The shape of the distribution of total views is very similar in these categories, but that of views over time is not. Music has very few videos below 20 views, but HowTo has almost 50 % of the videos below 20 views.

5   Towards a Workload Generator

5.1   Predicting Popularity

As an approach to predict future popularity of videos, Pearson's correlation coefficient (Eq. 2) is calculated between the added views[4] at different snapshots of the measurement period.

---

[4] Added views is the number of views on a particular day

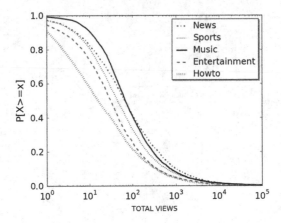

Fig. 7. Selected CCDF of total views.

$$r_{xy} = \frac{n \sum x_i y_i - (\sum x_i)(\sum y_i)}{\sqrt{n \sum x_i^2 - (\sum x_i)^2} \sqrt{n \sum y_i^2 - (\sum y_i)^2}} \qquad (2)$$

A high correlation coefficient between early views and the rest of the period implies that prediction of future views of individual videos is achievable [17]. We got very encouraging results for some of the categories including Sports, Travel, Howto, Tech and Games.[5] However, for other categories like Film, News, Entertainment the coefficients are very poor, indicating significant changes in the set of popular videos. Music shows a bit different characteristics than others (good correlation with the rest of the measurement period if we take first 10 days as our first snapshot). Figure 8 explains why early views of Sports (Film) videos can (cannot) be used as a good predictor of future views.

5.2   Three-Phase Characterization

The three-phase characterization of Borghol *et al.* [2] considers average viewing rate over time to be constant when the videos are grouped into at-peak, before-peak or after-peak on a particular day, because similar view distributions exist for the entire measurement period. This fairly simple approach requires only three fixed distributions plus the fixed peak distribution for the entire modelling.

Figure 9 shows the average viewing rate for News videos grouped at their peak phases. Showing results for only one of the three phases is enough, as the three-phase characterization method can only be applied when a constant rate is found for all three phases. We observed similar results for all other categories, which suggests that the viewing rates over time are not constant for any YouTube categories. The high and highly variable average views for News videos at the end of the measurement period is because very few videos reach peak popularity around that time. Otherwise, a decay in viewing rate is observed for the first

---

[5] Sports is 0.99 for the first day's views and the rest of the measurement period

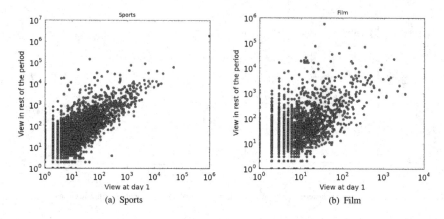

(a) Sports   (b) Film

Fig. 8. View changes of videos between two different snapshots.

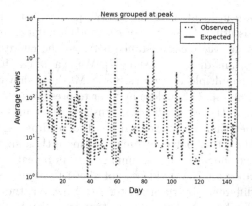

Fig. 9. Average views over time for News videos at peak.

two months, contradicting the time-invariant nature observed previously [2]. For some of the days, no videos were at their peak popularity.

5.3 Time-Series Clustering

This category variation led us to model the growth patterns differently. We decided to investigate whether the popularity growth patterns of videos in a specific category follow similar shapes. This can be considered as a time-series clustering problem and becomes challenging as different videos reach peak popularity at different times. Inspired by a study on viral videos [4], we translate all the time-series so that the x-axis is centred on the peak day, since most of the significant events happen around the peak periods.

Another challenging issue is to select the appropriate time-series clustering algorithm. We are particularly interested to identify similar shapes of the views per day, regardless of the time to peak. Moreover, the algorithm should not be affected much by outliers. We selected K-SC clustering [18], which has been

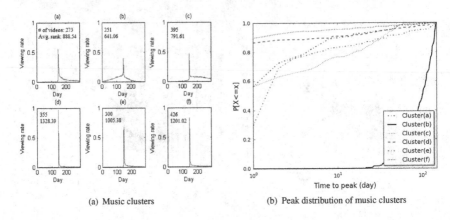

(a) Music clusters   (b) Peak distribution of music clusters

Fig. 10. Cluster information for music videos.

found to be accurate in identifying the growth patterns of other Web content. Unlike K-means clustering, K-SC cluster centroids are not distorted by outliers. Instead of considering Euclidean distance between the curves, K-SC applies a scale and shift invariant distance metric [7]. We evaluated the performance of K-SC algorithm for multiple categories. Only Music is shown. The clustering was performed for the top 2000 videos in order to present more accurate results.

Figure 10(a) shows the six clusters for Music videos found by K-SC. Forcing K-SC to select fewer than six clusters drops the accuracy significantly, as we lose some of the interesting patterns. However, more than six clusters does not significantly improve the accuracy as similar clusters repeat.

The cluster shapes for News videos (not shown) are very similar to Music, except very little difference between cluster *(a)*. However, the number of videos in each cluster differ between these two categories, complementing our earlier findings. 46 % of Music videos are contained within the slower-decaying clusters; this drops to 15 % for News videos.

An important question that must be answered is whether a particular cluster is more biased to popular videos than others. This can be answered by taking the average rank value of all the videos in a cluster. The central limit theorem suggests that the average rank of each cluster should be 1000 if it is not biased. For News videos, the average rank values are similar for each cluster (near 1000). For Music videos, the clusters with slower decay contain more popular videos, with average rank values of approximately 750. Popular Music videos observed a sharp decay with less frequency than popular News videos.

5.4 Performance of K-SC

In order to evaluate the performance of K-SC, we designed a synthetic workload generator for News and Music videos. The synthetic data should show similar characteristics to the empirical YouTube data if the clustering of K-SC is accurate. The workload generator can be described as follows. A rank value is

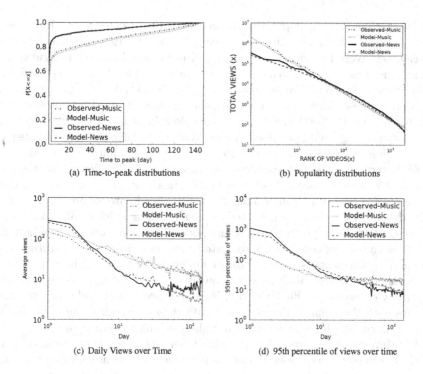

(a) Time-to-peak distributions

(b) Popularity distributions

(c) Daily Views over Time

(d) 95th percentile of views over time

Fig. 11. Modelling distributions.

assigned to each of the videos as suggested by the chosen distributions for Music and News respectively. Then centroid/cluster is assigned to the videos based on the distribution we observed earlier. We also imposed a little bias for the popular videos before selecting the appropriate cluster in order to match our observed average rank value. As the peak distributions are conspicuously different among the clusters in a category (Fig. 10(b)), each of them are considered separately in the request generator, so that the accuracy of K-SC can be verified.

We test similarity between the synthetic and empirical data from four different perspectives: (1) The total view distribution, (2) time-to-peak distribution, (3) Average daily views over time, and (4) 95th percentile of views over time. Figure 11(a) and (b) indicates very good matches between synthetic and empirical data for metrics 1 and 2, which does not in itself indicate high accuracy of K-SC. We imposed the distributions for these two cases from our observations,. Metrics 3 and 4 show, however, that the clusters found by the K-SC algorithm for both categories represent most of the videos growth patterns (Fig. 11(c) and (d), respectively).

6   Conclusions and Future Work

In this paper, we analyzed global daily viewing patterns of a representative subset of YouTube videos from upload time until they were 5 months old. We discovered significant time-varying popularity differences between categories. Most videos exhibit their peak viewing day very soon after publication and then there is a decay; relatively few videos ever approach peak popularity again. Video categories that reached their peaks later were more stable. This is expected and matches our intuitions. We developed an analysis method that permits quantification of these differences on a particular dataset. The confirmation of Zipf distributions for the total views of popular videos in nearly every category indicates that caching would be effective. One limitation is the accuracy of category identification, especially for those videos that belong to multiple categories.

We determined the relative trends of category-specific viewing patterns in the first few months since upload. Some categories contain a non-trivial number of videos which are still popular 5 months after upload date, whereas other categories dwindle to nothing. Some categories have videos which exhibit stationary behaviour that allows prediction of future popularity. Popularity changes around peak time can be captured by appropriate time-series clustering. Unfortunately, scale and deployment issues make direct applicability to YouTube impractical. Our methodology and analysis could be used to help design, configure, and deploy any category-specific UGC site. We developed a workload generator that matches with the empirical data for several categories; similar clusters exist in each category, but different numbers of videos belong to each cluster.

As future work, we are in the process of building a complete workload generator that encompasses more aspects of user-generated content video requests. In particular, we will incorporate category-specific introduction of new content over time to drive simulations and/or prototype content distribution networks to evaluate different design policies for storing and delivering videos.

Acknowledgements. The authors would like to acknowledge the support of the University of Saskatchewan's Dean's Scholarship Program.

References

1. Abhari, A., Soraya, M.: Workload generation for YouTube. Multimed. Tools Appl. **46**(1), 91–118 (2010)
2. Borghol, Y., Mitra, S., Ardon, S., Carlsson, N., Eager, D., Mahanti, A.: Characterizing and modelling popularity of user-generated videos. Perform. Eval. **68**, 1037–1055 (2011)
3. Brodersen, A., Scellato, S., Wattenhofer, M.: YouTube around the world: geographic popularity of videos. In: WWW, Lyon, France, pp. 241–250, April 2012
4. Broxton, T., Interian, Y., Vaver, J., Wattenhofer, M.: Catching a viral video. In: IEEE Data Mining Workshops, Sydney, Australia, pp. 296–304, December 2010
5. Cha, M., Kwok, H., Rodriguez, P., Ahn, Y., Moon, S.: Analyzing the video popularity characteristics of large-scale user generated content systems. IEEE/ACM Trans. Netw. **17**(5), 1357–1370 (2009)
6. Cheng, X., Dale, C., Liu, J.: Understanding the characteristics of internet short video sharing: YouTube as a case study. Technical report, Cornell University, arXiv e-prints (July 2007)

7. Chu, K.K.W., Wong, M.H.: Fast time-series searching with scaling and shifting. In: ACM PODS, Philadelphia, PA, pp. 237–248, May 1999
8. Ding, Y., Du,Y., Hu, Y., Liu, Z., Wang, L., Ross, K., Ghose, A.: Broadcast yourself: understanding YouTube uploaders. In: ACM IMC, Berlin, Germany, pp. 361–370, November 2011
9. Figueiredo, F., Benevenuto, F., Almeida, J.: The tube over time: characterizing popularity growth of YouTube videos. In: ACM WSDM, Hong Kong, China, pp. 745–754, February 2011
10. Gember, A., Anand, A., Akella, A.: A comparative study of handheld and non-handheld traffic in campus Wi-Fi networks. In: Spring, N., Riley, G.F. (eds.) PAM 2011. LNCS, vol. 6579, pp. 173–183. Springer, Heidelberg (2011)
11. Gill, P., Arlitt, M., Li, Z., Mahanti, A.: YouTube traffic characterization: a view from the edge. In: ACM IMC, San Diego, CA, pp. 15–28, October 2007
12. Gummadi, K.P., Dunn, R.J., Saroiu, S., Gribble, S.D., Levy, H.M., Zahorjan, J.: Measurement, modeling, and analysis of a peer-to-peer file-sharing workload. In: ACM SOSP, Bolton Landing, NY, pp. 314–329, October 2003
13. Khemmarat, S., Zhou, R., Gao, L., Zink, M.: Watching user generated videos with prefetching. In: ACM MMSYS, San Jose, CA, pp. 187–198, February 2011
14. Labovitz, C., Iekel-Johnson, S., McPherson, D., Oberheide, J., Jahanian, F.: Internet inter-domain traffic. In: ACM SIGCOMM, New Delhi, India, pp. 75–86, August 2010
15. Maier, G., Schneider, F., Feldmann, A.: A first look at mobile hand-held device traffic. In: Krishnamurthy, A., Plattner, B. (eds.) PAM 2010. LNCS, vol. 6032, pp. 161–170. Springer, Heidelberg (2010)
16. Siersdorfer, S., Chelaru, S., Nejdl, W., San Pedro, J.: How useful are your comments?: analyzing and predicting YouTube comments and comment ratings. In: WWW, Raleigh, NC, pp. 891–900, April 2010
17. Szabo, G., Huberman, B.: Predicting the popularity of online content. CACM 53(8), 80–88 (2010)
18. Yang, J., Leskovec, J.: Patterns of temporal variation in online media. In: ACM WSDM, Hong Kong, China, pp. 177–186, February 2011
19. Zink, M., Suh, K., Gu, Y., Kurose, J.: Characteristics of YouTube network traffic at a campus network - measurements, models, and implications. Comput. Netw. 53(4), 501–514 (2009)

Society, e-Business and e-Government

Enhancing the Modularity and Applicability of Web-Based Signature-Verification Tools

Thomas Lenz[1]([✉]), Klaus Stranacher[1], and Thomas Zefferer[2]

[1] E-Government Innovation Center, Inffeldgasse 16a, Graz, Austria
{thomas.lenz,klaus.stranacher}@egiz.gv.at
[2] Secure Information Technology Center - Austria, Inffeldgasse 16a, Graz, Austria
thomas.zefferer@a-sit.at

Abstract. Electronic signature are an important concept and crucial tool for security-critical applications. Employing the full potential of electronic signatures requires the availability of appropriate signature-verification tools. Today, a plethora of different signature-verification tools exist that allow users to verify electronically signed files and documents. Unfortunately, most of these tools have been designed for a special use case and lack support for various fields of application. This renders the development of applications based on electronic signatures difficult and reduces usability for end users. To overcome this issue, we propose an improved architecture for signature-verification tools. This architecture ensures flexibility and an easy extensibility by following a plug-in-based approach. The applicability and practicability of the proposed architecture has been assessed by means of a concrete implementation. This implementation demonstrates the proposed architecture's capability to meet requirements of various different application scenarios and use cases. This way, the proposed architecture and the developed implementation that relies on this architecture contribute to the security, usability, and efficiency of present and future electronic signature-based applications.

Keywords: Electronic signatures · Verification · Testing · Web services

1 Introduction

The concept of electronic signatures represents a basic building block of various security-sensitive solutions from different fields of application. Such solutions typically have strict requirements regarding data integrity, authenticity, and non-repudiation of origin. Electronic signatures are able to meet these requirements. The importance of electronic signatures has also been recognized by legislative bodies. For instance, the European Union has harmonized the use of electronic signatures in EU Member States through the Directive 1999/93/EC of the European Parliament and of the Council of 13 December 1999 on a Community

© Springer-Verlag Berlin Heidelberg 2014
K.-H. Krempels and A. Stocker (Eds.): WEBIST 2013, LNBIP 189, pp. 173–188, 2014.
DOI: 10.1007/978-3-662-44300-2_11

framework for electronic signatures [1], henceforth referred to as EU Signature Directive. The EU Signature Directive distinguishes between advanced and qualified electronic signatures. Compared to advanced electronic signatures, qualified electronic signatures have to fulfill several additional security requirements[1] and are defined to be legally equivalent to handwritten signatures.

The legal equivalence to handwritten signatures makes qualified electronic signatures especially useful for the realization of transactional e-government solutions provided by the public sector. Numerous countries are already issuing e-ID and e-signature tokens to their citizens. Citizens can use these tokens to remotely authenticate at e-government portals, to carry out electronic procedures, and to electronically sign documents. Smart card-based e-ID and e-signature tokens have for instance been issued to citizens in Austria[2], Belgium[3], Estonia[4], Germany[5], Portugal[6], or Spain[7]. A few countries such as Austria[8] and Estonia[9] additionally allow citizens to rely on their mobile phones as e-ID and e-signature tokens. This typically enhances usability, as citizens are not required to buy, install, and use appropriate smart card reading devices any longer.

In numerous countries, also service providers from the private sector rely on e-ID and e-signature tokens issued by the public sector. For instance, various e-banking portals support a secure user authentication based on available e-ID and e-signature tokens and allow users to authorize financial transactions remotely using electronic signatures. Additionally, electronic signatures are also frequently used in the private domain, e.g. to sign electronic contracts or similar bilateral agreements. Required signature tokens and signing certificates can usually be acquired from national certification authorities. Due to their various fields of application in both the public and the private domain, electronic signatures are gaining importance all over the world.

A key advantage of electronic signatures compared to handwritten signatures is their verifiability. Given a handwritten signature, its authenticity and originality is difficult to determine in practice. Additionally, subsequent modifications that have been applied to e.g. a signed contract might be difficult to detect in case of handwritten signatures. This is not the case for electronic signatures. The validity, authenticity, and originality of electronic signatures can be unambiguously determined by means of cryptographic methods that are based on strong mathematical foundations. Each electronic signature is unambiguously linked to the identity of a certain person by means of an electronic certificate that has been issued by a trusted third party, i.e. a certification authority. Additionally,

---

[1] These requirements basically cover the use of secure signature-creation devices (e.g. smart cards or similar secure elements) and reliance on qualified electronic signatures.

[2] https://www.buergerkarte.at/

[3] http://eid.belgium.be/en/

[4] http://www.id.ee/

[5] http://www.personalausweisportal.de

[6] http://www.cartaodecidadao.pt/

[7] http://www.dnielectronico.es/

[8] https://www.handy-signatur.at/Default.aspx

[9] http://e-estonia.com/components/mobile-id

each subsequent modification of a signed document immediately invalidates the electronic signature. Thus, by verifying its electronic signature, integrity, authenticity, and non-repudiation of origin of signed data can be reliably assessed.

In practice, the verification of electronic signatures is actually no trivial task as it requires the application of complex cryptographic methods. Hence, there is a need for appropriate tools that implement this functionality. Tools and Web-based services that allow for a convenient verification of electronic signatures have already been deployed in several countries. Austria is a representative example, since this country has started to rely on electronic signature-based solutions early [2]. Austrian citizens are provided with a Web-based verification tool that can be used to upload and verify electronically signed documents [3]. This tool supports various document and signature formats and is therefore able to act as single point of contact for the verification of arbitrary electronic signatures.

Unfortunately, the Austrian signature-verification tool has been optimized for manual use by citizens, i.e. the only opportunity to interact with this tool is by manually uploading signed documents through a Web-based user interface. This significantly aggravates an automated use of this tool, e.g. the integration of the tool's functionality into third-party applications, which for instance need to implement an on-the-fly verification of electronically signed documents. To overcome this issue, we present an improved signature-verification tool that enhances the existing solution by extended interfaces and communication capabilities. This way, approved components and key functionality of the existing solution are maintained, while access to the tool's functionality is eased for both users and external applications.

The remainder of this paper is structured as follows. In Sect. 2, general requirements of signature-verification solutions are defined. In Sect. 3, we show that existing signature-verification solutions are usually not able to meet all of these requirements. In Sect. 4, we present an enhanced architecture for the approved Austrian signature-verification tool that improves its functionality and accessibility. We demonstrate the practical applicability of the proposed architecture by presenting a concrete implementation relying on this architecture in Sect. 5. Finally, conclusions are drawn in Sect. 6.

2   Requirements

The secure and reliable verification of electronic signatures represents a key component of electronic signature-based applications and services. Signature-verification tools must meet various requirements in order to satisfy the needs of users and service providers. Requirements that need to be met by signature-verification tools have been identified and discussed in detail in [3]. However, these requirements mainly focus on the end-user perspective and do not cover aspects that are specific to providers of electronic signature-based applications and services. Considering the needs of both end users and service providers, the following requirements can be derived.

- **Security.** Electronic signatures are typically used in security-sensitive applications. If signature-verification tools process security-sensitive data, these data need to be protected appropriately in order to assure their confidentiality. Furthermore, signature-verification tools need to be resistant against attacks that threaten to illegally influence results of signature-verification processes.
- **Reliability.** End users and service providers that make use of signature-verification tools must be able to rely on the results of signature-verification processes. Thus, signature-verification tools must be able to correctly distinguish between valid and invalid electronic signatures at any time. Given the legal equivalence of qualified electronic signatures to handwritten signatures, the correctness of presented verification results is of particular importance.
- **Usability.** The requirement for usability covers several aspects such as simplicity of verification processes from the user point of view, hiding of complexity, platform independence, or avoidance of local software installations. An important aspect for both end users and service providers that make use of signature-verification tools is the requirement for a single point of contact. Signature-verification tools need to provide users and service providers a single interface, through which arbitrary document and signature formats can be verified.
- **Accessibility.** The functionality provided by signature-verification tools must be easily accessible for both end users and providers of third-party applications. To meet this requirement for end users, the provided user interface needs to comply with established usability and accessibility standards such as the Web Content Accessibility Guidelines (WCAG) [4]. In order to meet accessibility requirements for providers of third-party applications, signature-verification tools need to implement appropriate interfaces that can be accessed by external applications to carry out signature-verification processes.

The defined requirements are rather generic and not bound to a specific legal framework. Depending on the legal and organizational environment, in which a signature-verification tool is deployed, several additional requirements might apply. For instance, in the special case of Austria, signature-verification tools have to support proprietary signature formats that are frequently used in Austrian e-government solutions.

Different legal requirements of different countries have already led to the development of numerous signature-verification tools. In the next section, available signature-verification tools are briefly surveyed and their capabilities to meet the requirements defined above are assessed.

3   Existing Solutions

The growing importance of electronic signature-based solutions and the plurality of national legal requirements have led to the development of different signature-verification solutions. Depending on the context of their deployment, these solutions usually meet a subset of the requirements defined in Sect. 2.

For instance, Unizeto Technologies SA[10] provides a publicly available Web-based signature verification tool called WebNotarius[11]. Having its roots in Poland, WebNotarius supports the verification of public-key certificates issued by certified Polish certification authorities. Additionally, WebNotarius supports the verification of different document and signature formats including PKCS#7 [5], CMS [6], S/MIME [7], and XMLDSig [8].

A similar Web-based signature-verification tool is provided by the German company signagate[12]. Compared to WebNotarius, signagate is restricted to the PDF file format [9] and does not support different document and signature formats. Another Web-based verification tool for electronically signed PDF documents is provided by the company Secured Signing[13]. The company ascertia[14] offers Web-based tools for the verification of electronically signed PDF and XML files. A solution for the verification of XML signatures called MOA-SP[15] is also provided by the Austrian government to facilitate the integration of XML signatures into Austrian e-government applications. MOA-SP is available as open source and features API and Web service-based interfaces for the verification of electronically signed XML documents, namely XMLDSig [8] and XAdES [10].

There are also several activities related to the verification of electronic signatures on European level. The tool SD-DSS[16], commissioned by the EU Commission, supports the verification of signature formats defined by the Commission Decision on establishing minimum requirements for the cross-border processing of documents [11]. Additionally, the EU large scale pilots PEPPOL[17] and SPOCS[18] addressed issues concerning the validation of electronic signatures. PEPPOL developed a signature-validation service with focus on public procurement processes. Within SPOCS, signature verification is part of the validation of electronic documents concerning the issues raised by the EU Services Directive [12].

All above-mentioned solutions show very well the key problem of current signature-verification solutions. Most solutions are limited to the verification of certain document and signature formats such as XML or PDF. Hence, these solutions do not satisfy the usability requirement for a single point of contact for the verification of all document and signature formats. Even the tool Web-Notarius, which supports several different formats, only covers a limited subset of all possible document and signature formats. This is actually not surprising, as proprietary signature formats exist in several countries due to national legal requirements. For instance, in Austria a proprietary PDF signature format [13] has been introduced for the public sector in order to meet specific

---

[10] http://www.unizeto.pl/
[11] http://www.webnotarius.eu
[12] http://www.signagate.de/
[13] http://www.securedsigning.com/
[14] http://www.ascertia.com/
[15] https://joinup.ec.europa.eu/software/moa-idspss/description
[16] https://joinup.ec.europa.eu/software/sd-dss/home
[17] http://www.project.peppol.eu/
[18] http://www.eu-spocs.eu/

legal requirements [14]. Support for all national and international, standardized and proprietary signature formats rapidly increases the complexity of signature-verification tools.

This situation is even aggravated by the fact that especially proprietary signature formats are subject to frequent revisions and updates. As electronic signatures need to retain their validity even if the underlying signature format is updated, signature-verification tools have to maintain and support different versions of signature formats. This again increases the complexity of such tools and renders their development and maintenance difficult. As a first solution to this problem, Stranacher and Kawecki have proposed a mechanism to incorporate external verification services [15]. However, this proposal lacks an appropriate and efficient mechanism for the detection of different document and signature formats.

In order to cope with the growing diversity of different document and signature formats, a Web-based signature-verification tool has been developed in Austria. This tool features a modular design and implements an efficient format-detection engine that eases the integration of new document and signature formats. The signature-verification tool that has been discussed in detail in [3] has proven its practical applicability during several years of productive operation. Still, this tool suffers from several limitations. For instance, the tool is indented for manual use only. Users can upload documents to be verified through a Web-based user interface. As this is the only supported interface, the tool's functionality cannot be easily accessed by external applications to carry out signature verifications. Furthermore, the given limitation to a Web-based interface complicates the provision of the tool's functionality through new communication channels and emerging technologies such as mobile apps. Thus, this tool is obviously not able to meet accessibility requirements for service providers and third-party applications.

In summary it can be stated that there is currently no solution available that is able to meet all predefined requirements. From the Austrian perspective, powerful tools such as WebNotarius that have been developed in other countries are no alternative, as these solutions do not support proprietary document and signature formats that are specific to Austria. Hence, these solutions do not meet the predefined requirement for provision of a single point of contact for the verification of all document and signature formats. Unfortunately, the existing Austrian solution that supports these proprietary document and signature formats does not feature appropriate interfaces to meet the predefined requirement for accessibility. Hence, third-party applications are not able to access the functionality provided by the available tool in order to implement fully automated signature-verification processes of electronically signed documents.

To overcome this problem, we propose an enhancement of the existing Austrian signature-verification tool. The proposed enhancements improve the accessibility of this tool especially for third-party applications and facilitate access to the tool's functionality. The architectural design of the proposed solution is presented in the next section.

4   Architectural Design

The proposed solution is based on the Austrian Web-based signature-verification tool that has been discussed in the previous section. The Web-based approach followed by this tool has proven to be advantageous in terms of security and usability during several years of productive operation [3]. Figure 1 illustrates the general architecture of this tool. Key component of the entire solution is the *Process Flow Engine*, which coordinates the different steps of a signature-verification process. A signature-verification process basically consists of two steps. *First*, the document and signature format of the document to be verified is determined. This task is accomplished by the *Format Detection Engine*. For each supported format, an appropriate *Format Detection Plug-in* has been implemented. Internally, the different Format Detection Plug-ins are organized hierarchically in a tree structure. This way, the runtime for format-detection processes grows only logarithmically with an increasing number of Format-Detection Plug-ins. *Second*, the electronic signature is verified by the *Verification Engine*. Depending on the determined document and signature format, an appropriate *Verification Plug-in* is selected to accomplish this task. The selected Verification Plug-in extracts all signatures from the provided document and cryptographically verifies their validity based on the provided document data.

Files to be verified as well as verification results are exchanged with end users by means of a *Web Interface*. Users are provided with a Web form in order to upload signed documents to be verified. Results are directly presented in the users' Web browsers. After completion of the signature-verification process, users can additionally download an electronically signed version of the verification report in PDF format.

The concept shown in Fig. 1 has turned out to especially meet the expectations and requirements of end users. However, several problems arise when the functionality of this tool has to be accessed by third-party applications. As this tool has originally been developed for end users, its functionality can basically be accessed through the provided Web-based interface only[19]. This limitation renders an integration of the tool's functionality into third-party applications for automated signature verifications difficult.

In order to solve this issue and to facilitate an integration of the tool's functionality into third-party applications, we have enhanced the tool's general architecture. The resulting extended architecture of our solution is illustrated in Fig. 2.

The lack of appropriate interfaces to access the tool's functionality through different communication channels and technologies has turned out to be the main drawback of the existing solution. Our improved solution solves this issue by replacing the original Web interface by a more powerful I/O Engine. This I/O Engine supports different I/O channels and communication technologies.

---

[19] Actually, the tool provides also a command line based user interface. However, this interface is not appropriate for an integration of the tool's functionality into remote third-party applications either.

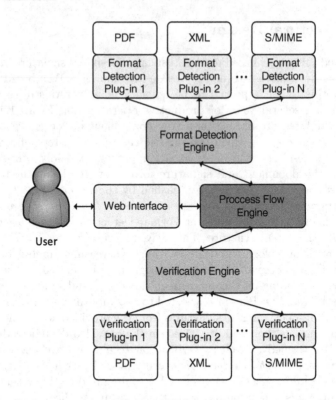

Fig. 1. Architecture of the Austrian Web-based signature-verification tool.

The I/O Engine adopts the approved plug-in-based approach that is already successfully followed by both the Format Detection Engine and the Verification Engine. This way, the entire solution remains modular and easily adaptable to future requirements.

The adapted architecture and the introduced I/O Engine enable the realization of various additional use cases. Figure 2 illustrates some of them. Of course, the approved Web-based interface is also compatible to the new architecture. A special I/O Plug-in can implement the required interface. However, the enhanced architecture is not limited to a Web-based interface any longer. For instance, the proposed architecture also allows the tool's functionality to be accessed through a SOAP-based Web-service interface provided by the tool's I/O Engine. The modular design also allows for efficient implementations of test frameworks that automatically run verification tests on well-defined test documents stored in local databases. This could be especially useful for the maintenance and further development of the tool. Finally, the proposed architecture also allows for the integration of new and emerging technologies such as smartphone apps that access the tool for an on-the-fly verification of electronic signatures.

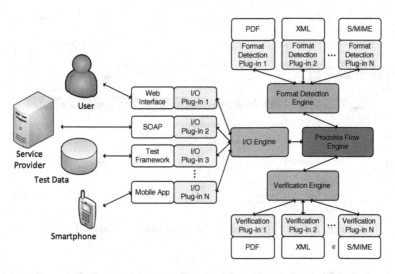

Fig. 2. Enhanced architecture of the Austrian Web-based signature-verification tool.

We have evaluated the practical applicability of the proposed architectural design by realizing the four above-mentioned use cases in practice. Details on the realization of these use cases are provided in the next section.

5   Use Cases

Core component of the proposed architecture is the I/O Engine that replaces the original Web-based user interface and allows for the implementation of different I/O Plug-ins. These plug-ins implement different communication technologies and make the signature-verification tool's functionality accessible through different communication channels. This way, the proposed tool can be used in different application scenarios. We have demonstrated the applicability of our solution by implementing solutions for four concrete use cases, which are discussed below in more detail.

5.1   Use Case 1: Web Interface

Use Case 1 covers the scenario, in which an end user accesses the tool's functionality in order to verify an electronically signed document. This is basically the scenario, which the predecessor of the proposed tool has been developed for. For this scenario, a Web-based user interface has turned out to be an appropriate solution. Therefore, our implementation relies on the approved Web-based interface of the original tool. Of course, it was necessary to redesign the existing API interface in order to connect the Web-based user interface to the new I/O Engine of our solution. While several internal components have been redesigned, the user interface itself has not been changed. This way, existing productive

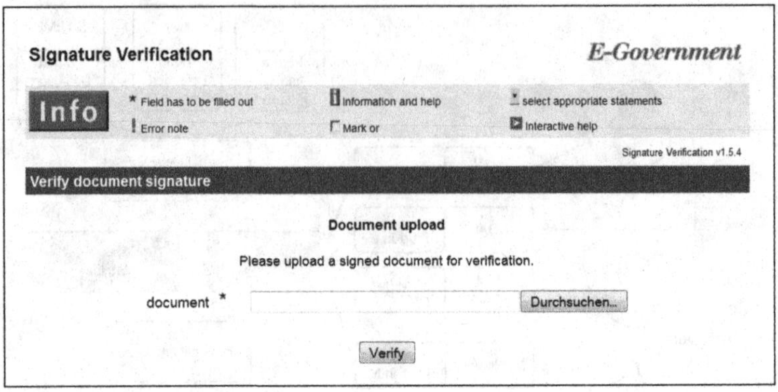

Fig. 3. Web front-end of the signature-verification tool.

instances of the tool can easily be upgraded and do not require end users to deal with new interfaces. Figure 3 illustrates the implemented Web interface that can be used by end users to upload and verify signed documents.

5.2 Use Case 2: Web-Service Interface

This scenario covers the case, in which a remote third-party application makes use of the signature-verification tool's functionality. In order to allow third-party applications to access the tool through a well-defined interface, another I/O Plug-in has been implemented. This plug-in provides a standardized interface, which can be used by remote applications to carry out automated signature-verification processes.

This is actually no completely new approach. There are already different standards that define appropriate interfaces for remote signature-verification services. Popular examples are the OASIS Digital Signature Service [16] and MOA-SP, which is mainly used in Austrian e-government solutions. However, these standardized interfaces specify the verification of a limited set of electronic

Listing 1.1. VerifyDocumentRequest XML schema.

```
<xsd:element name="VerifyDocumentRequest">
  <xsd:complexType>
    <xsd:sequence>
      <xsd:element name="Document"
          type="xsd:base64Binary"/>
      <xsd:element name="FileID"
          type="xsd:token"/>
    </xsd:sequence>
  </xsd:complexType>
</xsd:element>
```

signatures only. Consequently, these services are not suitable for scenarios, in which different document and signature formats need to be supported. Our solution specifies a new signature-verification interface, which fulfills these additional requirements.

The developed I/O Plug-in implements a Web service, which uses the SOAP protocol [17] to exchange information. Beneath the SOAP protocol, the Hypertext Transfer Protocol (HTTP) [18] is used as a carrier for SOAP messages. This is reasonable, because HTTP is popular, frequently used, and widely supported. SOAP messages being exchanged over the implemented Web-service interface rely on the Extensible Markup Language (XML) [19]. To meet all requirements of this use case, we have defined our own XML schema for document verification[20]. The XML schema, which defines the structure of a signature-verification request that is accepted by the tool's Web-service interface, is shown in Listing 1.1.

According to the defined XML schema, a signature-verification request consists of two XML elements. The *Document* element is mandatory and contains the signed file to be verified. The second element is optional and can be used to identify the signed file. When a schema-compliant SOAP request is received, a signature-verification operation is triggered.

The first step of the triggered verification process consists of a few preprocessing operations, like XML schema validation and BASE64 decoding. Afterwards, the provided document's format is determined using the tool's Format Detection Engine. Subsequently, the document's electronic signatures are verified using the tool's Signature Verification Engine.

Results of the format-detection step and the signature-verification step are collected to generate a verification report. This verification report contains information on the result of the format-detection process, as well as obtained signature-verification results.

The generated verification report is electronically signed in order to ensure its authenticity and integrity. The signed report is returned to the sender of the SOAP based verification request. Listing 1.2 shows relevant parts of the XML

Listing 1.2. VerifyDocumentResponse XML Schema.

```
<xsd : element  name="VerifyDocumentResponse">
  <xsd : complexType>
    <xsd : sequence>
      <xsd : element  name="VerificationReport"
          type="tns : VerificationReportType"/>
      <xsd : element  name="Signature"
          type="dsig : SignatureType"/>
    </xsd : sequence>
  </xsd : complexType>
</xsd : element>
```

---

[20] We were forced to define an own schema, since existing schemata were not able to meet our requirements.

schema, which specifies the structure of this SOAP response. The response consists of two parts, the *VerificationReport* and a *Signature* element, which contains the electronic signature of the verification report. This signature is created according to the XMLDSig standard using the enveloped-signature scheme.

The implemented SOAP-based Web-service interface provides third-party applications a common interface for on-the-fly signature verifications. Third-party applications can use this interface to efficiently carry out verification operations on different document and signature formats. This way, the provided solution facilitates the implementation of electronic signature-based applications by encapsulating and providing common functionality.

5.3   Use Case 3: Test Framework

The growing number of document and signature formats rapidly increases the complexity for developers and operators of the signature-verification tool. The situation is even more complicated by the fact that verification results are not only influenced by the input document and the implementation of the verification tool, but also by the tool's configuration. For instance, the validity of an electronic signature depends to a large extent on root and intermediate certificates that are configured in the tool's trust stores. Hence, extensive tests are not only required during development, but also after deployment. This use case describes how the tool's improved architecture is used to implement a comprehensive test framework that allows both developers and operators to verify the correct behavior of the tool.

The implemented test framework makes use of the tool's I/O Engine and implements an appropriate I/O Plug-in. Furthermore, the test framework makes use of a database containing signed test documents and corresponding expected verification results. By feeding the test documents as input into the signature-verification tool and comparing the obtained results with the stored expected results, the functional integrity of the tool can be verified. Figure 4 gives an overview of the test framework's general architecture.

The main part of the test framework is the *Automatic Test Engine*, which controls the entire automatic verification and test process. The Automatic Test Engine makes use of several additional submodules. These submodules implement an *User Interface*, an *Information Management* module, and a *Report Engine*. As interconnection to the signature-verification tool, we make use of the signature-verification tool's I/O Engine and its plug-in-based architecture.

The Information Management submodule is used to manage the signed test documents and the corresponding expected results. We use a file system-based method to manage the different files depending on their document type and signature format. The expected verification results are stored in XML files. This information is used to assess the correct behavior of the signature-verification tool during test runs.

Besides the Information Management submodule, the Report Engine represents another important component of the test framework. The Report Engine implements the entire report functionality. A report is created after each test

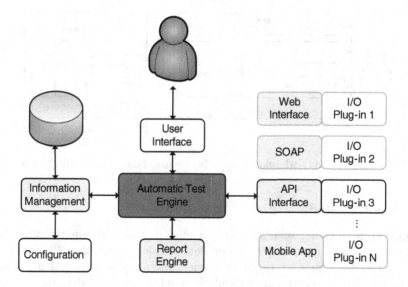

Fig. 4. Test framework with sub-modules and interconnections.

run and basically contains the number of tested documents and the number of documents, in which the signature-verification result matches the expected verification result. If the verification result of a test document does not match the expected result, a detailed report is generated. This detailed report contains an error description and shows, which part of the signature verification has caused the problem. By default, the report is rendered as HTML document and presented to the user via the user interface. Additionally, the Report Engine can generate an XML-based report or a textual report.

Developers and operators of the signature-verification tool can interact with the test framework by using a Web-based user interface. Access to this interface is protected by means of a secure user authentication based on the official Austrian national eID. After successful authentication, authorized users are redirected to the Web interface of the test framework. This interface provides users with a dynamic list that represents the directory hierarchy, in which test documents are organized. By selecting the corresponding directories, users can determine the set of test documents to be used for the automatic test run.

After selection of the desired test documents, the automatic test run can be triggered by the user through the provided Web interface. The Automatic Test Engine controls the entire test run and uses the Information Management submodule to get all documents from the selected directory. Each selected document is verified by the signature-verification tool. Obtained verification results are compared with the corresponding expected verification results stored in the database. The result of this comparison is stored and processed by the Report Engine. When all selected documents have been tested, the generated HTML report is displayed to the user through the Web-based user interface.

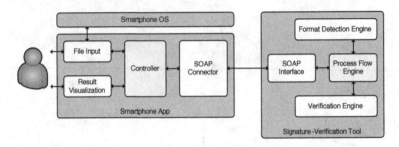

Fig. 5. Architecture of the developed smartphone-based signature-verification solution.

5.4   Use Case 4: Smartphone Application

During the past years, smartphones and related mobile end-user devices have gradually replaced tradional end-user devices such as desktop PCs and laptops. These developments requisite service providers to adapt their services and to make them compliant to and accessible by mobile devices. The proposed signature-verification tool can easily be made accessible to mobile end-user devices by relying on the tool's SOAP-based interface that has been introduced and discussed in Sect. 5.2. A first prototype implementation has been introduced in [20]. This prototype implementation comprises an Android app that accesses the proposed signature-verification tool through its SOAP interface and allows Android users to verify electronically signed documents on their smartphones.

Figure 5 shows the architecture of the developed prototype. The functionality of the entire solution is clearly separated between the central signature-verification tool and the smartphone app. The developed smartphone app has two main tasks. First, it interfaces with the mobile operating system to obtain signed files to be verified. Second, it provides a user interface, through which verification results are displayed to the user. The format-detection and signature-verification processes are implemented by the central signature-verification tool. Its functionality is accessed by the smartphone app through the provided SOAP interface.

In contrast to the other use cases that have been introduced in this section, this use case does not introduce a completely new I/O plug-in. Instead, this use case and the developed prototype mainly demonstrate the usefulness and the capabilities of the signature-verification tool's SOAP interface and show that the proposed modular architecture is well suited to support the development of new and innovative signature-verification solutions on arbitrary end-user devices.

6   Conclusions

The secure and reliable verification of electronic signatures is an integral component of security-sensitive applications from various fields of application such as e-government, e-banking, or e-business. The capability to assess the validity of electronic signatures can be important for both end users and service providers.

In this paper we have presented an improved solution for the verification of electronic signatures. The presented solution features a single point of contact for the verification of various document and signature formats and relies on a modular architecture that facilitates future extensions of the solution's functionality. Although the presented solution has been developed to meet the special requirements of the Austrian legal framework, its general architectural design and implementation is also applicable in other contexts.

We have demonstrated the practical applicability and flexibility of the presented architectural design by implementing solutions for different use cases. These use cases cover the use of the presented solution by end users through a Web-based user interface, the provision of the solution's functionality through a well-defined SOAP-based Web-service interface, the realization of a comprehensive test framework that assists is assessing the correct functionality of our solution, and the implementation of a smartphone app for the verification of electronic signatures on mobile end-user devices.

Due to its modular architecture, the presented solution is dynamically extensible especially with respect to new document formats and communication interfaces. This distinguishes the presented solution from other signature-verification tools that are available on the market. A conducted survey has revealed that these tools are typically limited to certain document and signature formats, or to certain communication interfaces. The presented solution removes these limitations and thereby contributes to the security, usability, and efficiency of present and future electronic signature-based applications.

References

1. The European Parliament and the Council of the European Union: Directive 1999/93/EC of the European Parliament and of the Council of 13 December 1999 on a Community framework for electronic signatures (2000). http://eur-lex.europa.eu/LexUriServ/LexUriServ.do?uri=OJ:L:2000:013:0012:0020:EN:PDF
2. Leitold, H., Hollosi, A., Posch, R.: Security architecture of the Austrian Citizen card concept. In: Proceedings of 18th Annual Computer Security Applications Conference (ACSAC'2002), Las Vegas, 9–13 December 2002, pp. 391–400 (2002). IEEE Computer Society, ISBN 0-7695-1828-1, ISSN 1063-9527 (2002)
3. Zefferer, T., Tauber, A., Zwattendorfer, B., Knall, T.: Secure and reliable online-verification of electronic signatures in the digital age. In: Proceedings of the IADIS International Conference WWW/INTERNET 2011, pp. 269–276 (2011)
4. World Wide Web Consortium: Web Content Accessibility Guidelines (WCAG) 2.0 (2008). http://www.w3.org/TR/WCAG/
5. RSA Laboratories: PKCS#7: Cryptographic Message Syntax Standard (1993). ftp://ftp.rsasecurity.com/pub/pkcs/ascii/pkcs-7.asc
6. Housley, R.: Cryptographic Message Syntax (CMS) (2009). http://www.ietf.org/rfc/rfc5652.txt
7. Ramsdell, B., Turner, S.: Secure/Multipurpose Internet Mail Extensions (S/MIME) Version 3.2 Message Specification (2010). http://tools.ietf.org/html/rfc5751

8. World Wide Web Consortium: XML Signature Syntax and Processing, 2nd edn. (2008). http://www.w3.org/TR/xmldsig-core/
9. Adobe Corporation: Document management Portable document format Part 1: PDF 1.7 (2008)
10. ETSI TS 101 903: Electronic Signatures and Infrastructures (ESI); XML Advanced Electronic Signatures (XAdES) V1.4.2 (2010)
11. European Commission: European Commission Decision, Establishing minimum requirements for the cross-border processing of documents signed electronically by competent authorities under Directive 2006/123/EC of the European Parliament and of the Council on services in the internal market, notified under document C (2011) 1081, 2011/130/EU (2011). http://eur-lex.europa.eu/LexUriServ/LexUriServ.do?uri=OJ:L:2011:053:0066:0072:EN:PDF
12. The European Parliament and the Council of the European Union: Directive 2006/123/EC of the European Parliament and of the Council of 12 December 2006 on services in the internal market (2006). http://eur-lex.europa.eu/LexUriServ/LexUriServ.do?uri=OJ:L:2006:376:0036:0068:en:PDF
13. Leitold, H., Posch, R., Rössler, T.: Media-break resistant eSignatures in eGovernment: an Austrian experience. In: Gritzalis, D., Lopez, J. (eds.) SEC 2009. IFIP AICT, vol. 297, pp. 109–118. Springer, Heidelberg (2009)
14. Leitold, H., Posch, R., Rössler, T.: Reconstruction of electronic signatures from eDocument printouts. Comput. Secur. **29**, 523–532 (2010). Challenges for Security, Privacy and Trust
15. Stranacher, K., Kawecki, T.: Interoperable Electronic Documents. In: Scholl, Flak, Janssen, Macintosh, Moe, Sbø, Wimmer, (eds.) Electronic Government and Electronic Participation - Joint Proceedings of Ongoing Research and Projects of IFIP EGOV and IFIP ePart 2012. Informatik, Trauner, vol. 39, pp. 81–88 (2012)
16. OASIS: Digital Signature Service Core Protocols, Elements, and Bindings Version 1.0 (2007). http://docs.oasis-open.org/dss/v1.0/oasis-dss-core-spec-v1.0-os.pdf
17. Gudgin, M., Hadley, M., Mendelsohn, N., Moreau, J.J., Nielsen, H.F.: Soap version 1.2 part 1: Messaging framework (2007). http://www.w3.org/TR/soap12-part1/
18. Fielding, R., Gettys, J., Mogul, J., Frystyk, H., Masinter, L., Leach, P., Berners-Lee, T.: Hypertext transfer protocol – http/1.1 (1999). http://www.ietf.org/rfc/rfc2616.txt
19. Bray, T., Paoli, J., Sperberg-McQueen, C., Maler, E., Yergeau, F., Cowan, J.: Extensible Markup Language (XML) 1.1, 2nd edn. (2006). http://www.w3.org/TR/2006/REC-xml11-20060816/
20. Zefferer, T., Golser, F., Lenz, T.: Towards mobile government: verification of electronic signatures on smartphones. In: Technology-Enabled Innovation for Democracy, Government and Governance - Proceedings of the 2nd Joint International Conference on Electronic Government and the Information Systems Perspective and International Conference on Electronic Democracy, pp. 140–151 (2013)

Status Quo and Best Practices of App Development in Regional Companies

Tim A. Majchrzak$^{(\boxtimes)}$ and Henning Heitkötter

Department of Information Systems, University of Münster, Münster, Germany
{tima,heitkoetter}@ercis.de

Abstract. Only a few years after their advent, smartphones and tablets are now used routinely by many people. While this has been bolstered by the fast innovation cycles of the hardware, mobile devices become versatile due to the applications developed for them. These apps are increasingly used for business purposes. In a research project we investigated whether apps are interesting for all businesses, how and for which activities they plan to use apps, and what kinds of challenges and problems they perceive. To this end, we conducted an interview-based survey with regional companies. Thoroughly analyzing the transcripts enabled us to draw conclusions on the status quo of apps. In this article we present the results from the project, including a set of early best practices. We also discuss our findings to derive directions for future research.

Keywords: App · Business app · Mobile application · Best practice

1 Introduction

A couple of years ago, the only mobile devices widely used were mobile phones, which focused on (speech) communication. Their functionality could be extended by e.g. installing small applications written in Java ME. This was seldom done, though. Other devices such as personal digital assistants (PDAs) were niche products. Within few years, smartphones and tablets have spread checklessly. They have replaced PDAs and many other mobile devices. A paradigm shift can be observed in the context of their increase in popularity. Communication is only *one* of many functions. While the hardware has become very powerful, it is the software of smartphones and tablets that makes them versatile and adaptable. Mobile applications – *apps* – are the key to mobile devices' success.

At first, apps were developed either by vendors of mobile platforms such as iOS (Apple) and Android (Google) or by enthusiastic individuals. With increasing awareness enterprises are now exploring the prospects of using apps. The number of apps developed with a commercial interest in mind grows. We set up a research project to find out *whether* apps are interesting for all businesses, *how* and *in which way* they think apps can be useful for them, and *what* kinds of challenges and problems they see. Business adoption is a phenomenon too recent to get insights from quantitative studies. Thus, we worked qualitatively in a project

© Springer-Verlag Berlin Heidelberg 2014
K.-H. Krempels and A. Stocker (Eds.): WEBIST 2013, LNBIP 189, pp. 189–206, 2014.
DOI: 10.1007/978-3-662-44300-2_12

with regional companies. While this seems like a limitation, it enabled us to keep close contact and conduct very detailed interviews.

This article presents results from our project. Whenever possible, general implications of our findings are given along with a discussion. Our work makes several contributions. Firstly, it depicts the status quo of app development as derived from a regional sample. Secondly, it presents a first set of best practices learned from the companies. Thirdly, it discusses aspects of app development that pose notable challenges. Fourthly, it theorizes about these findings. Results are specifically suited for businesses just beginning to examine mobile scenarios.

The remainder of the article is structured as follows. Section 2 motivates the importance of business apps and explains the background of our project. The status quo of app development as derived from our business partners is described in Sect. 3. In Sect. 4, early best practices for business app development and usage are compiled. Section 5 presents a discussion of our findings. An overview of related projects is given in Sect. 6. Finally, Sect. 7 draws a conclusion.

2 Project Background

Apps are, generally speaking, lightweight, easy-to-use, and optimized for the particularities of mobile devices, such as screen size and touch input. They are typically distributed via a mobile platform's app store. Demand for apps from consumers and businesses alike is very strong. Often, customers expect companies to be present on mobile devices in one way or another. They want to be able to use their smartphone to access a company's services. Increasingly, simply using existing Web sites on mobile devices is seen as unsatisfactory due to the low level of usability. There are apps of all conceivable categories, ranging from games over social media to shopping.

Our work focuses on *business apps*. We understand them as mobile applications that support business tasks. This definition is broad by intention. It for example includes apps that employ sophisticated graphics (or even are games) but serve a marketing function. However, in most cases apps with form-based input and output are concerned. They form the core of apps for business purposes [9]. Apps are interesting for enterprises with respect to several usage scenarios and target audiences. Firstly, a company may want to support its business processes and provide its employees with apps for this purpose. Secondly, it may offer apps to its customers for marketing, sales, or servicing activities. Thirdly, a company with a focus on software development may develop apps for and by order of its clients according to their requirements. For companies that support at least parts of their business processes with IT, the integration of mobile devices into these processes appears as the next logical step.

Developing apps poses several challenges, especially to small and medium enterprises, due to several particularities. Up to now, the mobile market is heavily fragmented into incompatible platforms like Android, iOS, and Blackberry. This leads to increased development and testing efforts. Furthermore, mobile operating systems are quite different from well-known desktop operating systems and limited in scope, requiring new concepts.

Small software development companies or businesses with small IT departments often lack the resources and expertise of larger enterprises, but are still eager to profit from the aforementioned benefits of apps. They often have no experience with app development and no department specialized in mobile marketing and similar activities. This was the starting point of our research. We contacted several regional companies that proved to be interested in the topic and set up the project *Business Apps*. As part of the project, status quo and best practices of app development were of particular interest. The participants were selected from a pool of companies managed by the local chamber of commerce. All of them either have IT-intensive business processes (e.g. as financial service providers), or offer IT services and software. In other words: they share an interest in supporting their business with IT. Participation was of course voluntary; therefore, not all companies we contacted actually took part in the project.

Our department was responsible for managing the project and conducting the research. Eleven regional firms of varying sizes and from different industries participated. We chose to first concentrate on a manageable number of regional companies in order to allow for in-depth conversations and insights. For a start, we regard this qualitative approach to be preferable compared to a quantitative survey, because a basic understanding of the current state of mobile development is still missing and is better elicited through personal interviews. With this article, we intend to examine the current state and provide results which can later be used to plan larger surveys.

In order to investigate the status quo, gather typical requirements of business apps, and recognize best practices, we conducted semi-structured expert interviews mainly with managers but also with developers. Based on a questionnaire that gathered quantitative data of the respective company prior to the interview, we discussed several areas: we first considered the company's current state of app development – how many apps, if any, had been developed already?; if none, why not?; which use cases did the apps support?; how (well) did the development process work from a business and from a technical point of view? This was followed by questions about the expectations and requirements concerning the development of apps. Finally, we asked our partners about their future plans.

Interviews were guided by an outline of questions that gave plenty of room for discussion. We did not ask the questions consecutively, but let our partners talk guided by intermittent inquiries from our side. This ensured a lively discussion, while still taking care of all important topics. The outline was developed based on our prior knowledge of the area and keeping in mind general criteria for developing software as described in the literature on software engineering. Moreover, we followed the approach chosen for a project in a similar setting: qualitative research with a small number of participants and long, open interviews [16,17]. This combination made sure that we did not leave out important aspects. At the same time, the openness of the interviews made sure that notable issues that could *not* be anticipated would still be captured because they would likely be named by the interviewees. As a consequence, interviews lasted on average about 90 to 120 minutes.

After the interviewing phase, we compiled information on the status quo from transcripts of the interviews and analyzed them for typical statements and often mentioned wishes and expectations. Section 3 describes the results. We also aggregated successful strategies mentioned during the interviews and analyzed them for general applicability, resulting in best practices (Sect. 4). Moreover, we found several topics of particular interest to smaller IT departments concerned with app development (Sect. 5), for which no satisfactory solution is available so far.

3   Status Quo

In this section, we describe the status quo broken down into the state of development, requirements, and future plans.

3.1   State of App Development

Apps Developed so Far. All participating companies had developed first apps. However, the number was small and typical projects were *proof-of-concepts* implementations. The level of heterogeneity was too high to categorize the apps. In general, most apps were designed to be used internally. Some of them would normally target customers but were implemented for internal assessment.

The described apps share a characteristic: very limited functionality. Only some of them represent *new* ideas. Many apps transfer existing functionality to the mobile realm. Interviewees often told us that functionality available as a Web site would be provided by apps more comfortably. These apps usually did not yet incorporate the full functionality of the considered Web site but only its core services or those of *one* of the Web site's parts.

Apps not based on existing functionality were very simple. Oftentimes, only a single function is provided, commonly supporting workflows or enabling easy access to information. A typical example is a calendar tool for trash collection days published by a local service provider. A majority of apps is concerned with providing access to information. Managing or even entering data still is negligible. We only learned of few app for that purpose. One was a kind of virtual clipboard used by mechanics to guide inspection activities and send data to a backend. It also made plausibility checks e.g. to make sure that all necessary inspection steps were followed during servicing. Another app was used by field staff equipped with tablets. It provided visualization and simple calculation of tariffs of financial service products.

Some apps did not even serve a purpose in terms of functionality. They were merely developed to assess functionality and especially development frameworks such as *PhoneGap* [19] (now *Apache Cordova* [2]) or the *Sybase Unwired Platform* [22]. The same applies for demonstration apps, e.g. a *management cockpit* provided for executives to observe real-time data.

Besides realized apps, many projects had been driven to the design phase but had not yet been implemented. This can be explained with the complexity of such apps. The participants described customer-centric apps; some of them were supposed to include cartographic services or make use of device-specific services such as the camera. Realizing these apps would be very valuable as novel services could be offered to customers. However, the companies found it very hard to estimate the actual effort required for doing so. Some companies also scrutinized the possibility of adopting or adapting apps by third-party vendors, specifically for Personal Information Management (PIM) functionality.

It has to be noted that the process for initiating apps was versatile. Instead of being launched by central management, several prototypic apps were built on employees' own discretion. These employees had acquired the necessary skills in their free-time and out of curiosity. Some companies provided support by assigning some time for free experimentation or by organizing workshops for experience sharing – the latter were partly held on weekends.

Platforms. Two approaches could be observed for platform choice. The first was to implement for one platform only: Android or iOS, sometimes Blackberry. Usually, this choice was made for apps that were designed for internal use or merely as prototypes. The second was to support Android *and* iOS. Quite notably, almost none of the projects targeting customers supported other platforms while companies stressed the importance of supporting these two. Not supporting the platform chosen by customers was perceived as a risk due to many peoples' quite emotional attitude towards "their" platform. One company noted that the choice of platforms should target to "win and safeguards the trust by customers".

Cross-platform development was only seen as important if customers were the target audience. The participants usually did not support a *bring your own device* (BYOD) policy fearing security problems due to employee-maintained smartphones and tablets. Particularly those companies that had provided staff with devices (usually Blackberry units) even prohibited BYOD. A common strategy for choosing multiple platforms was to take Android and iOS due to their market shares, and to develop an additional Web app to support all remaining platforms. Some companies argued that they still could develop an additional native version should another platform gain relevant shares among their customer base. Some companies refrained from multi-platform support despite its conceptual merits. Reasons were high effort, problems regarding usability and support of native appeal (e.g. due to differences in gestures such as swiping), and a highly increased administrative overhead.

We particularly wanted to learn whether compatibility to multiple platforms would be sought in the future. We found several, in parts strictly contrasting approaches: The *pragmatic* point of view is to support whatever platforms are demanded by customers. Several companies follow this paradigm. Prioritizing *usability* means to weigh up between Web apps and native apps while seeking to minimize effort. A *Web-based* strategy neglects native look & feel and waits for more device-support to be built into technologies such as HTML5 [13] (which can be used to build fancy apps already [25]). The *dual way* proposes to support the *most important* platforms natively while using a Web app as a fallback option to serve all others. The desire to *prevent effort* may strive for supporting relevant platforms but perceives additional effort with skepticism. Following an *observant* strategy, one platform is picked for now but market development is followed closely. Finally, for internal usage a deliberate decision for one platform in accordance with hardware investments could be made.

Decision Processes. The kind of developed apps and especially the selected platforms are strongly influenced by technological underpinnings. However, due to our business focus, we also wanted to understand which decision processes lead to the development of apps. Hence, we made this a topic in the interviews.

The simplest option is contract work for a customer. This is only relevant for some of the participating companies, though. Whether multiple platforms are supported solely depends on the customers' requirements – and budget.

In several cases, the companies developed apps proactively to reflect anticipated requirements. These apps were offered to key customers. Some companies also regularly conduct workshops with customers in which requirements are discussed. This in particular is popular if customers are shareholders at the same time (e.g. in cooperative legal entities).

Internally used apps are usually requested by the departments that want to use them to support business processes. Design is problem-driven in this case. The same is possible for external development, but not typical. App development projects initiated by management or even executives were not reported.

One large company had several app development projects initiated by their department for innovation management. The company provides IT services and tries to keep up with cutting-edge development to offer solutions that are mature and safe for business in alignment with rapid technological progress. Although this requires considerable effort among accepting the risk of following technologies that ultimately fail, this company had an edge in app development.

No clear picture can be drawn for technological specifications derived from business decisions. Most companies have not decided on a strategy, yet. Choice of technology is project-determined. Internal app development often is strongly influenced by the hardware strategy. If a company e.g. fixed to equip employees with Blackberry devices, platform and development frameworks are mostly predetermined. Only some companies have decided on an intermediate strategy for the next years; this usually stipulates the support of Android and iOS.

The interviews were used by several company representatives to utter criticism. For example, the closed nature of the iOS platform was seen as counterproductive while the importance of it prevented companies from not acquiring a developer's license from Apple. Other representatives complained about the level of investment security. The (hostile) coexistence of a number of platforms reminds them of the *browser wars* of the 1990s. To decide which platform is worth to acquire knowledge for is seen as a dilemma due to simultaneous customer demand. Finally, *security* was seen as a main concern with only Blackberry providing sufficient support (also see Sect. 5.1). It has to be mentioned, however, that all participants perceive profound chances in using the new technologies.

To conclude this phase of the interviews, we asked how satisfied the companies were with their current progress. Not all companies wanted to take a clear position but the general attitude was positive. This is remarkable since experiences are still very limited. At the same time, satisfaction reflects to some degree the potential seen in mobile devices.

It has to be noted as a final remark that some comments on technical issues were contrary to statements regarding decision processes. For example, iOS was praised for its ergonomics and the low effort in coaching employees in using it. Admittedly, this relates – at least partially – to the restricted nature of the platform that enforces design standards.

Distribution. Apps are typically distributed differently than desktop applications. Users sometimes download apps from Web sites but mainly access them via *app stores*. The latter are organized similarly to Web shops. They provide good overview and easy installation. For commercial purposes, software distribution tools are available. To our knowledge, these tools are not (yet) as powerful as their counterparts for distribution of software onto workstations and servers.

In common, companies are in favor of app stores. It is very comfortable for their customers to find and install apps. The possibility to rate apps is seen as a positive enforcing to develop *good* apps. However, if apps can be commented there also is the risk of unjustified criticism. Some companies regard app stores as the only interface to customers; providing apps for download on corporate Web sites is seen as awkward style. App stores are also considered for internal deployment (so called *enterprise app stores*). There have been critical remarks concerning the deployment duration in app stores. It would be "quite cumbersome" for Blackberry and require "up to two days" – for each deployment. The mandatory checks in Apple's app store were reported to take up to a week.

Automatically keeping employee-owned devices up-to-date is seen as a problem. It is vital to e.g. install security patches without user interaction. *Mobile Device Management* might be a solution (also see Sect. 5.1). Particularly Blackberry (or rather its vendor Research In Motion) was described as advanced in this regard. Apple is seen as focused on consumers but shifting to recognize business customers.

In contrast with our expectation, *virtualization* was not mentioned in the interviews. While virtualization on workstations is used routinely and employees connect to the corporate network using terminal servers, virtualization on mobile devices does not seem to be considered. It might, however, be a future way to offer access to resources and to increase security. This specifically applies to scenarios in which BYOD is allowed.

It has to be noted that none of the participating enterprises currently plan to offer premium services or to sell apps to end-customers (i.e. consumers). Such services might become available in the future but most of the companies see apps as an instrument for customer relationship management or to support processes.

Development. The next step was to have a look at the implementation of apps. No processes specifically tailored to apps could be observed. Development is conducted like for other application; due to the nature of apps particularity methods of graphical user interface (GUI) design are employed. It was noted that app development should be rapid; therefore, processes influenced by agile methods are used even if normally not utilized by a company.

A particularity is the team size: it typically is one, i.e. an app is developed by a single employee. If apps become larger, development processes ought to be adjusted. Roles might be aligned with the structure of apps as determined by the platforms. Android adheres to a modified model-view-controller (MVC) design pattern which would allow for differentiated developer roles. The "one developer" philosophy also leads to a rather unstructured proceeding. At the same time, there can be significant effort for learning technologies. Mastering powerful libraries such as jQuery Mobile [15] is not trivial [11].

Regarding the development for multiple platforms, it was noted that there should not be multiple parallel projects. Rather, a single project would ensure persistent quality on the different platforms. Moreover, it was noted that apps should strive for a native look & feel; Web apps would not be perceived as "real" apps by customers.

App testing poses novel challenges. In particular, coping with the different contexts an mobile application resides in is by no means easy [21]. An example is the transition between different network connections. Moreover, *device fragmentation* is a problem since functions change with devices and there are great differences in available performance.

A final observation is that only a small share of all developers has experience in app development, yet. This may be expected to change soon.

3.2 Requirements for Developing Apps

Requirements engineering is an essential activity [14]. If it is not done meticulously, the final application will be different from what was expected. Therefore, we discussed the role of requirements for app development. Mostly non-functional requirements (i.e., concerning an app's quality) were named, as we did not ask for requirements for one particular app but for expected general characteristics.

It was argued by the companies that requirements should be gathered in a context-dependent way. Device-specific functionality like acquiring GPS coordinates or using *Near Field Communication* is often important. A particularly named requirement was to develop apps that would enthuse users. However, we expect that this is just a temporary requirement and part of the hype. Some general requirements were named very often. Smartphones and tablets are easy to use; thus, apps should be easy to use. Apps should look good, provide sufficient performance and responsiveness, be adequately secure, and adhere to privacy standards. There was no clear line regarding a native look & feel. For several participants, this was the most important non-functional requirement; for some, however, it was negligible. Energy efficiency was a secondary requirement only but we expect it to become much more important in the future.

Special requirements could be observed for connectivity. Originally, apps were supposed to either be *online* at all times or to work *offline*. However, for many scenarios, it is required to load information if a proper connection is available but to be able to work without a connection as well. This is not trivial to realize and might furthermore require sophisticated synchronization mechanisms.

In general, apps need to be robust regarding improper input data due to the way they are used. Touching the display is considered to be more prone to erroneous input than using an application with keyboard and mouse.

To ease the usage of apps, they should ideally provide a *single-sign-on* functionality. This might lead to problems, though. Typically, smartphones and tablets are used by a single user – but this is not always the case. Problems might also arise if devices are used both in business and private settings.

Compliance with typical requirements for commercial software might be impossible. For example, many companies have policies that enforce anti-virus software. Hardly any products comparable to desktop software are available for mobile devices, though. It is unclear what the reaction to this situation will be, even though security software vendors seem to perceive a new market. Compromised customer data should be avoided at all cost. Moreover, there might be a need for specific privacy. An app that e.g. requests location-based services might seem harmless. If it, however, sends location data to a server regularly, an insecure connection or a data-leak in the server would be dramatic as it would allow for creating *movement profiles*.

Asked about practices for requirements engineering or the creation of requirements catalogs for apps, companies told us that is was too early to be specific.

3.3 Outlook and Conclusions

In the last part of the interviews, we asked companies about their future plans and scrutinized the overall importance they see in apps. For all participating companies at least the usage of IT but in many cases also the development of IT products has strategic relevance. Asked about the relevance of apps, some companies could directly take a position. Some companies see apps as part of their corporate strategy while others only consider them as operative tools. Some also emphasized that it is not their perception that matters but their customers'.

The companies for which apps have strategic importance usually share a set of expectations. Examples are the

- estimation that PCs and notebooks usage will decline,
- assumption that most people will have a permanent Internet connection in the near future,
- believe that Web-based solutions have extremely high accessibility, and the
- prediction that customer contact will increasingly be bi-directional, involving them in product design.

Seeing apps as a mean to improve processes underlines the great deal of optimism a number of companies have.

About half of the participants plan to increase investments to put more emphasis on apps. The other half plans to assign more budget to app development but to cut down equally on other activities. The companies do not expect apps to fully replace other instruments e.g. for marketing, though. In general, prices for mobile devices and app development infrastructure are expected to plummet.

When asking for a conclusion concerning the status quo of app development, the already reported satisfaction was acknowledged. However, this was mainly driven economically: *current investments were worth it.* Not all companies were completely contented with the technology. Particularly, the current compromises between quality and effort were seen as unsatisfactory. The economic satisfaction is driven by financial success: even some of the smallest app projects paid off; learning curves were steep. Unsuccessful projects were not necessarily seen as failures since the gained experiences had value. Acceptance of apps among customers and employees could not yet be fully assessed, though.

Finally, we asked the participants to name room for improvements and to provide us with their outlook. Progress was desired in several areas. Firstly, advanced language recognition would open up new possibilities. Secondly, security should be improved. Companies would specifically like to see more emphasize put on security on Android and iOS. At the same time, not all of them considered the concept of Blackberry as perfect since it was seen as a kind of *security by obscurity.* Thirdly, multi-platform support should be possible with small budgets. Fourthly, data throughput during mobile usage should be increased. Fifthly, synchronization of app and backend should be supported by sophisticated tools. Sixthly, enterprise support is trailing and needs to be improved.

In general, technological innovations were sought that would enable companies to accept less compromises when developing apps. Moreover, companies have a desire to learn about customer expectations. In addition, they would like to see studies and evaluations, e.g. of development frameworks.

4   Best Practices

In the following, best practices as derived from the experiences of the participating companies are described. Due to the early state of app development, they are mainly meant to be thought-provoking impulses. Best practices for cross-platform app development are not given as the level of knowledge about this is low in companies; work on cross-platform best practices has for example been described in [8].

The first best practice is to use apps to *motivate developers.* Several companies reported that some employees would acquire knowledge on app development on their own. Obviously, the topic is seen as *fun* rather than as work. While this cannot be universally assumed for any kind of app development, it might be utilized. If possible, app development projects should be seen as an incentive for employees willing to work on them. Ideally, developers should feel that they can contribute to the success of their company in adopting a new technology. However, incentives should be used with care. Employees that do not share the enthusiasm for apps should not feel that their work is considered subordinate.

Secondly, focusing on *component-orientation* and *service-oriented architectures* (SOA) is recommended. While many apps were build as single entities, they are suited to be constructed from standardized components and to use SOA.

Many commercial apps display information and are used to enter data. The functionality typically found is quite similar. For example, several types of diagrams will often be used for visualization and many apps need to process master file data of customers. Therefore, such apps should adhere to a common architecture and be built as far as possible from standardized components. The initial effort to create such components is higher than to develop a single app, but break even usually is reached with the second app already. As a positive side effect, the app landscape will become easier to overview. However, which components to provide as standardized artifacts and which to design individually has to be chosen with much care.

The usage of a service-oriented architecture makes sense if the company is using SOA anyway and apps rely on backend systems. At a first look, using services seems to be adverse for enabling apps to work without a reliable Internet connection. However, having orchestrated services can be beneficial. Instead of relying on a great number of single requests in a typical client/server-architecture, data is gathered by the backend and exchanged with the app client in few service requests. This could also save computational effort on the device and thus increase battery life. Relying on data processing in backend systems might also increase security. Securing the connection between app and backend is considered simpler than to design secure apps. A final critical remark has to be given, though: implementing SOA solely for apps is not considered to be a good strategy.

Thirdly, we found that enterprise apps might serve to increase *information availability*. Mobile devices are particularly suited for providing information. The first step should be to determine which information can be made available, and whether it makes sense to have it available mobile. *Mobile* in this case is an elastic word: it starts with an employee sitting at his desk and using a smartphone since data access is more convenient. It can mean that employees check their appointments for the next day after returning home. It goes as far as working completely remote.

The second step is to consider the level of criticality of information. The more critical they are, the more effort needs to be put into security for mobile access. The third step is to provide access by means of an app. It is advisable to make apps as customizable as possible. Employees will then be able to use them more effectively. While many companies describe this kind of usage as very rewarding, it is hard to assess its monetary value. An expected increase in employees' working precision and speed is hard to measure and even harder to attribute to such small changes as introducing apps on mobile devices.

Particularly due to having several financial service providers among the participating companies, a fourth best practice could be derived: the *support of field staff and sales*. Reports from usage of mobile devices in this area were very convincing. There are two possible usage scenarios: visualization and data entry. The first step usually is to provide visual access to information. Tablet computer are well suited for this task due to their larger screen, their convenient size, and the less person-attributed feel in comparison to a smartphone.

The vision of using tablets for visualization is to replace pen & paper. They are essential for field staff, e.g. in an insurance sales scenario. In the course of appointments with customers tariffs have to be shown, calculated, and adjusted. Calculating and visually demonstrating individual options requires either a large number of preprinted papers or using a laptop. However, the latter is a kind of barrier: while adjusting numbers, the customer only sees the back of the screen. Moreover, it will be perceived as the sales person's laptop and most likely not used without reluctance. In contrast, papers can be handed over and written onto. They do not allow for ad-hoc adjustments, though. Tablets provide the ease-of-use and low barrier of paper while enabling individual adjustments. They are easy to use and even accepted by people with low technical-affinity [18]. To keep calculated data, an additional app can be offered to customers that will synchronize with what has been worked on with the sales person.

Data entry has similar characteristics: paper is interactive and personal but forms usually have to be corrected once returned to the company; laptops are comfortable and powerful, and enable checking data in real-time. Again, using tablet computers can be a convenient solution. However, in this case more sophistication is required than for mere visualization: data entry by touchscreens is usually inferior to using keyboards – at least, if much text has to be entered.

Linking apps to a backend not only provides real-time verification but also allows most activities to be (pre-)computed on servers. This simplifies app implementation but again security concerns have to be taken into account. Moreover, apps needs to be designed to provide some kind of "user mode". The sales person might want to access data from all his customers using the app. However, when handing the tablet to a customer to show him some data, it should not be possible to easily browse to the file of another customer.

Despite all praises, investing into mobile technology for sales staff should be done carefully. A laptop provides a large set of possibilities typically including terminal-server access to company resources. A tablet in contrast is bound to the functionality realized in an app. Hence, sales processes have to be tailored to allow seamless work. However, this can be used for optimizations at the same time. It is advisable to keep laptops for a while after introducing tablets.

5   Discussion

Our findings regarding status quo and best practices are useful in several aspects. Having knowledge of the current state of mobile development in enterprises is important for research on new technologies. The design of mobile enterprise frameworks has to follow the needs of businesses. It also has to be based on the current situation typically found in software development departments in order to be capable of being integrated into their environment. Designing a product for mobile development without regard for the needs and capabilities of businesses will most likely prove unsuccessful. The following subsection highlights some of the needs recurringly mentioned during the interviews. They are the basis for the open research questions that we identify in the second subsection.

5.1   Topics of Particular Interest

We explicitly asked our interview partners for topics of specific concern. When analyzing the transcripts, we additionally looked for problems that were not considered successfully solved. As a result, we compiled the most often found topics of particular interest for which so far no universal solution exists, at least for small- or medium-sized software departments: security on mobile devices, mobile device management (MDM) in general, cross-platform app development, and testing mobile applications. They are discussed in the following.

Mobile security is a highly relevant topic. It subsumes the security of data and applications on mobile devices used in an enterprise context and is hence of utmost importance due to the critical information present on devices. Security has to be considered both in the administration of employees' devices and when developing apps for internal or external use. On the one hand, standard security considerations also known from PCs or laptops, for example regarding wireless communication and application permissions, are more prevalent on mobile devices. On the other hand, they require particular security measures due to their mobility, e.g., data protection in case of theft or loss. This unique combination of security risks along with a reduced awareness of users due to the playful nature of mobile devices poses severe challenges. Furthermore, users often blend private and business use to the point of using their private devices for work (BYOD).

First solutions to some of the problems are available as part of MDM (see below). MDM solutions often allow to specify security policies and provide means to react to device loss. Platform providers such as Google and Apple prepare guidelines for developing secure apps [1,4]. Nevertheless, a holistic security approach still requires considerable effort and knowledge, which poses a problem for smaller IT departments. Fast progress in this field can be expected, particularly since security software vendors increasingly target the affected market.

Commensurate to the scope and versatility of mobile devices, *mobile device management* increases in importance. Due the proliferation of apps, smartphones and tablets need to be administered similar to desktop PCs and laptops. This includes the configuration of (new) devices, installation of apps and updates, distribution of relevant enterprise data, and maintenance. Additionally, data should be synchronized with other devices and data sources. Most functions should be provided over-the-air, i.e., remotely without the need to hand in the device to administration. The heterogeneity of the mobile device market further complicates matters and necessitates a cross-platform MDM. However, developing suchlike products is hindered by the closed nature of mobile platforms with respect to administrative functionality.

The MDM market changes rapidly, which makes orientation especially for smaller companies difficult. Abstract, strategic overviews of the market like [20] do not offer enough insight for deciding on a MDM solution. In general, one can distinguish between *on-premise* and *cloud-based* MDM. Especially for smaller companies, cloud-based solutions might be viable, because they do not need to be installed and maintained by the company itself.

The mobile market is fragmented into largely incompatible mobile platforms, most importantly iOS, Android, Blackberry, and Windows Phone. In an enterprise context, at least the first two, but often more, need to be considered when developing apps. Implementing an app separately for each platform as a native app requires a lot of resources. *Cross-platform approaches* to app development promise to serve several platforms from a single code base. Several categories can be distinguished [8], but all of them have some limitations.

Depending on the particular app, a mobile Web app – essentially a Web site optimized for mobile use – might be sufficient, or a so-called hybrid app that has access to device-specific features can be used. However, Web-based approaches do not produce truly native apps with a native look & feel. No mature cross-platform solution with a native look & feel exists so far, although first steps in this direction emerge, such as Titanium Appcelerator [3]. A novel approach is to use model-driven software development (MDSD) to build apps. MD^2 for example can be used to describe apps as a model using a domain-specific language and to automatically generate native code from this model [9,10]. Similar to the MDM market, cross-platform approaches are an ongoing topic. Smaller development companies need help navigating the confusing market to pick a suitable approach.

During app development, *testing* is a particular concern to ensure a defect free and smooth user experience on all supported devices. Again, heterogeneity causes particular problems. Devices, even with the same mobile operating system, differ significantly with respect to screen sizes, input methods, and other device functionality. These features have direct impact on the functionality and user experience of apps. Hence, testing an app only on a single device type will not be sufficient, further increasing the testing effort. User interface tests, often manually executed, become more important compared to traditional applications. Due to the inherent mobility, apps have to be tested with respect to their reaction to context changes [21], e.g. regarding device orientation, loss of network connection, or relocation.

The emulators available for most mobile operating systems are not sufficient for thorough testing. Testers need access to several physical devices with different specifications. Provisioning such a set of current devices is not feasible for smaller app development teams. However, there are some cloud-based solutions that offer manual or automated remote control of mobile devices, e.g. [7]. Up to now, companies are on their own when developing a testing strategy that considers the particularities outlined above.

Topics of additional interest were mobile requirements engineering, motivating and training developers, energy efficiency, and coping with offline situations. They are not discussed here due to space restrictions.

5.2   Open Research Questions

While our project has led to insights regarding the status quo of using applications for mobile devices, it also has shown that there is a large number of open questions. This is a limitation of our work: we have worked qualitatively and with a small sample; findings cannot be statistically significant and are not necessarily true on a global scale. Therefore, open questions can be derived but answers need to be discovered in future research.

Some of the questions have a practical nature and stem directly from the findings and special topics discussed above. It is beyond the scope of this article to provide solutions to the questions that we can rise. In fact, there is much work to be done in a variety of directions and with a number of disciplines to contribute. Therefore, our idea is to rise questions and – if applicable – to give first ideas for paths to solutions.

Firstly, practical problems have to be solved to support companies. Several topics for research can directly be taken from the status quo drawn in Sect. 3:

- How can companies be supported in deciding whether app development should be pursued by them? How can the business value of apps be determined?
- For which areas does app development apply? What are particular requirements that apply to apps, and how can they be engineered?
- How should decision processes be adapted to allow efficient development?
- Which ways of distribution are reasonable? How can companies safely use app stores? How should companies react in case of problems (e.g. unfavorable comments)?
- What are the challenges of app development and what novel techniques might improve development processes?
- Which strategical underpinning could app development have for companies?

For many of the above questions, solution sketches already have been presented. It is our belief that there is no purely scientific answer to most of these questions. In fact, we deem a close observation of corporate practices along with scientific research to be the most adequate path to feasible solutions. This includes refraining from a hyped thinking about apps and seeing them as *one* instrument to support internal processes and customer-related activities.

Secondly, theory-driven work is required. This particularly applies to the purely economical and the purely technical topics. Regarding economical topics, the value-creation by apps has to be scrutinized. It is easy to estimate development effort and relate it to sales figures if apps are offered for a premium. Measuring the effect of process improvements by app usage or even of increased customer support is close to impossible. Therefore, ways have to be found to support the processes that lead to investment decisions. We consider this to be a theoretic question at first: explanatory models for the value of apps in different situations and for varying scenarios have to be identified in a first step. The second step is to evaluate them qualitatively and eventually quantitatively. This should be done in cooperation with enterprises.

Regarding technology, there are a number of questions that require profound theoretical work before assessing their application to corporate problems. There are four particular areas that we deem to be especially important:

Cross-platform development is supported by various approaches ranging from using Web apps over Web technology-based solutions to sophisticated frameworks based on cross-compiling or model-driven software development technology. Which framework to use in what situation is target of ongoing research [8]. The same applies to the development of improved frameworks with a focus on business problems.

There is no *sound background* for app development. Companies require guidelines, best practices, and a knowledge base similar to what they can draw from for classical software engineering.

Projects such as [25] have started with *scenario-based evaluation of technologies* applied to app development. Such work has to be extended, put into a greater structure, and eventually unified.

There is no *theory of app testing*. At the same time, testing apps is greatly different to testing desktop and server applications. Of course, many techniques can be transferred and there is no need to come up with completely new theories. After all, apps are computer programs and as such subject to similar factors as any other program. However, the context they run in and the changes in user interaction patters and runtime model ask for amendments to existing theories. Based on this, tools and techniques need to be developed and eventually evaluated by using practical examples.

Thirdly, a theoretical base for app development has to be worked on. This is the most open challenge, yet the hardest to pursue. While no strong differences to classical application development could be observed, *some* inherent particularities became obvious. The need to deal with context changes falls into this category. Moreover, the way that mobile technology is used poses some profound differences in terms of value to businesses and perception by humans. This even relates to the ongoing discussion of ubiquitous computing (cf. e.g. [5]). Finding suitable "small packets" for research and pursuing theoretization in an interdisciplinary way will be a challenge for the upcoming years.

6   Related Work

Due to the nature of our article and the novelty of the topic, relating to other work is no straightforward task. In a narrow sense, no directly related work that explores mobile strategies from a business point of view and surveys the status quo exists. In a wide sense, almost all papers considering app development are related due to their involvement in the early advances in the understanding of apps. Work that relates to particular aspects of our article has been cited at the appropriate locations. Therefore, we will only highlight a few approaches that relate in a closer sense.

WASSERMAN [24] gives an overview of software engineering issues prevalent when developing apps. He draws on a survey among mobile developers and highlights what makes mobile development different. The main part consists of a research agenda for software engineering, not a description of current practices, and hence is a worthwhile addition to our work. In contrast to our work, he focuses on the immediate environment of the developer himself, but not on the point of view of businesses that decide on mobile strategies. The work of DEHLINGER and DIXON [6] takes a similar direction. HOLZER and ONDRUS [12] study the mobile market from a developer's perspective as well. They intend to give advice to developers on how to engage in mobile app development. Similar to [24], their work has a narrower scope than our project, but provides additional insight.

TARNACHA and MAITLAND [23] take an entrepreneurial perspective on the opportunities of mobile commerce and analyze the dependencies between technology and business strategy. Hence, they focus on businesses for which mobility is a key factor, as their products entirely depend on it. Our work, instead, looks at enterprises with a modest relationship to software that want to expand towards mobile applications supporting their regular business. Published in 2006, the statements of [23] mostly apply to the pre-smartphone area and are in detail not applicable to today's situation.

7   Conclusions

We presented work on app development by enterprises. Our article summarized the status quo and best practices learned from regional companies, discussed findings, and proposed various topics for ongoing research.

Besides providing some insights, we hope to stimulate research with our work. Research has to keep pace with the extremely high speed the market for mobile apps evolves with. Moreover, there are many unsolved challenges for which solutions need to be provided.

Our own work is not finished. We are currently working on a project for cross-platform app development [9,10], one of the challenges presented earlier. Our idea is to provide a technically sound solution that still keeps a domain-specific focus (on business apps) in mind. Moreover, we keep contact to some of the enterprises we worked with. Thereby, we will tackle on some of the questions raised in this article. The medium-term goal is to provide business with answers to these questions while building the theory on app development.

Acknowledgements. We would like to thank the companies that filled out the questionnaire and particularly those that were available for interviews. Their participation made the underlying project of this article possible.

References

1. Android developers: Designing for security (2012). http://developer.android.com/guide/practices/security.html
2. Apache Cordova (2012). http://incubator.apache.org/cordova/
3. Appcelerator (2012). http://www.appcelerator.com/

4. Apple Inc.: iOS security (2012). http://images.apple.com/ipad/business/docs/iOS_Security_May12.pdf
5. Bell, G., Dourish, P.: Yesterday's tomorrows: notes on ubiquitous computing's dominant vision. Pers. Ubiquit. Comput. 11(2), 133–143 (2007)
6. Dehlinger, J., Dixon, J.: Mobile application software engineering: challenges and research directions. In: Workshop on Mobile Software Engineering (2011)
7. Deviceanywhere (2012). http://www.keynotedeviceanywhere.com/
8. Heitkötter, H., Hanschke, S., Majchrzak, T.A.: Comparing cross-platform development approaches for mobile applications. In: Proceedings of 8th International Conference on Web Information Systems and Technologies (WEBIST) (2012)
9. Heitkötter, H., Majchrzak, T.A., Kuchen, H.: Cross-platform model-driven development of mobile applications with MD2. In: Proceedings of the 2013 ACM Symposium on Applied Computing (SAC). ACM (2013)
10. Heitkötter, H., Majchrzak, T.A., Kuchen, H.: MD2-DSL - eine domänenspezifische Sprache zur Beschreibung und Generierung mobiler Anwendungen. In: Proceedings der 6. Arbeitstagung Programmiersprachen (ATPS 2013), No. 215 in LNI, GI (2013)
11. Heitkötter, H., Majchrzak, T.A., Ruland, B., Weber, T.: Evaluating frameworks for creating mobile web apps. In: Proceedings of the 9th International Conference on Web Information Systems and Technologies (WEBIST) (2013)
12. Holzer, A., Ondrus, J.: Trends in mobile application development. In: Hesselman, C., Giannelli, C. (eds.) Mobilware 2009 Workshops. LNICST, vol. 12, pp. 55–64. Springer, Heidelberg (2009)
13. HTML5 (2012). http://www.w3.org/TR/html5/
14. Hull, E., Jackson, K., Dick, J.: Requirements Engineering, 3rd edn. Springer, New York (2010)
15. jquery mobile (2012). http://jquerymobile.com/
16. Majchrzak, T.A.: Best practices for the organizational implementation of software testing. In: Proceedings of the 43th Annual HICSS. IEEE CS (2010)
17. Majchrzak, T.A.: Status quo of software testing - regional findings and global inductions. J. Inf. Sci. Technol. (JIST) 7(2), 3–20 (2010)
18. Majchrzak, T.A., Jakubiec, A., Lablans, M.,Ückert, F.: Towards better social integration through mobile web 2.0 ambient assisted living devices. In: Proceedings of 2011 ACM SAC, pp. 821–822. ACM, New York (2011)
19. Phonegap (2012). http://phonegap.com/
20. Redman, P., Girard, J., Basso, M.: Magic quadrant for mobile device management software. Technical report, Gartner (2012). http://www.gartner.com/DisplayDocument?id=2019515
21. Schulte, M., Majchrzak, T.A.: Context-dependent testing of apps. Testing Experience 19 (2012)
22. Sybase unwired platform (2012). http://sybase.de/products/mobileenterprise/sybaseunwiredplatform
23. Tarnacha, A., Maitland, C.: Entrepreneurship in mobile application development. In: Proceedings of 8th International Conference on Electronic commerce, pp. 589–593. ACM (2006)
24. Wasserman, T.: Software engineering issues for mobile application development. In: FoSER 2010 (2010)
25. Zibula, A., Majchrzak, T.A.: Developing a cross-platform mobile smart meter application using HTML5, jQuery Mobile and PhoneGap. In: Proceedings of the 8th International Conference on Web Information Systems and Technologies (WEBIST) (2012)

Web Intelligence

Vector Space Models for the Classification of Short Messages on Social Network Services

Ricardo Lage[1,2], Peter Dolog[1]([✉]), and Martin Leginus[1]

[1] Aalborg University, Aalborg, Denmark
dolog@cs.aau.dk
[2] LIP6, University Pierre Et Marie Curie (Paris 6), Paris, France
http://www.cs.aau.dk/

Abstract. In this chapter we review vector space models to propose a new one based on the Jensen-Shannon divergence with the goal of classifying ignored short messages on a social network service. We assume that ignored messages are those published ones that were not interacted with. Our goal then is to attempt to classify messages to be published as ignored to discard them from a set messages that can be used by a recommender system. To evaluate our model, we conduct experiments comparing different models on a Twitter dataset with more than 13,000 Twitter accounts. Results show that our best model tested obtained an average accuracy of 0.77, compared to 0.74 from a model from the literature. Similarly, this method obtained an average precision of 0.74 compared to 0.58 from the second best performing model.

Keywords: Information retrieval · Classification · Social networks

1 Introduction

Heavy users of social network accounts have to handle large amounts of information prior to deciding what to publish to their followers or subscribers. The New York Times, for example, publishes around 60 messages/day on Twitter to over 6.2 million followers[1]. A system or person behind this account must decide among a large number of news articles, which ones are worth broadcasting on the social network. Similarly, accounts that broadcast alerts and news about health outbreaks or natural disasters, must filter information in a timely manner in order to publish the most helpful content to all of their users. Deciding which messages to publish on those accounts is challenging because the users following them have different preferences and the amount of information available tends to be large. These accounts are also constrained by the limits in the number of requests imposed by the social network's API.

Prior work on recommendation and classification on social networks focused on improving the presentation of information to different types of users. For

---

[1] http://www.tweetstats.com/graphs/nytimes/zoom/2012/Sep

© Springer-Verlag Berlin Heidelberg 2014
K.-H. Krempels and A. Stocker (Eds.): WEBIST 2013, LNBIP 189, pp. 209–224, 2014.
DOI: 10.1007/978-3-662-44300-2_13

example, different works have proposed to predict the impact of a message [14], to rank them [2] or to provide better search functionality [12]. These studies, however, tend to focus on the consumer of information, disregarding the publisher. The publisher of a message on a social network has the challenge of addressing all of his or her followers or subscribers. That is, a message published in that account cannot be addressed to only one or a small subset of those followers. In a previous work [9] , we proposed a system to address the problem of publishing news articles on Twitter to a group of followers of a Twitter account. We did not consider, however, that prior to ranking which messages to publish, a number of them could be disregarded beforehand by being classified as irrelevant. This initial step could potentially filter out noise from a ranking algorithm aimed at recommending information to a group of people on a social network.

In this chapter, we propose such filtering method. Given a set of messages to be published by a user, we want to detect those that his or her subscribers would not interact with. We label those messages as "ignored" and filter them out from the original set. On Facebook, for example, these are published messages with no likes. On Twitter, they are those with no retweets. By identifying those ignored messages, a system can then move on to decide what to publish from a more likely set of messages to have an impact on the user's subscribers or followers. Our method is a supervised learning task where we propose a model to train a Naive Bayes classifier with messages from a user account labeled as "candidate" or "ignored". That is, given an initial set of labeled messages from one account, we want to classify subsequent messages of this same account. We restrict ourselves to single accounts to account for the limit on API requests imposed by social network services. Twitter, for example, restricts the number of requests to 350 per hour per IP address. Systems publishing messages on the platform already make use of the API to publish messages and to read user preferences. Using additional requests to gather extra messages to train a classifier could compromise this system's ability to publish messages frequently.

One of our challenges, therefore, is to deal with a small set of short messages often available on these accounts. To address it, we propose a vector space model that finds temporal latent relations in the existing vocabulary. We compare our model against existing ones for the same classification task on a dataset from Twitter. We repeat the same experiment of training the classifier and testing its accuracy on over 13,000 Twitter accounts of different characteristics, comparing the factors that affect performance. Results show that our best model tested obtained an average accuracy of 0.77, compared to 0.74 from a model from the literature. Similarly, this method obtained an average precision of 0.74 compared to 0.58 from the second best performing model.

The remainder of this paper is organized as follows. Section 2 reviews the literature on vector space models for classification and presents the models we compared ours against. Section 3 presents our method for classifying ignored messages and the models we propose to train the classifier. Section 4 explains our experiments on Twitter and presents our results. Finally, we present our conclusions and directions for future work in Sect. 5.

2   Related Work

Vector Space Models (VSMs) were first developed in the 1970s for an information retrieval system [18]. According to [18], the success of these models led many other researchers to explore them in different tasks in natural language processing. In one of its most traditional forms, the vectors of a vector space model are organized in a matrix of documents and terms. The value of a document's term is then computed with a weighting scheme such as the tf-idf which assigns to term t a weight in document d:

$$\text{tf-idf}_{t,d} = \text{tf}_{t,d} \times \text{idf}_t \tag{1}$$

There are different ways to compute the term frequency $\text{tf}_{t,d}$ and the inverse document frequency idf_t, depending on the task at hand. Lan et al. [10], for instance, compare different term weighting schemes in the context of a classification task.

In social networks, however, the contents of a document (i.e., a message published by a user) tend to be a short snippet of text. On Twitter, for example, although there is a limit of 140 characters per message, most of them have between 30 and 40 characters[2]. In this case, the use of these schemes to compute the documents' similarities has limitations due to the text size. Since there are few words in each snippet, the number of terms in common tends to be low.

One way to address this problem is to expand the term set of each snippet. This can be done, for instance, by stemming words instead of using their original forms or by expanding the term set with synonyms [21]. Following this approach, [16] proposes a kernel function to expand the term set with query results from a search engine. A short text snippet x is used as a query to a search engine. The contents of the top-n retrieved documents are indexed in a tf-idf vector v_i for each document d_i. Then, an expanded version, $QE(x)$, of x is computed as:

$$\text{QE(x)} = \frac{C(x)}{||C(x)||_2} \tag{2}$$

where $||C(x)||_2$ is the L_2-norm and

$$\text{C(x)} = \frac{1}{n} \sum_{i=1}^{n} \frac{v_i}{||v_i||_2} \tag{3}$$

Then the similarity $K(x,y)$ between two snippets of text x and y is defined as the dot product between the two expanded vectors:

$$\text{K(x,y)} = QE(x) \cdot QE(y) \tag{4}$$

---

[2] These numbers are based on discussions in blog posts such as in http://thenextweb.com/twitter/2012/01/07/interesting-fact-most-tweets-posted-are -approximately-30-characters-long/ and http://www.ayman-naaman.net/2010/04/ 21/how-many-characters-do-you-tweet/. But they do not provide an average. In our own dataset presented in Sect. 4.1, the average number of characters in a tweet is 84.

Yih et al. [21] further improve on this query expansion approach by weighting terms according to the keyword extraction system proposed by [20]. It modifies the vector v_i in Eq. 3 to one containing a relevancy score w instead of a tf-idf score. The authors also propose two machine learning approaches to learning the similarity between short snippets. They show better results compared to web-based expansion approaches. The latter has two main limitations, according to [21]. It relies on a static measure for a given corpus and have limitations in dealing with new or rare words existent in the original message, since they may not yield relevant search results. Web-based expansion approaches also have the obvious limitation of relying on third-party online resources to assist in the document expansion.

Alternatively, therefore, the term set can be expanded by deriving latent topics from a document corpus [3]. However, the authors still rely on an external set of documents, mapping the short text to an external topic space. In the opposite direction, [17] proposes a modification to the tf-idf scheme to reduce the number of words in a short snippet to fewer more representative ones. They introduce a clarity score for each word in the snippet, which is the Kullback-Leibler (KL) divergence between the query results and the collection corpus. The author, however, only compares the introduction of the clarity score with the traditional tf-idf scheme.

Approaches to expand the feature set can be combined with a method of feature selection. Feature selection has become an important procedure for various information retrieval tasks such as document clustering and categorization. Because of the large number of documents, corresponding feature vectors tend to be sparse and high dimensional. These properties result into poor performance of various machine learning tasks. Usually feature selection reduces the space of words by keeping only the top most relevant ones according to some predefined filtering or relevancy measure. Various filtering measures were exploited for feature selection tasks. The most simple measures [6] are document or term frequency which can be combined into tf-idf. The other family of measures are based on Information Theory. Such measures are Information Gain [19], Expected Cross Entropy for text [13] or statistic χ^2 [19]. Recently, a group of machine learning measures have emerged. These measures express to what extent a given term w belongs to a certain category c [4].

On Twitter in particular, where messages are restricted to 140 characters, a number of approaches that consider the text messages have been proposed for different tasks such as message propagation [14], ranking [2] and search [12]. These studies consider the words in a message as part of the feature set, which also includes other features from Twitter such as social relations. Their findings show poor results when using text features. However, they relied only on the actual terms from the messages, without considering, for example, the improvements discussed above to expand the vocabulary or find latent features.

In [14] a machine learning approach is proposed to predict which messages will be forwarded (i.e. retweeted). Similarly, [2] proposes a collaborative ranking approach to recommending Twitter messages to a user. Given a user u and an item i, the rating score can be predicted from a low dimensional representation of the users, $p_u \in \mathbb{R}^f$, and items, $q_i \in \mathbb{R}^f$:

$$\hat{y}_{u,i} = \mu + b_u + b_i + q_i^T p_u \qquad (5)$$

where μ is the overall average rating and b_u and b_i are respectively user and item bias on the score. This is an extension of a basic matrix factorization model which tries to separate the true interaction of items and users from biased variations in the data [1]. The authors then modify the model above in order to incorporate words w from the term set T_i of messages i:

$$\hat{y}_{u,i} = bias + p_u^T \left(\frac{1}{Z} \sum_{w \in T_i} q_w \right) \qquad (6)$$

where Z is the normalization term for features. The authors also propose other models incorporating other features available from Twitter.

3   Classifying Messages with No Interaction

Our task consists of filtering out messages likely to be ignored by users before they would be considered for publication on a social network account. This task can be considered as an initial step on a system aimed at recommending messages to a group of people following an account. In [9] we proposed such as system, called Groupmender, as depicted in Fig. 1. The system fetches news sources from any number of given urls. Based on collected preferences from users following the system's Groupmender account, it attempts to select and publish the set of news articles that will interest most users. An initial step in this selection process, therefore, could be the filtering of messages.

Given a set M of messages, we want to classify those that should not be published. We make the assumption that an "ignored" message is one that did not receive any feedback from users. For example, on Twitter, an "ignored" tweet would be one that was not retweeted by any of the account's followers. Similarly, on Facebook, an "ignored" status update would be one that did not receive any likes from the user's friends.

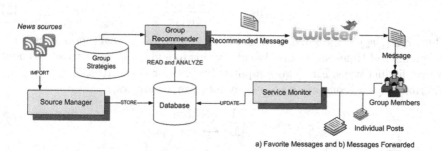

Fig. 1. Original architecture of the Groupmender system.

Assumption 1. An ignored message m published on a social network is one that did not receive any interaction $a \in A_m$ from other users ($A_m = \emptyset$).

This is a classification task where the positive labels are the messages without interactions. We use a Naive Bayes classifier to classify them into a positive or a negative class [11]. The algorithm takes as training set a feature matrix such as the ones described in Sect. 2 from labeled messages.

Our scenario is as follows. Given a social network account (e.g., a user on Twitter or Facebook) containing a set of messages M, we want to filter out the subset $B \subset M$ of messages where $\forall b \in B : A_b = \emptyset$. For that purpose we train a Naive Bayes classifier for that specific account. Our goal is to improve the classification task by improving the training model.

Initially, we use a simple tf-idf model as baseline. Given a social network account and its set of messages M, we extract the words from each message m_i and stem them. Next, we add the stemmed word w_i occurence to a term frequency vector $tf_m(w_i)$ for that message. The overall tf for the set of messages is computed as:

$$tf(w_i, m_i) = \frac{tf_m(w_i)}{max(tf_m(w_j) : w_j \in m_i)} \tag{7}$$

We compute the inverse document frequency idf using its traditional formula but we cache in $num(w_i)$ the number of messages m where word w_i occurs:

$$idf(w_i, M) = log\frac{|M|}{num(w_i)} \tag{8}$$

$$num(w_i) = |m : w_i \in m| \tag{9}$$

We do this to improve the performance of the computation. This way it is easy to expand the tf-idf model once a new message m' is added[3]:

$$num^*(w_i) = num(w_i) + 1 \rightarrow w_i \in m' \tag{10}$$

A simple improvement to the tf-idf model is to expand the set of words of a message with probable co-occurring words. Given a word w_1, we compute the probability of word w_2 occurring as:

$$p(w_2|w_1) = \frac{c(w_1, w_2)}{c(w_1)} \tag{11}$$

where $c(w_1, w_2)$ is the number of times w_1 and w_2 occur together and $c(w_1)$ is the number of times w_1 occurs. We apply this to a given social network account in two distinct ways. First, we compute $p(w_2|w_1)$ for all words $w \in m, \forall m \in M$. Alternatively, we compute $p(w_2|w_1)$ by message, as follows:

$$p(w_2|w_1) = \frac{1}{|M|} \sum_m \frac{c(w_1, w_2)_m}{c(w_1)_m} \tag{12}$$

---

[3] Note that we do not normalize our tf-idf model based on message length since all tend to have similar sizes [18].

Note that since all messages tend to be short, we consider all $\binom{|M|}{2}$ pairs of messages in the computation. Once this is done, given a word w_1 that occurs in message m, we add to the tf-idf model all the words w_2 where $p(w_2|w_1) > 0$:

$$\text{tf-idf}_{w_2,m} = \text{tf}_{w_1,m} \times \text{idf}_{w_1} \times p(w_2|w_1) \tag{13}$$

However, as [5] pointed out, $p(w_2|w_1)$ is zero for any w_1, w_2 pair that is not present in the corpus. In other words, this method does not capture latent relations between word pairs. Alternatively, [5] studies different similarity-based models for word cooccurrences. Their findings suggest that the Jensen-Shannon divergence performs the best. The method computes the semantic relatedness between two words according to their respective probability distribution. It is still considered the state-of-the-art for different applications [7,18] and we thus adopt it for computing the similarities between w_1 and w_2.

Given the time-sensitive nature of social networks, we also incorporate a time-decay factor determined empirically from our Twitter dataset described in Sect. 4.1. We assume that messages without any action for a longer period of time have less importance than more recent messages which did not have yet any actions from users.

Assumption 2. An older ignored message m has a higher probability of actually being ignored since most actions by users take place shortly after it was published.

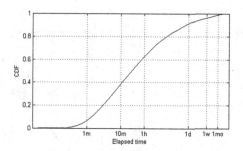

Fig. 2. Time difference between a published tweet and its first retweet.

Figure 2 shows the cumulative distribution function (CDF) of the time difference between a published tweet and its first retweet. Similar to the results of [8], it shows that over 60 % of retweeting occurs within the first hour after the original tweet was published. Over 90 % is within a day. When comparing with [8], it indicates that retweeting is occurring faster now than 2 years ago.

This distribution fits a log-normal distribution (standard error $\sigma_M < 0.01$; $\sigma_S < 0.01$) and we use it to model our time decay. Given the time elapsed t

between the original message and its first action a, the probability $p_m(a|t)$ of an action occurring on a message m is given by: s

$$p_m(a|t) = 1 - P(T \leq t) \qquad (14)$$

where $P(T \leq t)$ is the log-normal cumulative distribution function of elapsed times T with empirically estimated parameters $\mu = 7.55$ and $\sigma^2 = 2.61$. The lower the $p_m(a|t)$ is, the more likely the message is to be considered as ignored. Therefore, we add the inverse of $p_m(a|t)$ as an independent feature in our model.

4   Experiments

4.1   Experimental Setting

We test our method on a dataset from Twitter. We crawled a set of Twitter messages and associated information during one month, from september 17, 2011 until october 16, 2011. The crawler was built in a distributed configuration to increase performance since the Twitter API limits the number of requests per IP to 350/h. For each initial user crawled, we fetched all of his/her followers breadth-first up to two levels. Initial users were selected randomly using the "GET statuses/sample" API call [4]. To minimize API calls, we follow the results from [8] to filter out user accounts that are likely to be spam (those that follow over 10,000 other users) or inactive (those with less than 10 messages or less than 5 followers). In total, we crawled 137,095 accounts and 6,446,292 messages during the period.

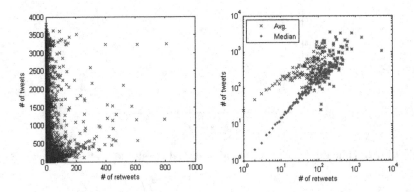

Fig. 3. Number of tweets vs. number of retweets of each Twitter account. The graph to the right shows the number of retweets in logscale and both the average and median number of tweets per log value.

Figure 3 plots the number of tweets and retweets for each of the accounts crawled. On the right side, the graph shows the number of retweets in logscale

---

[4] https://dev.twitter.com/docs/api/1/get/statuses/sample

and both the average and median number of tweets per log value. This shows that there is a correlation of tweets and retweets and, since the average is higher than the median, that there are outlier accounts which publish more tweets than expected given the number of retweets. Since many users publish a small number of tweets, we restrict ourselves to profiles that have at least 30 messages. In addition, many accounts have few or no tweets that were retweeted. So we similarly restrict ourselves to profiles that have at least 10 retweets.

This leaves us with 13,224 accounts to test our method, about 10 % of the original set. We test our method in each of these accounts individually. That is, for each individual account we proceed as follows:

1. We compute the account's tf-idf model and the modifications proposed in Sect. 3. We also compute the probability of action given the elapsed time $p_m(a|t)$. The result composes the feature matrix for the set of messages of the account.
2. We label all the tweets that did not have a retweet as "ignored", $B \subset M$, and all others as "candidates".
3. We split the feature matrix into training and test set. We experiment with 9 different training sizes, from 10 % to 90 % of the number of messages of the account. For each of these splits we:
4. Train the Naive Bayes classifier with the training set.
5. Test the classifier with the test set by computing its confusion matrix.

Once this done for each account, we aggregate the results in different manners. The overall results are presented in terms of precision and accuracy:

$$precision = \frac{tp}{tp + fp} \tag{15}$$

$$accuracy = \frac{tp + tn}{tp + tn + fp + fn} \tag{16}$$

where tp is the number of true positive messages, i.e., the messages correctly classified as "ignored", tn is the number of true negatives, fp is the number of false positives and fn is the number of false negatives.

We also test the following other models in order to compare our approach:

- **Twitter Message Features.** We train the classifier using features extracted from each individual message. These are its length, number of people mentioned, and number of tags. To evaluate the time decay, we test other two models. In the first, we compute a normalized time decay computed as $s(t_m) = (t_m - t_0)/max(\delta_t)$ where t_0 is the time of the most recent message and $max(\delta_t)$ is the time difference between the oldest message and the most recent one. In the second, we compute the $p_m(a|t)$ value for each message according to Eq. 14.
- **Okapi BM25.** We modify this ranking function [15] to compute the score of a word w in a tweet as a query Q:

$$S(Q = w) = idf_w \frac{tf_w \times (k_1 + 1)}{(tf_w + k_1 \times (1 - b + b \times \frac{N}{avgdl}))} \qquad (17)$$

where $k_1 = 1.2$ and $b = 0.75$ are parameters set to their standard values, and $avgdl$ is the average document length in the collection. We test the standard BM25 and a version expanded with co-occurrence of words by document using the formula from Eq. 12.

- **Web-Based Expansion.** We implement the approach described in Sect. 2, where the terms are expanded from search engine results. We query a search engine for each short message of a Twitter account and compute the tf-idf of the top-5 documents retrieved.

4.2   Results

Table 1 presents summary statistics for the accuracy results of the tested models. Mean values are computed across all Twitter accounts tested and all training sizes used. It shows slightly better performance overall for the tf-idf model expanded with the Jensen-Shannon method. All the methods to expand the tf-idf model performed better than the traditional tf-idf and BM25 models. After these two, the model with Twitter features follows with the third worse accuracy. Finally, the Web-based expansion method has slightly worse performance than the other methods of word expansion tested.

Table 1. Accuracy results for the different methods tested. *tfidfJS* is the tf-idf expanded with the Jensen-Shannon method, *tfidfCo* is expanded with the word co-occurrence probabilities from Eq. 11, *tfidfDoc* is expanded with the word co-occurrence probabilities by message from Eq. 12, *TwFeat* is the model with features from published messages and *WebExp* is Web-based expansion approach described in Sect. 2

	tfidfJS	tfidf	tfidfCo	tfidfDoc	BM25	BM25Doc	TwFeat	WebExp
Min	0.3339	0.1016	0.1016	0.1016	0.1016	0.1016	0.2607	0.2815
Q1	0.6078	0.3060	0.5150	0.6758	0.3060	0.6781	0.5886	0.5899
Median	0.7898	0.5731	0.5731	0.7761	0.5731	0.7745	0.6704	0.7308
Mean	0.7763	0.5310	0.5704	0.7557	0.5310	0.7560	0.6818	0.7422
Q3	0.9790	0.7158	0.6364	0.8787	0.7158	0.8786	0.7723	0.9222
Max	0.9999	0.9509	0.9867	0.9989	0.9509	0.9989	0.9882	0.9997
Std	0.1866	0.2438	0.1201	0.1661	0.2438	0.1657	0.1312	0.1811

Precision, on the other hand, as shown on Table 2 shows positive results for the tf-idf model expanded with the Jensen-Shannon method. Precision, in this case, measures how well the classifier identified the "ignored" tweets (i.e., the true positives), regardless of the classification of normal tweets (i.e., the true and false negatives). Classification using message features also has a high precision

Table 2. Precision results for the different methods tested.

	tfidfJS	tfidf	tfidfCo	tfidfDoc	BM25	BM25Doc	TwFeat	WebExp
Min	0.0079	0.0067	0.0256	0.0065	0.0205	0.0041	0.0159	0.0019
Q1	0.5542	0.1111	0.4308	0.1562	0.1112	0.1530	0.3920	0.2868
Median	0.8889	0.2146	0.5342	0.2552	0.2222	0.2552	0.5593	0.6047
Mean	0.7407	0.2189	0.5216	0.2839	0.2292	0.2829	0.5406	0.5875
Q3	1.0000	0.2222	0.6255	0.3843	0.2552	0.3825	0.7052	0.9017
Max	1.0000	0.6667	1.0000	1.0000	0.6667	1.0000	1.0000	1.0000
Std	0.3066	0.1564	0.1655	0.1691	0.1504	0.1695	0.2148	0.3241

compared with the poor accuracy performance. We show later in Fig. 8 that the classification using message features are further improved with the addition of a time decay factor. Note also the different standard deviation values of the models. Although the tf-idf model expanded with the Jensen-Shannon method has better accuracy and precision, its standard deviation is significantly higher than in most of the other models.

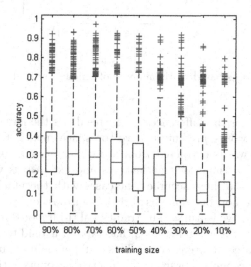

Fig. 4. Box plot showing the accuracy results for the different training set sizes tested.

Differences in the results across the different models and even within the models could be explained by different factors. First, a bigger training size yields better classification. Figure 4 shows the overall average accuracy over all models grouped by training size. The differences in the mean values, however, is relatively small between training sizes of 50 % and 90 % of the messages, and specially between 70 % and 90 %. A more significant drop is seen for training sizes of 40 % or smaller. One reason for these differences is the small number of retweets in many Twitter accounts as shown in Fig. 3. Hence, for training sets very small, there is a high a chance that no "ignored" messages are included in them. Similarly, for very large training sets, chances are that all "ignored" messages are included in them, simplifying the classification of the test set for those cases.

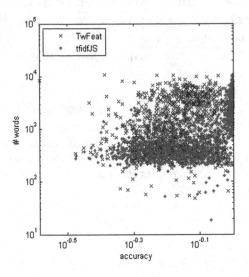

Fig. 5. Accuracy results based on the number of unique words of a Twitter account.

Another reason for the differences in the results is the large variation in the number of unique words present in a vector space model. Figure 5 plots the number of unique words extracted from a Twitter account and the accuracy values for the model using message features and expansions with the Jensen-Shannon method. Note how accuracy increases with the number of words for Jensen-Shannon method but remains varied, regardless of the number of words for the model of message features. The traditional tf-idf model remains limited to the original set of words while methods that expand it tend to improve over the addition of new related or latent words. This could explain the poor performance of certain types of accounts. For example, inactive accounts with few but similar messages and spam accounts that repeat the publication of similar messages are more difficult to model because the number of unique words tends to be small Fig 6.

A third reason that helps explain the variations in the results is the total number of messages published in a Twitter account as shown in Fig. 7. The plots are in log scale and represent respectively the average accuracy and average precision per number of messages. In almost all cases, accuracy and precision are higher in Twitter accounts with more messages published. The notable exceptions are the accuracy and precision of the tf-idf model and the precision of the tf-idf model

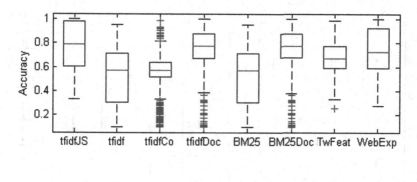

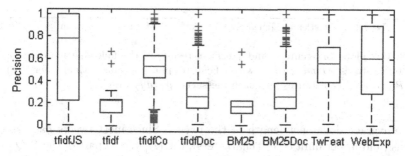

Fig. 6. Box plots for accuracy and precision results of the tested models.

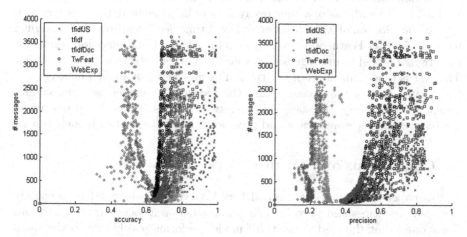

Fig. 7. Accuracy and precision results of the tested models according to the number of messages of each account.

expanded with co-occurrency by document. The poorer performance of the tf-idf could indicate that the extra messages do not add relevant extra features for the classification. These new features could be helpful to identify related or latent features in other models but may not be useful by itself. In the specific case of the BM25 approach, the similar results to the tf-idf models could be explained

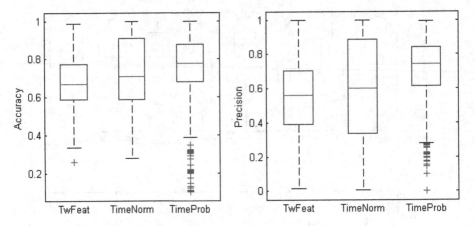

Fig. 8. Box plots for accuracy and precision results of the following models: *TwFeat* (Twitter Features), *TimeNorm* (Twitter Features plus normalized time difference) and *TimeProb* (Twitter Features plus each message's $p_m(a|t)$ value).

by the average document length of the tweets. Since most tweets have similar lengths (and upper limit of 140 characters), the $(N/avgdl)$ part of the $S(Q = w)$ score remains relatively unchanged. The score, then, boils down to a tf-idf model with parameters that do not seem to influence much the results.

Finally, the addition of a time decay feature helps improve the classification. To test the addition of it, we test two different time decay features on the original model of Twitter Features. Figure 8 shows the accuracy and precision results for the original model of message features and two other with time decay features. The first is a normalization of the time difference between a given message and the most recent of that account and the second, our model, is a probability measure of how likely a message is to be retweeted. Results show that our model has on average better accuracy and precision that the other two models tested.

5   Conclusions and Future Work

In this paper we proposed a method based on vector space models to classify "ignored" messages and prevent their publication on a social network account. We showed that the traditional tf-idf model performs poorly due to the small amount of messages in each account but it can be improved with different expansion techniques. We also tested different time decay parameters and showed that our model determined empirically from a Twitter dataset performs best. Overall, it is feasible to train a classifier for this task and reduce the amount of messages to evaluated for a recommendation process.

In future works, we plan to extend our method testing it with different feature selection algorithms. Furthermore, feature reduction could be performed with co-occurence cluster analysis where attained clusters would represent latent topics. These would result into low-dimensional vector space with more dense feature vectors that could help improve the classification further. We also plan to test how this classification could affect ranking algorithms aimed at recommending messages on a social network account.

References

1. Bell, R., Volinsky, C., Koren, Y.: Matrix factorization techniques for recommender systems. IEEE Comput. **42**(8), 30–37 (2009)
2. Chen, K., Chen, T., Zheng, G., Jin, O., Yao, E., Yu, Y.: Collaborative personalized tweet recommendation. In: Proceedings of the 35th international ACM SIGIR conference on Research and Development in Information Retrieval, pp. 661–670. SIGIR '12, ACM, New York (2012). http://doi.acm.org/10.1145/2348283.2348372
3. Chen, M., Jin, X., Shen, D.: Short text classification improved by learning multi-granularity topics. In: Proceedings of the 22nd International Joint Conference on Artificial Intelligence, IJCAI'11, vol. 3, pp. 1776–1781. AAAI Press (2011). http://dx.doi.org/10.5591/978-1-57735-516-8/IJCAI11-298
4. Combarro, E., Montanes, E., Diaz, I., Ranilla, J., Mones, R.: Introducing a family of linear measures for feature selection in text categorization. IEEE Trans. Knowl. Data Eng. **17**(9), 1223–1232 (2005)
5. Dagan, I., Lee, L., Pereira, F.C.N.: Similarity-based models of word cooccurrence probabilities. Mach. Learn. **34**(1–3), 43–69 (1999). doi:10.1023/A:1007537716579
6. Díaz, I., Ranilla, J., Montañes, E., Fernández, J., Combarro, E.: Improving performance of text categorization by combining filtering and support vector machines. J. Am. Soc. Inf. Sci. Technol. **55**(7), 579–592 (2004)
7. Halawi, G., Dror, G., Gabrilovich, E., Koren, Y.: Large-scale learning of word relatedness with constraints. In: Proceedings of the 18th ACM SIGKDD International Conference on Knowledge Discovery and Data Mining, KDD '12, pp. 1406–1414. ACM, New York (2012). http://doi.acm.org.zorac.aub.aau.dk/10.1145/2339530.2339751
8. Kwak, H., Lee, C., Park, H., Moon, S.: What is twitter, a social network or a news media? In: Proceedings of the 19th International Conference on World Wide Web, pp. 591–600. ACM, Raleigh (2010). http://portal.acm.org/citation.cfm?id=1772690.1772751
9. Lage, R., Durao, F., Dolog, P.: Towards effective group recommendations for microblogging users. In: Proceedings of the 27th Annual ACM Symposium on Applied Computing, SAC '12, pp. 923–928. ACM, New York (2012). http://doi.acm.org/10.1145/2245276.2245456
10. Lan, M., Tan, C.L., Low, H.B., Sung, S.Y.: A comprehensive comparative study on term weighting schemes for text categorization with support vector machines. In: Special Interest Tracks and Posters of the 14th International Conference on World Wide Web, WWW '05, pp. 1032–1033. ACM, New York (2005) http://doi.acm.org.zorac.aub.aau.dk/10.1145/1062745.1062854
11. Lewis, D.D.: Naive (Bayes) at forty: the independence assumption in information retrieval. In: Nédellec, C., Rouveirol, C. (eds.) ECML 1998. LNCS, vol. 1398, pp. 4–15. Springer, Heidelberg (1998)
12. Lin, J., Mishne, G.: A study of "Churn" in tweets and real-time search queries. In: 6th International AAAI Conference on Weblogs and Social Media, May 2012. http://www.aaai.org/ocs/index.php/ICWSM/ICWSM12/paper/view/4599

13. Mladenic, D., Grobelnik, M.: Feature selection for unbalanced class distribution and naive Bayes. In: Machine Learning-International Workshop then Conference, pp. 258–267. Morgan Kaufmann Publishers, INC (1999)
14. Petrovic, S., Osborne, M., Lavrenko, V.: RT to win! predicting message propagation in twitter. In: 5th International AAAI Conference on Weblogs and Social Media, May 2011. http://www.aaai.org/ocs/index.php/ICWSM/ICWSM11/paper/view/2754
15. Robertson, S.E., Walker, S., Beaulieu, M., Willett, P.: Okapi at TREC-7: automatic ad hoc, filtering, VLC and interactive track. In: TREC, pp. 199–210 (1998)
16. Sahami, M., Heilman, T.D.: A web-based kernel function for measuring the similarity of short text snippets. In: Proceedings of the 15th International Conference on World Wide Web, WWW '06, pp. 377–386. ACM, New York (2006). http://doi.acm.org/10.1145/1135777.1135834
17. Sun, A.: Short text classification using very few words. In: Proceedings of the 35th International ACM SIGIR Conference on Research and Development in Information Retrieval, SIGIR '12, pp. 1145–1146. ACM, New York (2012). http://doi.acm.org/10.1145/2348283.2348511
18. Turney, P.D., Pantel, P.: From frequency to meaning: vector space models of semantics. J. Artif. Intell. Res. **37**, 141–188 (2010). http://arxiv.org/abs/1003.1141. arXiv:1003.1141
19. Yang, Y., Pedersen, J.: A comparative study on feature selection in text categorization. In: Machine Learning-International Workshop then Conference, pp. 412–420. Morgan Kaufmann Publishers, INC. (1997)
20. Yih, W.T., Goodman, J., Carvalho, V.R.: Finding advertising keywords on web pages. In: Proceedings of the 15th International Conference on World Wide Web, WWW '06, pp. 213–222. ACM, New York (2006). http://doi.acm.org/10.1145/1135777.1135813
21. Yih, W.T., Meek, C.: Improving similarity measures for short segments of text. In: Proceedings of the 22nd National Conference on Artificial Intelligence AAAI'07, vol. 2, pp. 1489–1494. AAAI Press (2007). http://dl.acm.org.zorac.aub.aau.dk/citation.cfm?id=1619797.1619884

FactRunner: A New System for NLP-Based Information Extraction from Wikipedia

Rhio Sutoyo[1,2]([✉]), Christoph Quix[3,4], and Fisnik Kastrati[3]

[1] School of Computer Science, Bina Nusantara University, Jakarta, Indonesia
rsutoyo@binus.edu
[2] Thai-German Graduate School of Engineering,
King Mongkut's University of Technology North Bangkok, Bangkok, Thailand
[3] Information Systems and Databases, RWTH Aachen University, Aachen, Germany
quix@dbis.rwth-aachen.de, fkastrati@gmail.com
[4] Fraunhofer Institute for Applied Information Technology FIT,
St. Augustin, Germany

Abstract. Wikipedia is playing an increasing role as a source of human-readable knowledge, because it contains an enormous amount of high quality information written by human authors. Finding a relevant piece of information in this huge collection of natural language text is often a time-consuming process, as a keyword-based search interface is the main method for querying. Therefore, an iterative process to explore the document collection to find the information of interest is required. In this paper, we present an approach to extract structured information from unstructured documents to enable structured queries. Information Extraction (IE) systems have been proposed for this tasks, but due to the complexity of natural language, they often produce unsatisfying results.

As Wikipedia contains, in addition to the plain natural language text, links between documents and other metadata, we propose an approach which exploits this information to extract more accurate structured information. Our proposed system *FactRunner* focusses on extracting structured information from sentences containing such links, because the links may indicate more accurate information than other sentences. We evaluated our system with a subset of documents from Wikipedia and compared the results with another existing system. The results show that a natural language parser combined with Wikipedia markup can be exploited for extracting facts in form of triple statements with a high accuracy.

Keywords: Information extraction · Semantic search

1 Introduction

Managing structured information as, for example, in relational database systems (RDBMS) has been the main method for information management in the recent decades. With the growing popularity of the World Wide Web (WWW), a huge

© Springer-Verlag Berlin Heidelberg 2014
K.-H. Krempels and A. Stocker (Eds.): WEBIST 2013, LNBIP 189, pp. 225–240, 2014.
DOI: 10.1007/978-3-662-44300-2_14

amount of data collections in form of unstructured and semi-structured sources became available (e.g., webpages, newspaper articles, blogs, scientific publication repositories, etc.). These sources contain useful information which can be easily read and understood by humans. Wikipedia is a good example of this case; with more than 3.8 million articles, it has become one of the main sources of human-readable knowledge repository in the modern information era.

Keyword search is still the dominating way of search in large document collections. Keyword search is quite efficient from a system-oriented point-of-view (relevant documents can be found very quickly using a traditional keyword-based search engine) and user friendly (users do not have to learn a query language such as SQL). However, finding a certain piece of information is often an iterative, time-consuming process of keyword searches. An initial set of keywords is tried first; if relevant documents are returned, then the user has to read parts of the retrieved documents in order to find the information of interest. If the answer is not found, the user has to refine her query, and look for other documents which might contain the answer. This process of querying, reading, and refining might have to be repeated several times until a satisfying answer is found.

Therefore, the search process would be simplified if it could be supported, at least partially, by some system that actually understands the semantics of the searched data. Such systems are called semantic search engines and various approaches have been proposed [1,2]. They range from approaches which replace the original keywords with semantically related terms (e.g., [3]) to more complex approaches which require a query in a formal language as well as semantically annotated data (e.g., SPARQL endpoints for Linked Data [4]).

The latter search paradigm is geared towards data retrieval as the system is only able to answer concepts or documents which contain semantic annotations. This is fine as long as the documents have been annotated with semantic information (e.g., RDF statements). However, most information which is available today is stored in unstructured text documents which do not contain semantic annotations. Annotating the entire web, is at this time an unattainable task. Web documents, in contrast to plain text documents, contain other useful information such as links, tables, and images. Especially, links connecting documents can be exploited to extract more accurate information from text documents. We apply this idea to the Wikipedia collection.

The task of converting information contained in document collections into formal knowledge is addressed in the research area of Information Extraction (IE), but it is still an unsolved problem. Approaches such as Open Information Extraction [5] are able to extract information in form of triples (e.g., statements of the form subject – predicate – object) from unstructured documents, but the extracted triples require more consolidation, normalization and linkage to existing knowledge to become useful to the extend where one could find information of interest by means of simple queries. In order to fulfill such an aim at a large scale (such as world wide web), this task has to be done in unsupervised and fully-automatic manner. A particular challenge for information extraction from Wikipedia articles is the lack of redundancy of sentences describing a particular fact.

Redundancy has been greatly leveraged by systems that perform IE over the web (e.g., TextRunner [5] and KnowItAll [6]) to increase their quality of extracted facts. Furthermore, redundancy is important for the scoring model as frequently occurring facts get a higher score, i.e., these facts are assumed to be correctly extracted with a high probability. A strong scoring model is fundamental towards ensuring the accuracy of the extractor (i.e., for filtering out incorrect triples). This is not the case with Wikipedia, as articles generally address only one topic, and there are no other articles addressing the same topic. This feature reduces information redundancy greatly; if a fact is missed while extracting information from one article, the probability is very low that the same fact will be encountered in other articles.

The contribution of this paper is a novel system called *FactRunner* for open fact extraction from Wikipedia. The primary goal of this system is to extract high quality information present in Wikipedia's natural language text. Our approach is complementary to other approaches which extract structured information from Wikipedia infoboxes [7] or the category system [8]. Our method utilizes the existing metadata present in Wikipedia articles (i.e., links between articles) to extract facts with high accuracy from Wikipedia's English natural language text. Extracted facts are stored in form of triples (subject, predicate, object), where a triple is a relation between subjects and objects that is connected by a predicate [9]. These triples can then later be queried using structured queries, and thereby enabling the integration of structured and unstructured data [10].

The paper is structured as follows. We first present in Sect. 2 the main components of our system. Section 3 describes the preprocessing step of our system, which actually does most of the work for the triple extraction, as it simplifies and normalizes the natural language text input. Because of this simplification, the triple extraction method (Sect. 4) is quite simple compared to the preprocessing steps. Section 5 then presents the evaluation results for our system which we applied to a subset of documents from Wikipedia. Related work is discussed in Sect. 6 before we conclude our paper.

2   System Overview

Wikipedia contains a vast amount of information stored in natural text. There is much valuable information hidden in such text, but computers cannot directly reason over the natural text. Wikipedia is designed to be read by humans. To tackle this problem, we introduce a solution which utilizes Wikipedia metadata to detect high quality sentences in the Wikipedia data and extract valuable facts from those sentences. Metadata surrounds important text fragments located in Wikipedia articles. Metadata provides a link pointing to separate Wikipedia articles devoted to the highlighted text, this way giving more information (e.g., general definition, biography, history, etc.), and emphasizing the importance of such text. Wikipedia contributors have invested efforts to create such metadata, and they inserted them manually, giving a good hint on importance of such fragments. To this end, we treat metadata as an indicator of

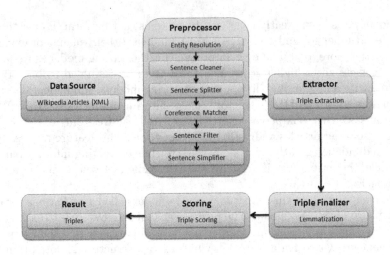

Fig. 1. System architecture.

importance of sentences where they occur, and we invest efforts into exploiting such sentences, with the ultimate goal of producing high quality triples.

The system architecture of our system is represented in Fig. 1. The architecture consists of six components, namely, the data source, the preprocessor, the extractor, the triple finalizer, the scoring, and the result producer. The main components are the preprocessor and the triple extractor. The preprocessor does most of the work; it prepares the natural language text in such a way that the extractor can easily extract the triples from the transformed input. Preprocessor and triple extractor will be described in more detail in Sects. 3 and 4.

2.1   Data Source

While YAGO [11] exploits the Wikipedia category system and KYLIN [7] uses Wikipedia infoboxes as their data source for extracting facts, we use the natural language text of Wikipedia articles because there are more facts embedded in the text. Furthermore, not all Wikipedia articles have infoboxes because the use of infoboxes in Wikipedia articles is optional. Thus, although the idea of providing articles' general information through Wikipedia infoboxes is favorable, many Wikipedia articles do not have infoboxes. On the other hand, most Wikipedia articles belong typically to one or more categories. Unfortunately, these categories are usually defined for quite general classes and are not as detailed as a classification which can be found in Wikipedia's natural language text. Another reason for choosing Wikipedia is that the articles are rich with markup around text fragments that can be utilized to extract facts with a higher precision.

3   Preprocessor

The preprocessor is responsible for generating a set of sentences to be passed to our triple extractor. There are six steps, which are explained in the following subsections.

3.1   Entity Resolution

Entity resolution is a component in our system that utilizes metadata in order to synchronize multiple occurrences of the same entity expressed with different textual representations, e.g., "Albert Einstein" vs. "A. Einstein" . This component is invaluable towards reconciling different variants of an entity representation. For all cases, we always replace entities with their longest text representation in order to preserve information. In our current approach, we consider for reconciliation only entities corresponding to persons.

3.2   Sentence Cleaner

This component is responsible for cleaning sentences in articles from brackets and similar text fragments. We realized during the testing of our system that words inside brackets are often supplementary facts which give additional details about the words occurring before the brackets. Moreover, it is also difficult for the triple extractor to understand linguistically the semantic relationship of the brackets and to correctly extract facts from them. Furthermore, we also extract metadata from the articles before we remove them completely from the texts. For each entity surrounded with metadata, we store its textual representation and its URL, e.g., `<harry potter, http://en.wikipedia.org/wiki/Harry_Potter>`, into our metadata collection. This collection will be later used to remove unwanted sentences in the filtering process.

3.3   Sentence Splitter

After the text is filtered and cleaned, we split our input from paragraphs into a set of sentence chunks. Generally, one sentence may contain one or more triples. Sentence splitting is a crucial process towards ensuring that only qualitative sentences are fed to the system, this way ensuring triple extraction with higher precision. For this purpose, we rely on the sentence detection library provided by LingPipe[1].

3.4   Coreference Matcher

The need for coreferencing surfaces when multiple entities or pronoun words in a text refer to the same entity or have the same referent. In the first sentence of Wikipedia articles, an author typically introduces a person or an object with

---

[1] http://alias-i.com/lingpipe

his full name (e.g., Albert Einstein). Then, in the following sentences the writer will begin using a substitute word (e.g., he, his, him, Einstein) for that person. Building the connection between these entities, e.g., *Albert Einstein* and *Einstein*, is what we refer to as coreferencing. Triples extracted from sentences with coreferences are fuzzy, because the context of the sentence is lost once the triple has been extracted. Even a human cannot understand the meaning of a triple such as (he,received,Nobel Prize in Physics) without a given context. Thus, we need to replace entities that have different representation forms into one single representation, i.e., full name. In order to do so, we apply the LingPipe's coreference resolution tool.

Although the purpose of the coreference matcher is similar with the entity resolution, which is to synchronize different associated entities into the same representation form, they work in a different way. In our approach, entity resolution only affects entities which are marked as links. Such links have been entered by humans manually and are highly accurate, therefore they can be used to correctly replace entities to their original representation (i.e., the title of the article describing the entity). On the other hand, the coreference matcher is able to catch entities which are not covered with metadata including pronoun words. However, its accuracy might not be as precise as entity resolution because LingPipe's coreferencer is a machine-based prediction system.

3.5   Sentence Filter

We remove invalid sentences which are caused either by the sentence splitting tool or by human errors. For example, sentences that do not start with a proper text or end with inappropriate punctuation symbols are ignored. Furthermore, we also exclude sentences which have a length over the defined threshold. This step is necessary as with a deep parsing techniques that we employ, long sentences demand high memory resources, and they ultimately slow down significantly the runtime of the whole system. This is a system constraint, our algorithm nevertheless supports long sentences given that the system has enough resources. Sentences with less than three words are removed as well, because a sentence at least needs to have a subject, a predicate, and an object to form a proper triple. After making sure that all sentences are valid by employing the above mentioned methods, we use the extracted metadata provided by the sentence cleaner to use those sentences with metadata only for triple extraction. Based on our observations, sentences with metadata are more likely to produce high quality triples.

3.6   Sentence Simplifier

An important step towards improving the performance of the system is sentence simplification. The purpose of this step is to split complex sentences into subsentences. Wikipedia authors sometimes use rich stylish writing (e.g., list of items, dependent clauses, etc.) this way making some sentences complex and hard to understand. Therefore, complex sentences need to be simplified in order to produce simple and clear triples as final result. We borrow the concept of sentence simplification processes from [12].

We utilize the Stanford parser [13] to get the grammatical structure of sentences. The result of this parsing tool is a parse tree which will distinguish noun phrases (NP), verb phrases (VP), and group of words that belong together (e.g., dependent clauses (SBAR), prepositional phrases (PP), etc.) in the sentences. We use the generated parse tree to understand the correlation between words in a sentence and to split the sentences correctly. Nevertheless, parsing of natural language text is a challenge for any kind of NLP tool. Thus, not all generated parse trees are correct. Because our simplification process is really dependent on parse trees, the simplification results will be wrong if the provided parse trees are wrong. However, the overall results of this step are still decent and useful for the extraction process.

The sentence simplification has four steps:

Split Coordinating Conjunctions. Coordinating conjunctions are words like "and", "or", and "but" which are used in enumerations or to connect sub-sentences. An example from Albert Einstein's Wikipedia article is: '*his travels included Singapore, Ceylon, and Japan.*' As we aim at supporting structured queries, we should extract three triples from this sentence and not only one. This would enable us to answer a question like 'Who travelled to Ceylon?' and not only the question 'Who travelled to Singapore, Ceylon, and Japan?'. Such simple enumerations could be still handled in a post-processing after the triples have been extracted, but we also want to handle more complex sentences like '*Welker and his department paved the way for microwave semiconductors and laser diodes*' (from the Wikipedia article about Heinrich Welker). The coreferencing step described above transforms 'his' into 'Welker's'. To extract the complete factual information from this sentence, we have to extract four triples from the sentence which correspond to the following statements:

- *Welker paved the way for microwave semiconductors.*
- *Welker paved the way for laser diodes.*
- *Welker's department paved the way for microwave semiconductors.*
- *Welker's department paved the way for laser diodes.*

Metadata in this step are used to filter text fragments. If a text fragment is a link to another article, then this text fragment is not processed by this method.

Extract Dependent Clauses. In this simplification step, we will separate a dependent clause (SBAR in the terminology of the Stanford parser) from its main clause and create a new sentence which contains the SBAR clause and the subject from its main clause. There are two types of SBAR clauses: subordinate conjunctions (for adverbial clauses) and relative pronouns (for relative clauses) [12]. Our approach handles each type differently. The first type will be extracted into sub-sentence modifiers, while the second type will create a new sentence. Sub-sentence modifier is a part of sentences that generally explain more about the main idea of the sentences. In order to produce simple triples, we need to separate these modifiers from the sentences. We attach these modifiers to the main sentences using the concept of *zero-to-many* to preserve the connection of the sentences and their modifiers. Hence, one sentence could have zero or more sub-sentence modifiers. Nevertheless, we will not discuss further about these modifiers because the focus of this work is triples. With extract dependent clauses, the sentence *'Albert Einstein also investigated the thermal properties of light which laid the foundation of the photon theory of light.'* that contains a relative clause is translated into *'Albert Einstein also investigated the thermal properties of light.'* and *'The thermal properties of light laid the foundation of the photon theory of light.'* Nevertheless, there are some cases where the relative pronoun (for relative clauses) twists the true meaning of sentences. For example, the second sub-sentence of the sentence "Anarchism is a political philosophy which considers the state undesirable." is "Political philosophy considers the state undesirable". This result is true when viewed only from its grammatical structure, but the meaning of the sentence become inverted and wrong. In order to avoid these kinds of results, we add the subject and the predicate from their first sub-sentence to the second sub-sentence as an additional subject. This exception is applied if the predicate of the first sub-sentence is a *to be* ("am", "is", "are", "was", or "were") forms. Thus, the final result of the triple from the second sub-sentence is: ((Anarchism is) political philosophy, considers, state undesirable).

Extract Adjective Phrases. In this step, we extract adjective phrases from their main phrase. Adjective phrases generally appear in the middle of two phrases, i.e., a noun phrase and verb phrase, which are separated by comma. Adjective phrases could be a noun phrase (e.g., *'Planck's oldest son, Karl Weierstrass, was killed in action in 1916.'*) or a verb phrase (e.g., *'Jacques Vergs, born 5 March 1925 in Siam, is a French lawyer...'*. We handle those two cases differently. For the noun phrases, we extract them from their main sentence and make them as the subject in the new sentence (e.g., we would get *'Planck's oldest son was killed...'* and *'Karl Weierstrass was killed...'*). Verb phrases will be used as the predicate (including the object) in the new sentence (e.g., *'Jacques Vergs born 5 March 1925 in Siam.'* and *'Jacques Vergs is a French lawyer...'*).

Extract Secondary Verbs. Finally, we extract all secondary verbs from the given sentences. These kinds of sentences contain two verb phrases with the same noun phrase. The second verb phrase is nested in the first verb phrase (e.g., *'Amy Lee Grant is an American singer-songwriter, best known for Amy Lee Grant's Christian music.'* would be translated into *'Amy Lee Grant is an American singer-songwriter.'* and *'Amy Lee Grant best known for her Christian music.'*

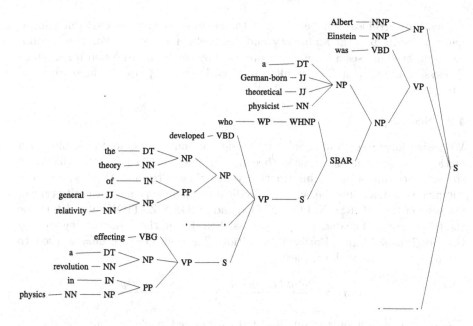

Fig. 2. Phrase structure tree.

4   Extractor

Triple extractor is responsible for extracting facts and representing them in the form of triples. Triples are stored in the form of (subject, predicate, object). We extract the triples by using the parse tree approach introduced in [9]. We use the Stanford parser [13] to generate the parse tree. The main idea of this approach is to utilize the parse tree as a helping tool to extract subjects, predicates, and objects from sentences, then combine them to produce a triple. In order to find the subject of a sentence, we have to search for it in the noun phrase (NP) tree. Furthermore, the predicate and the object of a sentence can be found in the verb phrase (VP) tree (Fig. 2).

By applying the simplification method of extracting dependent clauses and extracting secondary verbs described above, we get these following results for the sentence '*Albert Einstein was a German-born theoretical physicist who developed the theory of general relativity, effecting a revolution in physics.*':

- (Albert Einstein, was, German-born theoretical physicist)
- ((Albert Einstein was) German-born theoretical physicist, developed, theory of general relativity)
- ((Albert Einstein was) German-born theoretical physicist, effecting, revolution in physics)

4.1   Triple Finalizer

The triple finalizer converts the predicates of the triple results into their lemmatized form. The lemmatized form is a base form of a verb, for example, the word *receiving* or *received* will be changed to the word *receive* as its lemma form. Lemma results prevent ambiguity and are useful for queries. For this component, our system uses a lemmatizer provided by the Stanford Natural Language Processing Group [14]. The results produced in this step are the final triples of our system.

4.2 Scoring

We assign lower scores for triples which do not contain metadata. Triples with metadata deserve a higher score because the metadata ensure the quality of the sentence and also the information which they surround. Furthermore, the completeness of a triple (i.e. subject, predicate, and object) and the entity type of the subject (i.e., PERSON, LOCATION, and ORGANIZATION) also determine the triple scores. The entity types are assigned during the coreferencing step by the LingPipe's Named Entity Recognition. The following formula is used to compute the score of the triples:

$$score = \frac{metadata + completeness + entity}{3}$$

The score is a hint on the quality of the extracted triple; it could be used in further processing steps (e.g., in ranking results of a structured query). However, this was not the focus of our work, and we are aware that a more sophisticated scoring mechanism might be required which includes more factors that indicate the quality of the extracted triple. This is an issue which we intend to address in future work.

5 Evaluation

We have performed system evaluation in two directions: a user-based evaluation (Sects. 5.1 and 5.2) and a system-based evaluation which compares our system with a state-of-the-art IE system: ReVerb [15] (Sect. 5.3). ReVerb performs open information extraction and has shown very good performance.

5.1 User-Based Evaluation: Setup and Dataset

Wish user-based evaluation we verify the correctness of the extracted triples, as our goal is extracting high quality triples. As there is no golden standard for the task of triple extraction over Wikipedia, we had to take a subset of documents from the english version of Wikipedia, apply the FactRunner algorithm, and rate the correctness of the extracted triples manually. In order to avoid a very subjective rating of correctness of the extracted triples, several users were involved in the evaluation. A triple was considered as correct when all users agreed on its correctness.

The evaluation was done using a web-based interface. For each sentence, the list of extracted triples was presented. For each triple, the user could state whether the triple is correct or not. As stated before, we consider only correctness

Table 1. Statistics of the dataset and the extracted triples.

	American Actors	American Physicists
# Articles	2,483	1,298
Total # triples	51,088	26,967
Triples with full score	39,313	19,975
Contains entity	46,735	23,394
Contains metadata	42,140	22,524
Triple completeness	48,510	25,587

and not completeness; therefore, we did not ask the user for other triples that could have been extracted from the sentence.

We conducted our evaluation by using two categories of articles in Wikipedia: *American Actors* and *American Physicists*. Table 1 summarises the statistics about the dataset and the extracted triples.

5.2   User-Based Evaluation: Results

For the user-based evaluation, we picked randomly 15 articles from each category as the predefined documents that we presented to the users. The overview of this evaluation is shown in Fig. 3. The y-axis of the figure shows the number of triples extracted (total, correct, and incorrect). The average precision of the used-based evaluation system is 77 %. It shows promising result where 6 from 30 predefined articles have precision equal or greater than 90 %. We believe the complex process of the sentence preprocessing, especially the sentence filtering and the sentence simplifier component, are the main reason for this high score. Nevertheless, three articles from our datasets scored a precision below than 60 %. After we looked into our result, we found that the main reason for this low precision is because the subjects of the triples are not clear (e.g., he, she, her, these, their, etc.). The reason for this is that the coreference matcher failed to map pronoun words into the corresponding entities in subjects of the triples. This resulted with vague triples, therefore the users were confused and evaluated those triples as incorrect.

5.3   System-Based Evaluation

Table 2 summarises the results of the comparison of our system with ReVerb. The dataset is the same as for the user-based evaluation. The numbers show how many triples our system was able to extract for the dataset in contrast to ReVerb. Thus, it is indicator for the recall of the system; however, computing exact recall values for such a large dataset is a very tedious and time consuming process, therefore exact computation of the recall value is not possible. Although we used the same datasets for both systems, our system considered only sentences which have metadata and are shorter than 200 characters. Thus, the number of sentences considered by our system is smaller than that in ReVerb. The evaluation

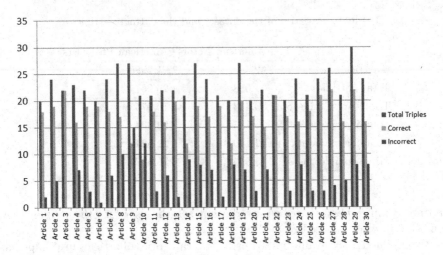

Fig. 3. Overview of user-based evaluation.

Table 2. Comparison of FactRunner and ReVerb.

	FactRunner		ReVerb	
	American Actor	American Physicist	American Actor	American Physicist
# Articles	2,483	1,298	2,483	1,298
# Considered sentences	27,489	15,371	40,760	25,625
# Extracted triples	51,088	26,967	52,817	33,620
Triples/sentence	1.86	1.75	1.30	1.31

shows that both systems are able to extract multiple facts from one sentence. In average, FactRunner is able to extract 1.81 triple/sentence and ReVerb is able to extract 1.3 triple/sentence. Thus, our system is able to extract more triples with fewer sentences. The reason behind this result is that FactRunner uses a deep-parsing technique in order to extract its triples. However, the cost of this technique is a slow processing speed (about 7–8 times slower than ReVerb on the same machine).

5.4 Performance

We tested our system on a PC with a installed Windows XP 64 bit, and CPU Intel Core2 Quad (2.83 GHz), with 8 GB RAM. The system is implemented in Java and uses the aforementioned libraries (LingPipe, Stanford Parser, etc.). Due to the heavy NLP processing for parsing the texts, our system needs about 3 s to process one document. The runtimes for the American actors dataset were about 128 min, and about 64 min for the American physicists dataset. This results in

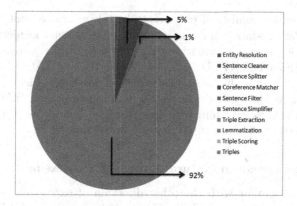

Fig. 4. Distribution of processing time.

an average time of about 20 documents per minute, or 3 s per document. In contrast, ReVerb achieved a value of about 160 documents per minute. However, we must emphasize that the performance was not yet the focus of our system. For example, we do not make use of the multicore CPU by using parallel threads. Parallelization or distribution in a cluster of the application would be easily possible, because each document can be processed independently, in this context, a Hadoop style processing would be very much applicable using convenient machines.

Figure 4 shows the distribution of the processing time for each step of the FactRunner system. Most of the time goes in the sentence simplification because it requires the analysis of the natural language text (deep parsing) using an NLP tool. Nevertheless, the additional effort pays off as the extraction is simplified to a great extend. In a previous version of the system, the extractor required much more resources because it had to apply the NLP techniques on more complex sentences.

6 Related Work

There are two major bodies of work in the area of information extraction (IE). The first body of work relies on pattern-based techniques, whereas the second relies on natural language processing methods.

6.1 Pattern-Based Techniques

The pattern-based techniques, as the term implies, are techniques used to identify patterns in order to extract information in the target corpus. Patterns are skeletal frames of text fragments which can be used to extract relations in a given text corpus. Such pattern-based extraction systems are able to extract relations if a given pattern is matched with an existing relation in the document collection [16]. Before the extraction process, pattern-based techniques generally need to prepare a limited number of patterns to be taken into account in the extraction process. Pattern-based approaches perform well when considering precision, but they cannot capture information that does not use the predefined patterns. KnowItAll [6], Snowball [17], DIPRE [18], WOE [19], and YAGO [11] are all successful existing systems which use this extraction paradigm. The YAGO ontology uses Wikipedia as their source, as we do it in our approach. YAGO combines the Wikipedia category system with the WordNet lexical ontology in order to extract information which in turn creates a larger ontology.

6.2   Methods Based on Natural Language Processing

Our approach is similar with the other direction of extraction technique, i.e., natural language processing (NLP). This technique relies on NLP tools which focus on analyzing natural language text. The NLP approach is able to handle an unbounded number of relations because it does *pattern recognition* and not *pattern matching*. An NLP-based approach can capture a large amount of information from many sources, for instance the World Wide Web. Nevertheless, natural language processing is a complex and ambiguous process. To the best of our knowledge, there are no NLP tools that can perfectly understand natural language text, thus resulting errors cannot be avoided. Our approach is a combination of NLP techniques, as well as proliferation of the already existing metadata in the text, in order to perform a precise relation extraction from English natural text.

TextRunner [5] is a good example showing the benefits of NLP-based techniques. It is assembled based on the idea of Open Information Extraction (OIE) paradigm. OIE is a newly developed approach of information extraction system that could provide relation independence and high scalability, handling a large corpus such as the Web corpus. Similar to our approach, TextRunner is able to extract information from a vast variety of relations located in a given corpus with only a single pass. However, our approach is mainly targeting Wikipedia articles and its metadata; not the World Wide Web. In short, our goal is to further enhance the extraction process by utilizing the already existing metadata available in the Wikipedia collections.

Another good representative of the NLP-based approach is KYLIN [7]. KYLIN uses Wikipedia infoboxes as a training dataset in order to extract information from Wikipedia and the Web. The result of this approach is a system that automatically creates new infoboxes for articles which do not have one, as well as completing infoboxes with missing attributes. Unfortunately, not all Wikipedia articles have infoboxes. Infoboxes also suffer from several problems, which are: incompleteness, inconsistency, schema drift, type free system, irregular lists, and flattened categories [20]. In contrast to KYLIN, our approach uses the existing metadata available in almost every Wikipedia article. Our approach treats each sentence with metadata individually, thus we are not relying on any specific limited resources for training datasets. Furthermore, although KYLIN can learn to extract values for any attributes, their attribute sets are limited to those attributes occurring in Wikipedia infoboxes only.

7 Conclusions and Future Work

In this paper, we have presented a novel approach for extracting facts from the Wikipedia collection. Our approach utilizes metadata as a resource in order to filter 'important' sentences in Wikipedia documents. We have also implemented techniques to resolve ambiguous entities (i.e., persons) in such sentences. Furthermore, we simplify complex sentences in order to produce more accurate triples as final result of our system. This simplification plays important role towards improving the runtime of our system, as well as memory requirements, this way making our system runnable in convenient machines. We applied lemmatization to the triples' predicates in order have a uniform representation, which simplifies querying and browsing of the extracted information. The evaluation has shown that we can achieve a relatively high precision at about 75 %.

For the future work, we have several ideas to improve the current version of the system. The first idea is to improve our scoring component. Triples extracted from the first sentences of a document could get higher scores as these sentences usually contain very clear facts. Furthermore, the transformations which we have applied during the preprocessing step should be taken into account when scoring a triple (e.g., a triple with a subject derived from coreferencing is less certain). Another important issue is the consolidation and normalization of the triples. We already apply lemmatization and entity resolution, but further consolidation according to the semantics of predicates would be helpful for querying. Nevertheless, we think that our proposed system provides a good basis for extracting high quality triples from Wikipedia.

Acknowledgements. This work has been supported by the German Academic Exchange Service (DAAD, http://www.daad.org) and by the DFG Research Cluster on Ultra High-Speed Mobile Information and Communication (UMIC, http://www.umic.rwth-aachen.de).

References

1. Mangold, C.: A survey and classification of semantic search approaches. Inl. J. Metadata Semant. Ontol. **2**, 23–34 (2007)
2. Dong, H., Hussain, F., Chang, E.: A survey in semantic search technologies. In: Proceedings of 2nd International Conference on Digital Ecosystems and Technologies (DEST), IEEE, pp. 403–408 (2008)
3. Burton-Jones, A., Storey, V.C., Sugumaran, V., Purao, S.: A heuristic-based methodology for semantic augmentation of user queries on the web. In: Song, I.-Y., Liddle, S.W., Ling, T.-W., Scheuermann, P. (eds.) ER 2003. LNCS, vol. 2813, pp. 476–489. Springer, Heidelberg (2003)
4. Heath, T., Bizer, C.: Linked data: evolving the web into a global data space. Synthesis Lectures on the Semantic Web Theory and Technology. Morgan & Claypool Publishers, San Rafael (2011)
5. Banko, M., Cafarella, M.J., Soderland, S., Broadhead, M., Etzioni, O.: Open information extraction from the web. In: Veloso, M.M. (ed.) Proceedings of 20th International Joint Conference on Artificial Intelligence (IJCAI), Hyderabad, India, pp. 2670–2676 (2007)

6. Etzioni, O., Cafarella, M.J., Downey, D., Kok, S., Popescu, A.M., Shaked, T., Soderland, S., Weld, D.S., Yates, A.: Web-scale information extraction in knowitall: (preliminary results). In: Proceedings of WWW, pp. 100–110 (2004)
7. Weld, D.S., Hoffmann, R., Wu, F.: Using Wikipedia to bootstrap open information extraction. SIGMOD Rec. **37**, 62–68 (2009)
8. Hoffart, J., Suchanek, F.M., Berberich, K., Lewis-Kelham, E., de Melo, G., Weikum, G.: Yago2: exploring and querying world knowledge in time, space, context, and many languages. In: Proceedings of WWW (Companion Volume), pp. 229–232 (2011)
9. Rusu, D., Dali, L., Fortuna, B., Grobelnik, M., Mladenic, D.: Triplet extraction from sentences. In: Proceedings of 10th International Multiconference on Information Society, vol. A, pp. 218–222 (2007)
10. Halevy, A.Y., Etzioni, O., Doan, A., Ives, Z.G., Madhavan, J., McDowell, L., Tatarinov, I.: Crossing the structure chasm. In: Proceedings of 1st Biennal Conference on Innovative Data Systems Research (CIDR), Asilomar, CA, USA (2003)
11. Suchanek, F.M., Kasneci, G., Weikum, G.: Yago: a core of semantic knowledge. In: Proceedings of WWW (2007)
12. Defazio, A.: Natural language question answering over triple knowledge bases. Master's thesis, Australian National University (2009)
13. Klein, D., Manning, C.D.: Accurate unlexicalized parsing. In: Hinrichs, E.W., Roth, D. (eds.) Proceedings of 41st Annual Meeting of the Association for Computational Linguistics (ACL), Sapporo, Japan, pp. 423–430 (2003)
14. Toutanova, K., Klein, D., Manning, C.D., Singer, Y.: Feature-rich part-of-speech tagging with a cyclic dependency network. In: Proceedings of International Conference of the North American Chapter of the Association for Computational Linguistics on Human Language Technology, Stroudsburg, PA, USA, vol. 1, pp. 173–180 (2003)
15. Etzioni, O., Fader, A., Christensen, J., Soderland, S., Mausam: open information extraction: the second generation. In: Proceedings of IJCAI, Barcelona, Spain, pp. 3–10 (2011)
16. Blohm, S.: Large-scale pattern-based information extraction from the world wide web. Ph.D. thesis, Karlsruhe Institute for Technology (KIT) (2010)
17. Agichtein, E., Gravano, L.: Snowball: extracting relations from large plain-text collections. In: Proceedings of 5th ACM International Conference on Digital Libraries, pp. 85–94 (2000)
18. Brin, S.: Extracting patterns and relations from the world wide web. In: Atzeni, P., Mendelzon, A.O., Mecca, G. (eds.) WebDB 1998. LNCS, vol. 1590, pp. 172–183. Springer, Heidelberg (1999)
19. Wu, F., Weld, D.S.: Open information extraction using Wikipedia. In: Hajic, J., Carberry, S., Clark, S. (eds.) Proceedings of 48th Annual Meeting Association for Computational Linguistics (ACL), Uppsala, Sweden, pp. 118–127 (2010)
20. Wu, F., Weld, D.S.: Autonomously semantifying wikipedia. In: Silva, M.J., Laender, A.H.F., Baeza-Yates, R.A., McGuinness, D.L., Olstad, B., Olsen, Ø.H., Falcão, A.O. (eds.) Proceedings of 16th Conference on Information and Knowledge Management (CIKM), Lisbon, Portugal, ACM, pp. 41–50 (2007)

Mobile Information Systems

Context and Activity Recognition
for Personalized Mobile Recommendations

Toon De Pessemier[⊠], Simon Dooms,
Kris Vanhecke, Bart Matté, Ewout Meyns, and Luc Martens

Dept. of Information Technology, iMinds - WiCa - Ghent University,
Gaston Crommenlaan 8, Box 201, 9050 Ghent, Belgium
{toon.depessemier,simon.dooms,
kris.vanhecke,luc.martens}@intec.ugent.be

Abstract. Through the use of mobile devices, contextual information about users can be derived to use as an additional information source for traditional recommendation algorithms. This paper presents a framework for detecting the context and activity of users by analyzing sensor data of a mobile device. The recognized activity and context serves as input for a recommender system, which is built on top of the framework. Through context-aware recommendations, users receive a personalized content offer, consisting of relevant information such as points-of-interest, train schedules, and touristic info. An evaluation of the recommender system and the underlying context-recognition framework demonstrates the impact of the response times of external information providers. The data traffic on the mobile device required for the recommendations shows to be limited. A user evaluation confirms the usability and attractiveness of the recommender. The recommendations are experienced as effective and useful for discovering new venues and relevant information.

Keywords: Context · Activity recognition · Mobile · Recommendation · Personalization

1 Introduction

Contextual information is used in many application domains to offer users a service that is adapted to their location, needs, and expectations. Also in recommender systems, the user context has gained an increased interest from researchers [1]. For instance, various tourist guide applications use the location of the user to personalize and adapt their content offer to the current user needs. An interesting example is a mobile recommender system proving personal recommendations for Points Of Interest (POI) based on the user ratings [13]. User ratings can be weighted higher to differentiate between users that rate POI using the mobile tourist guide application in direct proximity of the POI and others using the Internet away from the POI. Still via mobile devices such as smartphones, more contextual information can be retrieved than currently exploited by traditional recommendation algorithms. Users are carrying

© Springer-Verlag Berlin Heidelberg 2014
K.-H. Krempels and A. Stocker (Eds.): WEBIST 2013, LNBIP 189, pp. 243–262, 2014.
DOI: 10.1007/978-3-662-44300-2_15

their mobile device on them, resulting in additional information such as their location, speed, environment, etc. This additional information can revolutionize the role of recommender systems from topic oriented information seeking and decision making tools to information discovery and entertaining companions [17].

To ease the development of mobile context-aware applications, frameworks have been introduced to provide an abstraction for sensors and actuators. Such a framework assists application developers in gathering data from various sensors, represent application context, and reason efficiently about the context, without the need to write complex code [3]. However, most of these frameworks provide only low-level sensor data and do not interpret the data over a longer period of time to deduce high-level context information such as the user's activity.

Various attempts have been made to recognize user activity from accelerometer data. Wearable sensors have been used to measure acceleration and angular velocity data in order to recognize and classify sitting, standing, and walking behavior [15]. An experiment with five biaxial accelerometers worn simultaneously on different parts of the body, showed that it is possible to recognize a variety of different activities like walking, sitting, standing, but also watching TV, running, bicycling, eating, reading etc. [2]. Moreover, the recognition performance drops only slightly if data of only two biaxial accelerometers are available - thigh and wrist.

Also through a single triaxial accelerometer worn near the pelvic region, user activities can be recognized with fairly high accuracy. Nevertheless, experiments showed that activities that are limited to the movement of just hands or mouth (e.g., brushing teeth) are comparatively harder to recognize using a single accelerometer [16]. Although most mobile devices contain only a single triaxial accelerometer, these results indicate the ability to detect user activities through this built-in accelerometer.

In this research, we present a framework for recognizing the user's context and activity based on sensor data originating from the user's mobile phone in a daily user environment. The developed framework (Sect. 2) first detects basic contexts and activities such as walking and cycling by analyzing the acceleration of the mobile device. By analyzing these basic activities over a longer period of time, recognizing more complex contexts, such as "walking to a station while it is rainy", is possible. This contextual information is used by the recommender system (Sect. 3) in order to achieve the main goal of this research: providing personalized information and suggestions that are adapted to the current context and activity of the user. The response time of the information providers as well as the data traffic required for the recommendations are evaluated. The accuracy and usefulness of the recommendations is assessed via a user study (Sect. 4).

2   Context and Activity-Recognition

Because of its rapid growth in popularity and widespread use, we opted for Google Android as implementation platform of our framework. Nowadays, almost every Google Android device has several built-in sensors, such as an accelerometer and GPS. But sensor data are also available in many other operating systems for mobile devices.

The context-recognition framework consists of three successive phases: (1.) *Monitoring* the (sensor) data, i.e., logging the raw data from the accelerometer, GPS, battery, proximity sensor, cell-ID, etc. (2.) *Processing* the sensor data and recognizing basic activities. (3.) *Analyzing* the successive basic activities and recognizing the overall context.

2.1 Monitoring

This phase involves the gathering of all available raw data from the device. GPS data provides location updates. If no GPS data are available (e.g., in indoor environments), the cell-ID can give an indication of the location through the ID of the cellular tower that is currently providing reception to the device. Further, the battery status (e.g., charging) of the device as well as the battery level can be retrieved. The accelerometer of most Android devices is capable of capturing the device's acceleration on three axes every 20 ms. This accelerometer data are used to recognize the activity of the user. The proximity sensor is used by the Android operating system to detect if an object is in the vicinity of the device. Its main purpose is to detect if the user is holding the device next to the ear for making a phone call. In that case, the screen can be switched off to save power. In this research, the proximity sensor is used to detect where the user carries the device. If the proximity sensor detects no object in the vicinity of the device, then the device is not in the pocket of the user, and recognizing basic activities based on accelerometer data is not reliable. The framework can easily be extended with additional sensor data in order to add additional contextual information.

2.2 Processing

In this phase, each type of data obtained in the monitoring phase, is converted into basic contextual information by a processing unit. For some sensor data, such as data from the proximity sensor, this conversion is straightforward. Other sensor data, such as data from the accelerometer, require a more intelligent processing to obtain contextual information. If additional sensor data become available, the framework can be extended with a new processing unit to extract valuable information from it.

Points-Of-Interest. Matching the current location of the user to the location of POI enables the framework to identify the nearest POI or the POI within a specified range. The location of the user is retrieved via GPS data or (if GPS is not available, or switched off) estimated by the current cell-ID. Different services are used to retrieve data about the POI in the current neighborhood of the user. E.g., the location of the Belgian railway stations is retrieved via the iRail API [19], a service that provides information about railway stations, schedules, and delays in Belgium. Via the Foursquare API [7], the framework retrieves data about various other types of POI such as restaurants, bars, shops, etc.

Urbanization. The POI that are retrieved by the Foursquare API are used to estimate the urbanization of the current location of the user. The more POI in the neighborhood of the device, the higher the urbanization level of the neighborhood.

Weather. To find out the weather conditions, the location of the user is first converted into an address via the Google Geocoding API [8]. Subsequently, the ZIP code of the address is used to retrieve weather information from the Google Weather API. This information is refreshed after a change in location or if more than 2 h have elapsed. To retrieve data about the current weather and urbanization level, GPS data are not strictly required since an estimation of the location of the device by the cell-ID is sufficiently accurate.

Movement. Based on location updates of the GPS data (or cell-ID info) and the coupled timestamps, the framework calculates the current speed and future position of the user. Together with the information about the POI, the framework can detect if the user is approaching a POI. For this detection, the framework considers the type of POI, the direction of the movement, the distance between the user and the POI at successive times, and the movement speed to estimate to which POI the user is on the way.

Company. In the application, users can add other users as friends and specify their relationship with these friends, e.g., husband, child, buddy etc. Besides, users can opt to share their location data in order to enable the framework to detect whether different users are in another's company or whether some of their friends are in the neighborhood.

Battery. Information about the status of the battery can be used to deduce contextual information about the user, e.g., charging the battery indicates a fixed position of the user. (Many users charge their phone while they are at home.) Data about the battery level can be used to decide to switch off the framework to extend the battery lifetime.

Available Time. By checking the user's appointments in the calendar application of the phone, the framework can estimate the availability of the user. Appointments in the near future can influence the behavior of the user. E.g., if the user has an appointment within one hour, (s)he might choose a nearby restaurant to have lunch.

Physical Activity. Recognizing physical activities based on patterns in the data originating from the accelerometer is the most complicated processing task of the framework. The framework tries to distinguish four basic activities: standing still, walking, running, and cycling. These different activities induce different

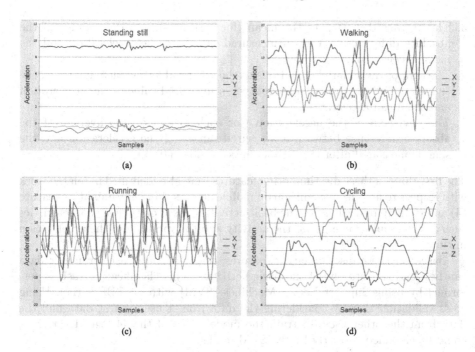

Fig. 1. Visualization of the data of the accelerometer obtained while doing physical activities.

accelerations along the three dimensions (X-axis, Y-axis, and Z-axis); and these patterns in the accelerometer data are used to distinguish the basic activities. An important requirement is that users have to carry the mobile device in their pocket, so that the movement of the user's leg can be registered by the device.

Learning to recognize patterns in the accelerometer data is done by training the framework with samples of real physical activities. To obtain these training data, accelerometer data from 11 different users (between 16 and 50 years old) performing the four activities were collected. Every user was asked to perform one of the basic activities during a 5-s time frame while a mobile device recorded the accelerometer data. This was repeated for all four basis activities, thereby yielding 44 training samples. These training data clearly showed different patterns for the four activities, as shown in Fig. 1. Standing still induces the least activity on the accelerometer, cycling produces a data pattern with a periodic variation in time, and running shows more energy than walking.

These training data were used for determining the five discriminating features based on which the four basic activities are distinguished:

1. The average resultant acceleration, i.e., the average of the square root of the sum of the values of each axis squared $\sqrt{x_i^2 + y_i^2 + z_i^2}$.
2. The difference between maximum and minimum acceleration (for each axis).

3. The average deviation to the mean (for each axis), i.e., the average of the absolute difference between a measured sample of the acceleration and the mean acceleration.
4. The sum of the squared deviations to the mean value (for each axis), i.e., the sum of the squared differences between a measured value of the acceleration and the mean acceleration.
5. The deviation of the acceleration (for each axis), i.e., the average of the absolute difference between a measured sample of the acceleration and the sample measured after three time units (so after 60 ms).

The first three of these discriminating features were also identified in related work with respect to activity recognition on mobile devices [14]. Discriminating feature (4) and (5) help to distinguish the basic activities based on typical characteristics such as the required energy for the activity and the variation of the acceleration in time.

Based on these discriminating features, newly-acquired accelerometer data can be classified into one of the basic activities. This classification task is performed by using Support Vector Machines (SVM) with an RBF-kernel. Using cross validation thereby considering the data from 1 user as test data and the data from the other users to train the model, each of the 44 logged activities could be classified correctly by the SVM model.

Proximity. As explained in Sect. 2.1, the data of the proximity sensor can indicate that the device is not in the pocket of the user. Since the recognition of physical activities requires the user to carry the device in his/her pocket, this proximity data can indicate if the activity recognition is reliable.

2.3   Analyzing

Based on the basic activities that are recognized by processing the accelerometer data and the additional contextual information gathered in the processing phase, the framework can recognize more complex user behavior. The underlying idea of the analyzing phase is that complex user behavior consists of different basic contexts which have some relation with each other. E.g., "The user is walking home while it's rainy" consists of "The user is walking", "The user is approaching his/her house" and "it's rainy". The common conditional relationship between these basic contexts is the timing; they have to occur at the same time.

So to recognize complex user behavior, these complex activities are first decomposed into different basic contexts that have a conditional relationship to each other. A basic context can be: the current weather, the current time and day, the battery status and level, being located in an urbanized area, being located in the neighborhood of a specific POI, approaching a specific POI, being in the company of another user, traveling with a specific speed (range), the distance traveled in a specific time interval, or a physical activity such as standing still, walking, running, or cycling. For each potential complex activity, the framework checks if the first basic context matches the data that are gathered in the processing phase. If this is the case, the framework checks the conditional relationship of this basic context to the second basic context. The conditional relationship can indicate that the second basic context has to occur in parallel with the first basic context or within a specified time frame (e.g., within the next 60 min after the first context was detected). So upon detecting the first context, until the conditional time frame has elapsed, the framework monitors the sensor data and tests if the processed data match the pattern of the second basic context. This procedure of matching the processed sensor data to the basic contexts and testing the conditions, is repeated for all basic contexts and conditions of the complex activity.

As soon as one of the basic contexts of the complex activity cannot be matched to the processed sensor data or one of the conditions between the basic activities is not met, the complex activity cannot be recognized. Only if all basic contexts are recognized and all conditions are met, the complex activity is flagged as recognized.

An example of a complex activity is "taking the train" which is composed of the following subsequent basic contexts: (1) The user is approaching a railway station. (2) The user is in the neighborhood of a railway station. (3) GPS connection is lost. Although GPS data are available inside a car, GPS data are in most cases not available inside the train. (4) The user is traveling with a minimum speed. In this case, location updates are based on the cell-ID, because GPS info is not available. (5) In parallel with (4), the user is traveling in the direction of another (nearby) railway station. As soon as these basic contexts and conditions are recognized, the framework believes that user is traveling by train. This complex activity does not include the act of arriving at the railway station of the destination. If the destination would be included in the complex activity, then the activity could only be recognized after the train journey. Nevertheless, for many applications such as personalized information and recommendations, the recognition has to be performed as soon as possible during the user activity. In the current implementation, a set of complex activities is defined, but depending on the use case, the framework can also be extended with new complex activities by composing existing or new basic contexts and conditions.

3   Context-Aware Recommendations

Based on the contextual information that is provided by the context-recognition framework, we developed a context-aware recommender system that offers personalized information according to the preferences and current context of the user.

To enable the use of community knowledge (i.e., data regarding user behavior, feedback, and contextual information from all users of the system) in the recommendation process, personalized recommendations are calculated on a centralized server. Based on this community knowledge, Collaborative Filtering (CF) techniques can be used to assist in the recommendation process [4]. The mobile client can send the server a request for recommendations combined with the current context that is retrieved from the context-recognition framework. Based on the stored preferences of the user and the contextual information, the server calculates the most appropriate context-aware recommendations tailored to the user's (current) needs.

As shown in Fig. 2, the recommendation process consists of three successive phases:

1. *Determining the categories* of information that are most suitable according to the current context of the user.
2. *Retrieving the information* of the items of these selected categories.
3. *Recommending the most suitable items* from the retrieved information according to the context and preferences of the users.

After determining the categories and selecting the items, an aggregator combines the partial results.

3.1   Determining the Categories

In the first phase, the recommender system receives the current context of the user as input, and predicts the information categories that match this context. One obvious example: if the user is approaching a railway station, information regarding the train schedule might be interesting for the user. To determine the suitability of an information category, four information models work together: the activity model, preferences model, popularity model, and history

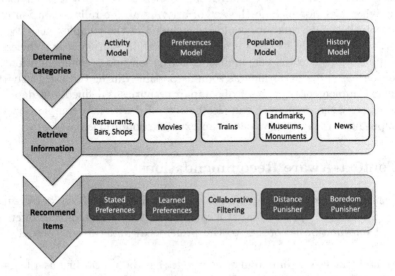

Fig. 2. Schematic overview of the recommendation process, which consists of three successive phases: determining the categories, retrieving the information, and recommending the items. The activity model, population model, and collaborative filter are based on the knowledge of all users of the system; the other models are based on a single user's personal data.

model. Each of these models assigns a probability score to each information category. This score estimates the conditional probability that the user is interested in information of the specific category, given the current context of the user. The information categories that are used are: Food (restaurants, bakeries, etc.), Movies (schedules, descriptions, etc.), Trains (schedules, delays, etc.), Monuments (info about churches, statues, etc.), and News (newspaper articles, RSS feeds, etc.); but the system can easily be extended with other categories.

Activity Model. The activity model is a knowledge-based system, consisting of a set of general rules that apply to all users. These rules connect a context to an information category that may be interesting for the user in that context. E.g., the context "being in a new city" and "sunny weather" is linked to the information category "Monuments", since users might be interested to do some sightseeing if the weather is good. The context "Evening" is linked to the information category "Food", since information about restaurants for having dinner might be interesting. These rules are stored as triplets (context, category, score), in which the score estimates the probability that users are generally interested in a category, given the specified context.

These general trends of the activity model also offer a solution to the cold start problem, the initial situation in which no information about the preferences

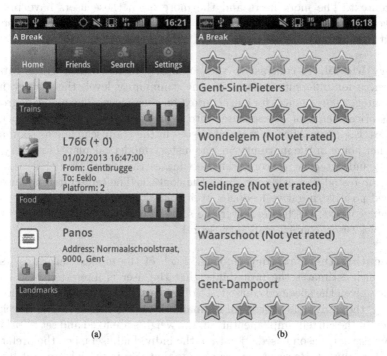

Fig. 3. Screenshots of the mobile application, showing the list of recommended information items (a) and the possibility to provide explicit feedback (b).

of the user is available. If no personal preferences are known, the user receives recommendations based on the knowledge of these general trends.

Preferences Model. The activity model defines rules for the whole community; but via the preferences model, rules can be specified for each individual user. This way, user preferences for a specific information category, given a specific context, can be specified. E.g., user "Alice" always wants to receive items of the category "News", if she is traveling by train in the morning. These personal rules are stored as 4-tuples (user, context, category, score), in which the score indicates how important this rule is for the user. An initial explicit questionnaire can be used as input to compose these rules.

Popularity Model. This model keeps track of the historical behavior of users and learns in which information categories users are interested, given the context. This learning process is based on the feedback that users can provide for information categories. Figure 3 shows two screenshots of the user interface of the mobile application and illustrates the possibility to provide feedback. The popularity model collects feedback information from all users to discover general relations between a context and an information category. The result of this model is a set of triplets (context, category, score) in which the score estimates the probability that users are generally interested in a category, given the specified context. The more users and the more often these users have provided positive/negative feedback on a content item of a specific category in a specific context, the higher/lower the score.

History Model. In contrast to the popularity model, which learns category preferences for different contexts on the community level, the history model learns category preferences for each context on a user level. The model aggregates the historical behavior of each user into a profile to learn the user's personal practices. E.g., user Alice may be interested in the train schedule as soon as she leaves her home in the morning. So, the history model calculates for every user, context, and category, a score which estimates the probability that a specific user is interested in a category, given the context. The more often the user has provided positive/negative feedback on a content item of a specific category in a specific context, the higher/lower the score. These personal habits are stored as 4-tuples (user, context, category, score).

Aggregating the Category Scores. Each of the models generates its own score which estimates the probability that the user is interested in a specific category, given the specified context. To obtain a single probability value for each category, the individual scores are normalized and aggregated using a weighted average. In the current implementation, the weights are fixed and set to prioritize the models that reason based on data of the individual users, i.e., the preferences and history model. However, one can argue that varying weights might be more efficient: assigning more importance to the models that are based on community knowledge if a limited amount of personal preferences are available; and raising the importance of the models that use individual data if more knowledge about the user's individual preferences becomes available.

The resulting scores determine the importance of each information category for the user. Therefore, the user receives a proportional number of items of a specific information category as recommendations. Items of an information category with a high score are more common in the recommendation list, whereas items of an information category with a low score are rare or even not present in this list.

3.2 Retrieving the Information

As soon as the most suitable categories are determined, given the preferences and context of the user, information items belonging to these categories can be retrieved. Because this information has to be up-to-date (e.g., for the train schedule or newspaper articles) and because this information is dependent on the context of the user (e.g., the neighboring POI are determined based on the current location of the user), the information items are retrieved at the moment of requesting the recommendations.

Various services are used to retrieve information items of the different information categories. Information regarding locations or POI (e.g., information about monuments, restaurants, shops, bars, trains, etc.), is selected based on the current location of the user. Potentially interesting data about nearby railway stations, train schedules, and delays are retrieved via iRail [19]. General information about POI in the current neighborhood of the user is retrieved via the Foursquare API [7] and the Google Places API [9]. WikiLocation is the service that is used for additional information about monuments and landmarks that might be interesting for the user [6]. Information about (cultural) events is available through the service of CultuurNet Vlaanderen [5]. CultuurNet gathers all information about cultural activities, movies, and events in Flanders (i.e., the Northern part of Belgium). This service is used to retrieve e.g., information about movie theaters and the scheduled movies. Various comparable services that offer news feeds exist. Because of its structured metadata, the RSS feed of HLN [11] is used to obtain the latest news articles of different categories such as sports, business, local news, international news, etc.

3.3 Recommending Items

The last phase of the recommendation process is to select the most appropriate items from the retrieved information of the relevant categories. To accomplish this task, five models for selecting items cooperate: the stated preferences model, learned preferences model, collaborative filtering model, distance punisher model, and boredom punisher model. Each of these models assigns a score for the usefulness to each item, thereby indicating how interesting or important the item is for the user. Some of these models consider the preferences of the user, whereas others are merely based on the current context of the user.

Stated Preferences Model. Through explicit feedback for an item or an attribute of the item, users can state their preference for a particular item (e.g., the user's favorite restaurant) or for a set of items characterized by the attribute they have in common (e.g., all Italian restaurants). In the user's profile, explicit feedback for an item propagates to the attributes and the category of the item. E.g., a positive evaluation of a news article about soccer induces a positive assessment for the attributes "Sports" and "Soccer" as well as for the category "News". As shown in Fig. 3, users can specify these preferences via a star-rating mechanism in the user interface, thereby creating a personal profile consisting of triplets (user, item or attribute, score). Based on this explicit profile, the stated preferences model assigns a score to each candidate item by considering the user's rating for the item and/or the attributes describing the item. The context is not considered in the stated preferences model because of the large number of combinations of context and attribute. Specifying preferences for all these different context-attribute combinations can put a heavy burden on the user.

Learned Preferences Model. Whereas the stated preferences model is based on explicit preferences for items and attributes of items, the learned preferences model extracts these preferences from implicit data and learns the user behavior. By saving the implicit preferences as 4-tuples (user, context, item or attribute, score), this model can also take into account the context of the user. This way, the recommender can learn for example that the user likes fast-food for lunch, a hot soup on a cold winter day, or a soda after running. Also in this model, feedback for an item propagates to the attributes and the category of the item.

Implicit feedback is gathered by tracking the user's location. If the user is approaching a POI, such as a restaurant or a pub, the framework will monitor the time that the user is staying at that POI. The hypothesis is that users stay longer at a POI, e.g., a bar, if they are having fun, whereas they leave the POI early if they do not like it. Together with the number of visits to the POI, these data provide some insights into the user's preference for the POI. The more a user visits a POI, and the longer (s)he stays there, the better the implicit feedback for that item. In the current implementation, the implicit feedback is a linear function of the time of the visit and the number of visits, in which the coefficients are determined by the information category of the item. These coefficients specify for instance that spending time in a shop has a different impact than spending time in a railway station. For items of the category "News", implicit feedback is based on the view-time of an article.

Collaborative Filtering Model. This model predicts a score for each item by using a standard user-based collaborative filtering algorithm, thereby yielding triplets (user, item or attribute, score). Collaborative filtering is a technique to estimate the preferences of a user for not-evaluated items, by using the preferences of many similar users for these items. These similar users are defined as users with similar preferences on a set of previously-evaluated items and are identified by using a similarity metric [4]. Here, the Pearson correlation metric is used for calculating similarities. Using the preferences of the community, the collaborative filtering model assigns the highest scores to the items that best match the preferences of the user, but neglects thereby the contextual information.

Distance Punisher Model. Since the recommender system has to suggest location-based items, such as restaurants, shops, train info, or the cinema schedule, the location of these items with respect to the current location of the user is especially important. The rational behind the distance punisher model is the users' preference for nearby items. E.g., if the user is traveling on foot, faraway places are not attainable and recommendations for these places are undesirable. Therefore, this model favors items in the direct neighborhood of the user at the expense of more distant places.

The distance that the user is willing to cover in order to reach a POI depends on the travel mode of the user. By bicycle, the user can move faster than on foot; and by car or train, even distant places can be reached. So the physical activity of the user is important contextual information that is used in the distance punisher model. Also the weather is a contextual aspect that influences the distance that users are willing to cover. Traveling on foot or by bicycle in combination with snow or rain will strengthen the users' preference for nearby places; whereas in sunny weather conditions, users might like to walk to their destination.

A measure of the accessibility of a place can be obtained by using distance decay curves for the different travel modes. For multiple travel modes and different purposes, the distance decay function fits a negative exponential curve, as demonstrated by research focusing on the detailed relationship between actual travel behavior and the mean distance to various services [12]. However these proposed distance decay functions cannot be adopted in this research (without changes), since the weather is not included as contextual parameter.

Table 1. The factors that influence the results of the distance punisher model, a factor determined by the travel mode and a factor for the current weather condition.

Standing/walking	Running	Cycling	Car/train
10	5	3	1
Snow	Rain	Cloudy	Sunny
6	4	2	1

So in this research, the usefulness of an item was estimated by a negative exponential function of the distance, d, weather, w, and physical activity of the user, a, as shown by Eq. 1.

$$usefulness = e^{-f(d,w,a)} \qquad (1)$$

Ideally, the function f should be determined based on actual measurements of the distance user travel in the various contexts (i.e., weather conditions in combination with transport modes). However in the current implementation, f is simplified to the product of the distance, a factor determined by the weather, and a factor determined by the travel mode. Table 1 shows the values of these factors for illustration. Faster travel modes and better weather conditions are associated with smaller factors. Smaller factors in combination with the negative exponential curve induce that additional, further located items can also be considered as recommendations.

Also the availability of the user can be a limitation and is therefore checked by this model. Items that are not attainable within the time frame of the user's calendar (i.e., before the next appointment), given the user's transportation mode, are excluded as potential recommendations.

Boredom Punisher Model. Recommendations should not only reflect the personal preferences of the user (in a specific context), but also help the user to find surprisingly interesting items (s)he might not have otherwise discovered. E.g., recommending the user's favorite restaurant over and over again might not be useful. In the domain of recommender systems, serendipity is used as a measure of how useful and surprising the recommendations are [10]. To increase the serendipity of the recommendations, the boredom punisher model favors the items that are new for the user at the expense of items that are already explored by the user (i.e., evaluated or selected for more information).

The information category of the item is an important characteristic that is taken into account by the model. The schedule of the movie theater for a movie that the user has already seen and evaluated is not useful, since people normally do not go to the movie theater twice to see the same movie. Likewise, recommendations for news articles that the user has already read are not desirable. In contrast, it might be interesting to provide information on a regular basis about the schedules and delays of a train that the user regularly catches. In conclusion, new, unexplored items receive the maximum score from the boredom punisher model. Items that the user has already interacted with, are disadvantaged by a specified penalty in accordance with the category of the item.

Aggregating the Item Scores. Each of the models discussed above generates a score that estimates the usefulness of each item based on the current context and preferences of the user. For each item, these scores are then aggregated into a single estimation of the usefulness, which is used to select a subset of the items within each information category as recommendations. Similar to the aggregation of the category scores, the item scores of the individual models are normalized and aggregated using a weighted average. In the current implementation, the weights are fixed and set to prioritize the model that estimates the usefulness based on the explicit preferences of the user, i.e., the stated preferences model.

Also this aggregator can be extended with varying weights to anticipate the development and improvement of user profiles during service usage. For new users of the service who have a limited profile, the stated preferences and distance punisher model may be the most consistent models. As a user utilizes the recommendation service more often, his/her profile becomes more detailed, and as a result, the collaborative filtering, learned preferences, and boredom punisher model are able to make a valuable contribution. So the weights associated to the models can be made variable in accordance with the advancement of the user profile in order to generate more accurate recommendations.

So to conclude, the category score determines the importance of an information category and the corresponding amount of slots for that category in the recommendation list. For each information category, the items with the highest estimated usefulness are filling these slots and offered as recommendations to the users.

4 Evaluation

4.1 Response Time

The response time of the recommender system is dependent on the available processing power and can be improved by hardware upgrades or parallelization of the calculations. However since the system queries various services during operation and information of different content providers is retrieved for the recommendations, the response time of the system is also strongly influenced by the response times of these information providers, which are beyond our control. Therefore, the response times of the various information providers was evaluated by means of 3000 measurements at different times of the day.

Table 2. Response times of the different information providers.

Provider	Type of info	Mean response time (ms)	Standard deviation
Foursquare	Bars, shops, restaurants	144	169
HLN	News	201	296
CultuurNet	Events, movies	861	217
WikiLocation	Landmarks, monuments	1450	614
iRail	Trains	5810	11028

Table 2 shows for all the information providers the type of information they offer, the mean response time, and the standard deviation on the measurements. Foursquare showed to be the fastest information provider, but also news of HLN can be retrieved with a short response time. The response times of CultuurNet and WikiLocation are longer than the response times of Foursquare and HLN but still less than 1.5 s and so acceptable for the recommender system. The slowest information provider is iRail with a mean response time of almost 6 s for retrieving information about train schedules, railway stations, and delays. The large standard deviation (approximately 11 s) illustrates that the response times of iRail are highly varying with peaks up to 30 s.

Since the recommender system relies on these information providers, the response times of these information providers directly influence the response time of the recommender system. Caching data can be a partly solution for static information about bars, shops, restaurants, landmarks, and monuments but is not appropriate for rapidly changing information such as train delays and movie schedules.

4.2   Data Traffic

Mobile data communication is necessary for the proper functioning of the recommender system and the underlying context-recognition framework, e.g., for retrieving information about the POI. Given that some mobile subscriptions are charging users based on their data traffic, the recommender application (combined with the framework) was evaluated on this criteria.

In this evaluation, we distinguished intensive and non-intensive use of the application and measured the data traffic for both scenarios. Intensive use of the application is defined as "very frequently requesting recommendations and providing feedback". The scenario of intensive use is simulated in the context of "walking in a city center", whereby recommendations are requested for the current location, and feedback on one of these recommended items is provided once per minute. The duration of the test was one hour. So during this walk, recommendations are requested 60 times for different districts of the city, and as many times feedback on one of these items is processed. Non-intensive use of the application differs from intensive use by less-frequently requesting recommendations and sporadically providing feedback. During the one hour walk, recommendations are requested 5 times and feedback is provided for 3 of these items.

Table 3 shows the average (avg) and standard deviation (std) of the data traffic in download and upload direction for intensive and non-intensive use of the application. These results indicate that even in the case of intensive use of the application, the total data traffic is only 2.29 MB on average. As a results, the data traffic required for the functioning of the application is acceptable and in the range of the data traffic induced by similar mobile applications.

Table 3. Evaluation of the recommendation application and the underlying framework in terms of data traffic.

	Intensive	Non-intensive
Avg download (MB)	1.97	1.17
Std download (MB)	0.03	0.08
Avg upload (MB)	0.32	0.12
Std upload (MB)	0.02	0.01
Avg total (MB)	2.29	1.29
Std total (MB)	0.04	0.08

4.3 User Evaluation

To evaluate the usefulness and effectiveness of the application and the personal recommendations, a small user evaluation was performed. The test panel consisted of 16 test subjects (12 men and 4 women) who are representative for the target users of the applications. All test subjects were between 21 and 32 years old and make daily use of a smartphone. They were asked to download and install the application on their own smartphone and use it during one week to retrieve recommendations in their daily environment. To ensure that the test subjects are sufficiently familiar with the application for an evaluation after the test, we asked to use the application at least once a day and at least three times outdoors. The latter requirement stimulates test subjects to use the application on the move, or for exploring new places.

After one week, test subjects received a questionnaire to evaluate the application by means of 9 multiple choice questions and 3 open questions. The multiple choice questions consisted of statements that test subjects had to assess on a 5-point rating scale ranging from "1: totally disagree" to "5: totally agree". The goal of the open questions was to inquire for potential improvements or extensions to the application.

Figure 4 visualizes the answers to the most interesting multiple choice questions as histograms. The first histogram, Fig. 4(a), indicates that all test subjects experienced the application as "easy to use". Because of the automatic context recognition and the straightforward way to retrieve recommendations, no test subject provided a negative evaluation regarding the usability. Future work may comprise more comprehensive user tests to obtain a more detailed evaluation of the usability and functionality of the application and the interface by using adaptive user-interface techniques [18].

The second histogram, Fig. 4(b), gives an indication about how pleasant it is to use the application. Only three test subjects disagreed with the statement "I like to use the application". Detailed feedback of the test subjects explained their dissatisfaction with the application or the recommendations. According to one test subject, loading the recommendations takes too much time. Two other test subjects would like to have more detailed sub-categories. Besides, two test subjects mentioned the battery drain as a serious drawback. One test subject did not understand the added value of a recommender system for selecting information on a mobile device.

The accuracy of the recommendations is assessed by asking the test subjects if the recommendations are interesting. Except for two people, the test subjects agreed with the statement that the recommendations of the application are really interesting for them, as illustrated in the third histogram, Fig. 4(c). The test subject who totally disagreed with this statement had a data connection problem during the test, which explains why he did not receive (interesting) recommendations. The ability to help users discovering new and interesting information or POI, i.e., the serendipity of the recommendations, is assessed via the last histogram, Fig. 4(d). Except for two people (one of them had a connection prob-

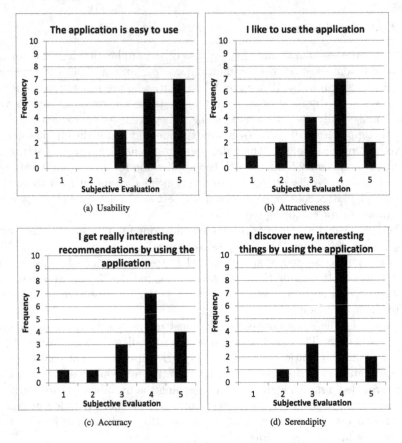

Fig. 4. Histograms of the answers on the multiple choice questions of the user evaluation.

lem), test subjects confirmed that they can find new and interesting information or POI via the recommendations.

To summarize, the application that offers context-aware recommendations based on the automatically-detected context of the user, is easy to use. According to the test subjects, the personal recommendations are a valuable asset in the context of information retrieval: these recommendations are interesting and help them to discover new content and places.

Via the open questions, test subjects were asked if additional features should be added to the application, and which existing features should be removed. Four test subjects suggested to extend the friend-functionality of the application. Besides adding and removing users from their friend list, they would like to see the context of their friends. They also mentioned the possibility to recommend items to friends and to see their friends' feedback on items. One test subject would like to receive detailed information for additional categories, such as detailed info about the articles in supermarkets. Another feature on the wish list of the test subjects is "changing their own current context".

E.g., manually changing the location would be useful to plan a holiday and retrieve the recommendations for the holiday destination before arriving. At last, also a more detailed feedback mechanism consisting of check-ins, likes, and reviews, was mentioned.

Three test subjects indicated that the items of the category "News" might be superfluous. The friend-functionality was also mentioned two times as a feature that can be removed from the application, since it was not clear for the test subjects that this information is used by the recommender.

5 Conclusions

In this research, we investigated how the current context and activity of the user can be recognized based on sensor data and the accelerometer of his/her mobile device. The context-recognition framework first monitors and processes the sensor data to recognize basic activities or context changes. Then these successive basic activities are analyzed to recognize the overall context of the user. An evaluation of the framework proved that physical activities and the context of the user can be recognized with a high accuracy and that this contextual information can be valuable knowledge for a context-aware recommender system. Besides, the framework can be used for other applications, e.g., for monitoring the physical activities of the user in the context of health care.

Several challenges, such as the response time and the data traffic, are associated with the development of the context-recognition framework and the recommender on top of it. Experiments demonstrated that the response times of information providers can have a big influence on the response time of the recommender system. The data traffic required for the recommender is limited to a couple of MB per hour, even in the case of intensive use, by constraining the recommendations to the current context of the user.

A user study showed that context-aware recommendations are effective and helpful for discovering new places and interesting information. Moreover, users like to receive information tailored to their current needs and consider the recommender application as easy to use. These results confirm the necessity to adapt (mobile) applications and services to the activity and context of the user in order to improve the effectiveness and the user experience.

References

1. Adomavicius, G., Sankaranarayanan, R., Sen, S., Tuzhilin, A.: Incorporating contextual information in recommender systems using a multidimensional approach. ACM Trans. Inf. Syst. **23**(1), 103–145 (2005). http://doi.acm.org/10.1145/1055709.1055714
2. Bao, L., Intille, S.S.: Activity recognition from user-annotated acceleration data. In: Ferscha, A., Mattern, F. (eds.) PERVASIVE 2004. LNCS, vol. 3001, pp. 1–17. Springer, Heidelberg (2004). http://dx.doi.org/10.1007/978-3-540-24646-6_1

3. Biegel, G., Cahill, V.: A framework for developing mobile, context-aware applications. In: Proceedings of the Second IEEE International Conference on Pervasive Computing and Communications (PerCom'04), PERCOM '04, pp. 361–365. IEEE Computer Society, Washington, DC (2004). http://dl.acm.org/citation.cfm?id=977406.978672

4. Breese, J.S., Heckerman, D., Kadie, C.: Empirical analysis of predictive algorithms for collaborative filtering. In: Proceedings of the Fourteenth Conference on Uncertainty in Artificial Intelligence, UAI'98, San Francisco, CA, USA, pp. 43–52 (1998). http://dl.acm.org/citation.cfm?id=2074094.2074100

5. CultuurNet-Vlaanderen: Uitdatabank developer tools (2012). http://tools.uitdatabank.be/docs

6. Dodson, B.: Wikilocation (2012). http://wikilocation.org/

7. Foursquare: Foursquare API (2012). https://developer.foursquare.com/

8. Google: Geocoding API (2012). https://developers.google.com/maps/documentation/geocoding/

9. Google: Places API (2012). https://developers.google.com/places/documentation/

10. Herlocker, J.L., Konstan, J.A., Terveen, L.G., Riedl, J.T.: Evaluating collaborative filtering recommender systems. ACM Trans. Inf. Syst. 22(1), 5–53 (2004). http://doi.acm.org/10.1145/963770.963772

11. HLN: Rss news feed (2012). http://www.hln.be/rss.xml

12. Iacono, M., Krizek, K., El-Geneidy, A.: Access to destinations: how close is close enough? estimating accurate distance decay functions for multiple modes and different purposes. Technical report. University of Minnesota, Twin Cities. Minnesota Department of Transportation (2008). ref.: MN/RC 2008–11

13. Kenteris, M., Gavalas, D., Mpitziopoulos, A.: A mobile tourism recommender system. In: Proceedings of the IEEE Symposium on Computers and Communications, ISCC '10, pp. 840–845. IEEE Computer Society, Washington, DC (2010). http://dx.doi.org/10.1109/ISCC.2010.5546758

14. Kwapisz, J.R., Weiss, G.M., Moore, S.A.: Activity recognition using cell phone accelerometers. SIGKDD Explor. Newsl. 12(2), 74–82 (2011). http://doi.acm.org/10.1145/1964897.1964918

15. Lee, S.W., Mase, K.: Activity and location recognition using wearable sensors. IEEE Pervasive Comput. 1(3), 24–32 (2002)

16. Ravi, N., Dandekar, N., Mysore, P., Littman, M.L.: Activity recognition from accelerometer data. In: Proceedings of the 17th Conference on Innovative Applications of Artificial Intelligence, IAAI'05, vol. 3, pp. 1541–1546. AAAI Press (2005). http://dl.acm.org/citation.cfm?id=1620092.1620107

17. Ricci, F.: Mobile recommender systems. Inf. Technol. Tourism 2(3), 205–231 (2010). http://www.ingentaconnect.com/content/cog/itt/2010/00000012/00000003/art00002

18. Savidis, A., Stephanidis, C.: Software refactoring process for adaptive user-interface composition. In: Proceedings of the 2nd ACM SIGCHI Symposium on Engineering Interactive Computing Systems, EICS '10, pp. 19–28. ACM, New York (2010). http://doi.acm.org/10.1145/1822018.1822023

19. Tiete, Y., Schmitz, S., Colpaert, P.: iRail API (2012). http://project.irail.be/wiki/API/APIv1

Author Index